The Contemporary Singer

Elements of Vocal Technique

Anne Peckham

Berklee Press

Director: Dave Kusek
Managing Editor: Debbie Cavalier
Marketing Manager: Ola Frank
Sr. Writer/Editor: Jonathan Feist

ISBN 0-634-00797-1

DISTRIBUTED BY

HAL•LEONARD®
CORPORATION
7777 W. BLUEMOUND RD. P.O. BOX 13819
MILWAUKEE, WISCONSIN 53213

1140 Boylston Street
Boston, MA 02215-3693 USA
(617) 747-2146

Visit Berklee Press Online at
www.berkleepress.com

Visit Hal Leonard Online at
www.halleonard.com

Table of Contents

YOU CAN PERFORM the material on the audio CD without the book—just put it on and follow along. Do track 1 and the Level One Workout for your voice type and you should be thoroughly warmed up for performance. More in-depth exercises follow the Level One for each voice type.

Performers: Jude Crossen, voice
Tamara Gebhardt, voice
Anne Peckham, voice
David Shrewsbury, piano

Track 1   Introduction

VOCAL WORKOUTS

Track 2.   Beginning Warm-up for All Voices
Track 3.   Level One Workout for High Voices
Track 4.   Advanced Workout for High Voices
Track 5.   Level One Workout for Low Voices
Track 6.   Advanced Workout for Low Voices

**DEMONSTRATION TRACKS: PERFORMANCE
OF BOOK EXERCISES**

Track 7.   Balanced Onset Exercise 1
                     Example 3.1
Track 8.   Balanced Onset Exercise 2
                     Example 3.2
Track 9.   Resonance Exercise 1
                     Example 4.1
Track 10.   Resonance Exercise 2
                     Example 4.2
Track 11.   Blending Exercise 1
                     Example 5.1
Track 12.   Blending Exercise 2
                     Example 5.2
Track 13.   Blending Exercise 3
                     Example 5.3
Track 14.   Blending Exercise 4
                     Example 5.4
Track 15.   Onset Exercise 1
                     Example 6.1
Track 16.   Onset Exercise 2
                     Example 6.2
Track 17.   Articulation Exercise
                     Example 6.5
Track 18.   Humpty Dumpty Etude
                     Example 6.6
Track 19.   Sliding Warm-up
                     Example 7.1

THE CONTEMPORARY SINGER discusses the elements of singing, addressing the specific needs of singers of popular music. It is intended for singers of all levels who want to improve their stamina, increase their range, develop a better sound, and enhance their overall vocal health. *The Contemporary Singer* and its companion CD are the ideal tools for creating a singing course for students of almost any age group, from junior high school to college to professional. ■ Since 1987, I have been teaching voice at Berklee College of Music, where I developed a course called "Elements of Vocal Technique." This book is the result of these efforts and of my teaching experiences.

Acknowledgments

THANKS TO Sharon Brown, Sean Carberry, Debbie Cavalier, Jonathan Feist, Matt Marvuglio, Yumiko Matsuoka, Donna McElroy, Rick Peckham, Jo-Ann Ross, Jan Shapiro, and Dr. Steven Zeitels.

1

KNOWING YOUR INSTRUMENT

PART

A VOICE IS A COMPLEX INSTRUMENT, capable of a wide range of expression. There are many singers who have a wonderful natural sound without studying singing. However, singers who acquire a vocabulary to describe their vocal mechanism and an understanding of their instrument reap many benefits. You can improve and maintain your vocal sound through years of singing, and learn to prevent and correct problems.

This book will help you learn to take care of your voice and advance your singing to the next level. Studying its techniques will help you understand and develop your voice by describing the basic elements of your instrument and teaching you how to practice. It can help you isolate the physical elements of singing, master them, and then expand this mastery of the details to a more holistic technical and musical whole.

In my teaching experience, I have encountered many myths surrounding vocal training. One myth is that singers of popular music don't need training. Many young singers are surprised to learn that careers of untrained singers can be cut short prematurely due to vocal injuries. Even seasoned performers who have bad habits sometimes must relearn how to sing, or else risk permanent vocal damage.

Music styles such as pop, rock, gospel, country music, and musical theater can involve loud singing for extended periods of time, which can be very tiring to your voice. You might have the added problem of performing in venues that may be dry, dusty, and smoky, and have to project over a background of noise.

Comprehensive voice study will help you develop proper breath management and a resonant tone, improving your voice by building stamina and vocal power. You can learn to minimize vocal tension and understand how your environment affects your voice. Understanding your voice will help you eliminate any bad vocal habits that are holding you back.

Your voice is subject to the effects of your emotions, eating and sleeping habits, use of medications and drugs, and speaking. It is dependent upon your overall good health and vitality. Learning how to take care of your voice and developing good practice habits can help you maintain your singing voice for a lifetime.

Another myth about vocal study is that it leads singers to lose the unique, natural sound of their voices. On the contrary, studying voice can help you build your instrument and enhance its best natural qualities. Mastering the elements of singing, such as breath control, will help you make the most of your natural sound. It will also make you aware of areas that need improvement and habits that are detrimental to vocal longevity. In fact, many successful, professional pop singers take lessons to improve and maintain their voices. Lessons won't make you lose your unique sound. Instead, you will gain control and enhance your instrument.

What is the best vocal method? Every singer explains the complex process of singing differently, using dissimilar terms, and emphasizing different body parts and pedagogical concepts. A good singing method is one that is practical, relevant, has a basis in scientific fact, and uses exercises targeting specific, nuts-and-bolts issues for a singer.

Don't be intimidated by technical details when you are learning to sing. Information about your body and voice will help you become a smart singer, knowing how to make the most of your natural instrument.

TIPS FOR GETTING STARTED

■ Focus on long-term goals

As you begin to study voice, keep your long-term goals in mind. Learning to sing is both an intellectual and a physical process. Training your muscles to "remember" how to react when approaching a leap or when sustaining a phrase takes time and practice. You must train your muscles by repeating a task correctly many times so your instrument responds effectively when you perform.

Singers commonly understand technical concepts intellectually long before they are able to perform the skills, so practicing is important. Throughout the process, remember that singing well requires skill. You can develop this through practice and patience. Think positively and acknowledge your successes.

■ Choose your repertoire carefully

Singers need to build a base of positive performance experience in order to develop confidence. Early in vocal development, avoid songs that spotlight your weaknesses. It is better to sing a simple song well than to sing a difficult song poorly. Challenge yourself, but be ready to recognize when you need to put a song away to give your voice the time to develop.

■ Sing for fun

Stay in touch with your love of singing. As you work to improve your singing in practice sessions, make sure you have outlets for performing that are purely pleasurable. Group singing can enhance your joy of making music, so get together with friends, join a choir, and sing for fun. Performing can be very satisfying, even while you work to fulfill your highest potential.

The following overview presents in a nutshell how your voice works. Each of these elements will be described in detail, along with exercises that will develop each specific component of your voice.

AN OVERVIEW OF THE SINGING PROCESS

All musical instruments have three common elements: a generator, a vibrator, and a resonator. Your voice, for example, is powered by breath from your lungs (generator) that makes your vocal cords (vibrator) move. The sound produced by your vocal cords is colored and amplified by resonance in your throat, mouth, and nasal cavity (resonators).

In addition to these three common elements, singers also have *articulators* (the mouth, teeth, tongue, lips, cheeks, and palates) that give singers the unique capability of combining words with music. Skillful articulation is a mark of good vocal technique.

■ Breath (generator)

Air powers your singing, and controlling the inflow and outflow of air requires the skilled use of breathing muscles and organs. These include the trachea, lungs, diaphragm, ribs (and associated muscles), and abdominal muscles.

Many vocal problems originate with these two problems: lack of sufficient breath support, and/or excessive muscular tension. The delicate balance of energy and relaxation is essential to good singing. When you manage your breath well with energy and relaxation, you will see a totally positive effect on your singing. Breath management is one of the most important practices you will learn in vocal study. It affects your intonation, tone quality, sustaining power, range, dynamics, expression, flexibility, phrasing, and stylistic interpretation. This is why good breath management is often the primary focus from the beginning in voice study.

■ **Sound production** (vibrator)

The larynx is comprised of cartilage, ligaments, muscle, nerves, and mucus membranes. The vocal cords are situated in the larynx and comprised of the arytenoid cartilages, the vocalis muscle (thyroarytenoid), ligaments, and membranes. Activated by the brain with the thought of speaking or singing, nerves control the muscles that close the arytenoid cartilages, bringing the vocal cords together. This closure offers a resistance to airflow, which results in a "buzz tone," the fundamental tone of vocal production.

You can feel your vocal cords vibrating if you place your fingers lightly on the small protrusion at front of your throat (Adam's apple). Say "hoo!" at a moderately high pitch. You will feel a buzzing sensation at your fingers. This is where your vocal cords are.

Your vocal cords do not have nerves that tell you when they need rest or that they are swollen or injured. When you have a sore throat from vocal misuse or illness, you feel the inflammation or infection of surrounding tissues or tired muscles from incorrect singing, not the vocal cords themselves. That is why it is important to listen to your body and stop singing before you get to the point of hoarseness or voice loss.

I had a student years ago who had her upcoming senior recital scheduled when she came down with laryngitis. She could make sound but was very hoarse. She was very anxious to finish her college work so she could start a singing job after graduation. She insisted on singing her recital despite admonishments from her laryngologist and me. A couple of weeks later, she called me from her home, just having been diagnosed with vocal nodules caused by singing with laryngitis. She lost her gig because she couldn't sing, was put on vocal rest for a time (no singing), and then gradually began to recover her voice with voice therapy and much work. This singer could have avoided developing nodules that seriously impaired and set back her singing by resting her voice when she had laryngitis.

■ **Resonance** (tone enhancer)

The throat, mouth, and nasal cavity are all parts of the vocal tract. The buzz produced by the vibrating vocal cords (the fundamental tone) reverberates in the resonators and enhances the tone. This resonance colors and amplifies tone.

When I work with young men who want to sing rock, they often ask how to get a more powerful sound on high notes. A powerful sound can be developed with energetic breath support, and an awareness of resonance, taking into account variables, such as age and voice type, which will affect your sound output. It is tough for young singers to have the patience to wait to grow into their voices, but it is important to approach your vocal development like an athlete. Runners don't train for a marathon in a week, or in a semester. Learning to sing is a long-term commitment to becoming the best that you can be.

■ **Words** (articulators)

The tongue, jaw, cheeks, teeth, lips, and palates coordinate to produce speech sounds. Adding words to music makes your voice a unique musical instrument.

Some of my students who are nonnative English speakers must work hard to produce natural sounding English diction. As their pronunciation becomes more smooth and clear, their singing tone often becomes more relaxed and natural as a result.

All basic elements of tone production are interconnected, and mastering them in order to sing freely is the goal of understanding the singing process.

**Cross-section of
upper body**

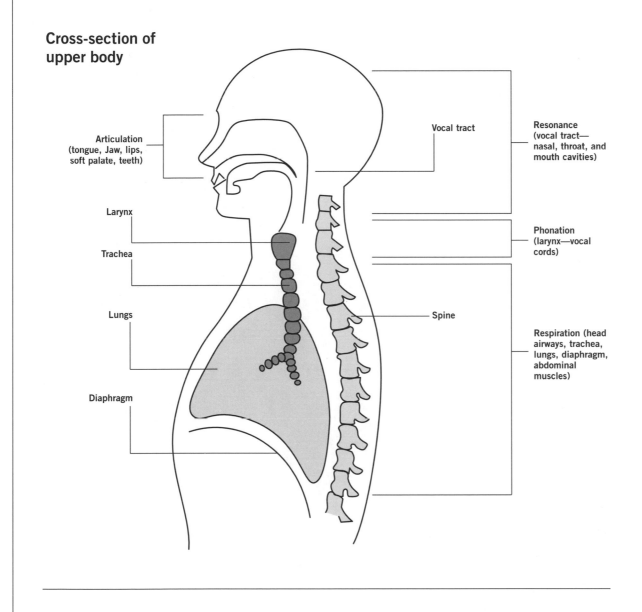

Articulation
(tongue, Jaw, lips,
soft palate, teeth)

Larynx

Trachea

Lungs

Diaphragm

Vocal tract

Spine

Resonance
(vocal tract—
nasal, throat, and
mouth cavities)

Phonation
(larynx—vocal
cords)

Respiration (head
airways, trachea,
lungs, diaphragm,
abdominal
muscles)

 OUR VOICE IS A WIND INSTRUMENT that needs breath to produce sound. Training your body and unconscious mind to manage the breathing process will give you the control you need to sing longer phrases, to sing high and low notes well, and to gain better control over dynamics.

POSTURE

Good posture is the first step to making your body work for you because it provides alignment that maximizes lung capacity and releases tension. But posture that feels "natural" to you, even if relaxed, may not provide a high enough chest position for effective singing. You may need to learn what it feels like to stand with correct posture. A collapsed chest makes it difficult to control breath when singing, and it diminishes breathing capacity.

Correct and incorrect posture

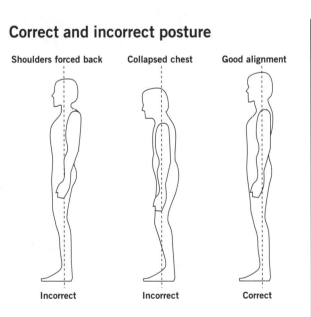

Shoulders forced back   Collapsed chest   Good alignment

Incorrect   Incorrect   Correct

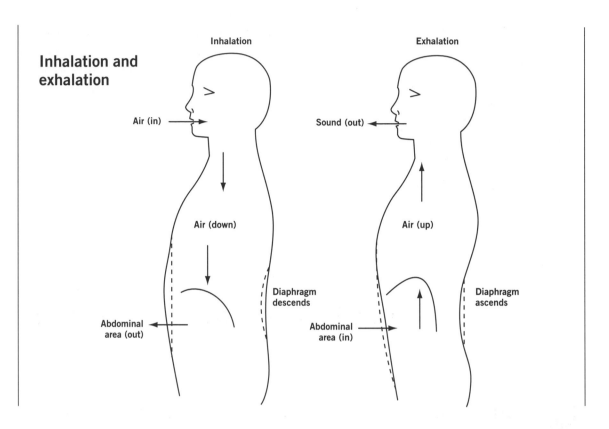

Inhalation and exhalation

To establish good posture, start with a comfortably high chest, relaxed knees (not locked), and feet hip-distance apart. As you become familiar with good posture it will feel more natural to you. During singing, be sure to keep your chest comfortably high. Beginners should practice while standing in front of a mirror because it is easier to see good posture than to feel it, when you are starting out.

Singers of pop and rock music sometimes resist good posture habits because they are afraid of appearing formal or "classical." But since contemporary music can be strenuous to voices, it is especially these singers who need good posture to reduce tension and increase breath capacity. If you do not actively involve your body in breath support, you will be more likely to strain or injure your vocal cords.

■ Moving while singing

Singers need to be able to manage their breath without actively thinking about it so they can focus their energy on performing. Experienced performers can sing while vigorously dancing and in almost any position, including lying down. While you are training your voice, however, correct posture allows you to focus on breath management and helps free tone production.

Begin by working on breath management while standing still and looking in a mirror. Once you understand the concepts and master the physical coordination, movement will not compromise your singing. Practicing makes correct breathing natural and automatic, so that you don't always have to think about it. Of course, to sing and move without becoming winded, you must be in good physical condition, which may require maintaining a regular exercise routine.

■ Everyday breath vs. singing breath

Breathing as an automatic, natural function is usually taken for granted. Singing, however, requires deep, relaxed breathing that has been refined to minimize tension and maximize efficiency. Studying the respiratory mechanism and the way it functions will help you master your breathing.

FOUR STEPS OF EFFECTIVE BREATHING

Try this simple exercise that outlines four steps of the breathing process.

1. Stand with your body aligned, your feet hip-distance apart, and your chest comfortably high.

2. Inhale through your nose and mouth by expanding around your waistline and relaxing your lower abdominal muscles.

3. Allow your lower abdominal muscles to contract slightly as you start to sing a long tone in the middle of your range.

4. Maintain your comfortably high chest position, and try to keep your ribs open as you sing. Don't let your chest collapse.

When inhaling, don't overfill your lungs. Stuffing your lungs creates tension in your throat and jaw before you even make a sound. Inhale completely by expanding around your waistline and in your lower abdominal area, taking care not to create tension by lifting your shoulders.

■ Practice makes perfect

Singers, like athletes, must develop physical skills in order to perform well.

Almost anyone can run, but athletes train to run a marathon. In the same way, you are training to use your breath in a more demanding way than the average person does, developing special skills the non-singer does not need. Moreover, breath management and tone quality are interconnected, so if you want to improve your tone, work on breath management.

The diaphragm

The *diaphragm* is a flat muscle, curved in a double-dome shape, separating the chest cavity from the abdominal cavity. It connects to the bottom of your ribs and is the floor of your rib cage.

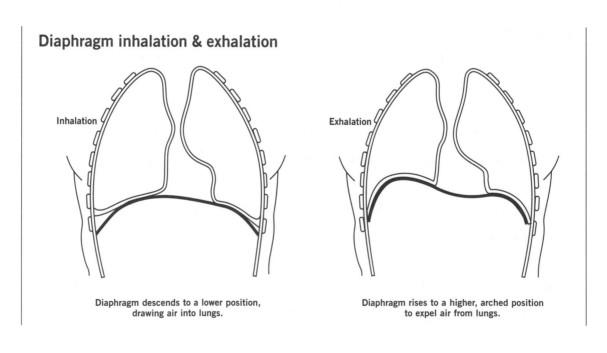

Diaphragm inhalation & exhalation

Inhalation

Exhalation

Diaphragm descends to a lower position,
drawing air into lungs.

Diaphragm rises to a higher, arched position
to expel air from lungs.

In a relaxed position, your diaphragm is slightly arched upward. When you expand your midsection by relaxing your abdominal muscles, your diaphragm descends into a more flattened position, creating a vacuum in your lungs that causes air to rush in. During exhalation, your firm abdominal muscles cause the diaphragm to arch upward in a double-dome shape and expel air. Your diaphragm is not consciously controlled during singing, but rather moves with its associated rib and abdominal muscles.

Most people have the erroneous idea that the diaphragm is located in the same position as the abdominal muscles, across the front of the belly. The instruction to "sing from your diaphragm" accompanied by a pat on your tummy may direct your attention to the right general area, but is misleading as to where your diaphragm is actually located. In fact, it is positioned horizontally inside your body and cannot be felt by placing your hand on your belly. You can find the general location of your diaphragm by feeling along the bottom of your rib cage and imagine that it is inside your body, under your ribs in the position of an upside-down bowl.

■ Ribs and lungs

Your rib cage is comprised of bone and cartilage. During breathing, the attached intercostal muscles open and close your rib cage, filling and emptying your lungs. The external intercostals expand your rib cage during a full breath, while the internal intercostals force air out during exhalation. Singers try to resist the contraction of the internal intercostals to avoid running out of air. When you sing, steady flow of air to your vocal cords is achieved by opening your ribs and slightly contracting your abdominal muscles.

This exercise will help increase your awareness of the expansion of your rib cage.

1. Place your fists on your sides above your waist.

2. Take a full breath and feel the expansion of your rib cage.

3. Exhale and feel your rib cage become narrow.

4. Take a second breath, spreading your ribs as wide as you can. Try to not lift your shoulders.

5. Hold your breath but keep your throat open. Slowly, count to four. Maintain an open rib cage as you hold your breath. You will feel the external intercostal muscles of your ribs working to stay open.

6. Exhale and allow your ribs to become narrow again.

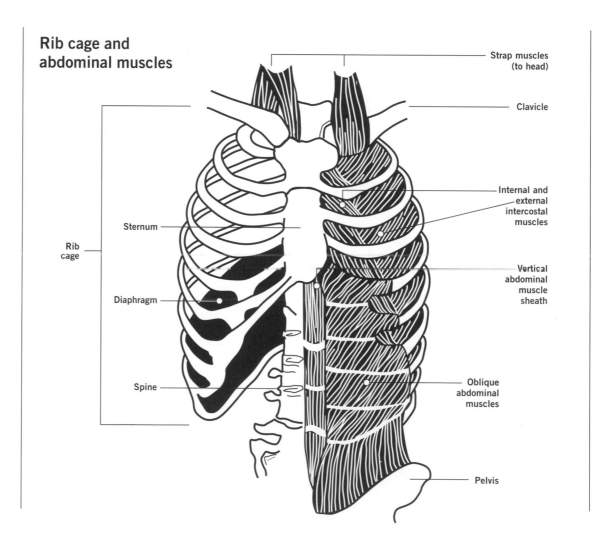

Rib cage and abdominal muscles

Strap muscles (to head)

Clavicle

Internal and external intercostal muscles

Sternum

Rib cage

Vertical abdominal muscle sheath

Diaphragm

Spine

Oblique abdominal muscles

Pelvis

■ **The abdominal muscles**

These powerful muscles cover the entire abdominal region running vertically and

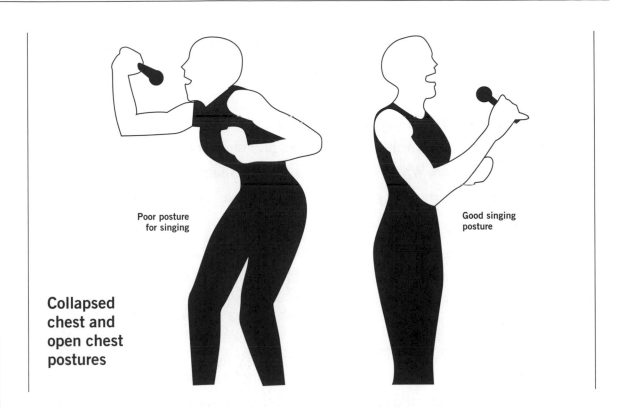

Poor posture
for singing

Good singing
posture

**Collapsed
chest and
open chest
postures**

diagonally across your belly. Your lower abdominal muscles relax outward during inhalation and contract inward slightly during exhalation.

During singing, your rib cage should stay open while your abdominal muscles move in slightly. This is called *support*; it enables your diaphragm to ascend to its high position at a slower rate, allowing you to sustain longer phrases and maintain better pitch control. If your ribs descend immediately, air will rush out too quickly for good phrasing, or a breathy tone may result. Collapsing your ribs and chest tightens your neck and throat muscles, preventing your larynx from functioning freely. This can cause your singing to sound and feel constricted.

DIFFERENT APPROACHES TO BREATHING

There are three main ways that singers tend to breathe, but only one of them is widely considered to be effective. The others can lead to poor intonation (singing out of tune), lack of sustaining power, poor tone quality, and a host of other vocal problems. In fact, many vocal problems are rooted in either inadequate breath support or excessive muscular tension caused by chest breathing or rib breathing.

■ Chest breathing (very limited effectiveness)

Chest breathing involves raising the shoulders and chest for inhalation and lowering the chest for exhalation. While this allows air to move in and out very quickly, singers should not use this technique because it is difficult to control the airflow for phrasing, and the pumping motion of the chest and shoulders creates tension. When your neck and shoulder muscles are tight, the internal muscles of the larynx cannot function freely. This kind of breathing can produce tone that is overly breathy, strained, weak, and out of tune.

■ Rib breathing (somewhat limited effectiveness)

Rib breathing involves expansion in the ribs, but not the lower abdominal muscles. Some singers tend to breathe this way to maintain a trim profile or because of admonitions from classical ballet training to hold in the tummy or to "pull up." Others have not developed the awareness required to release these muscles. Also, some singers have highly developed abdominal muscles that are difficult to relax outward during inhalation. Because contracted abdominal muscles restrict full inhalation, rib breathing is not recommended for singing. Rib breathing can lead to lack of sustaining power and throat tension, and can revert to chest breathing.

■ Rib/abdominal breathing (most effective)

The most effective breathing method for singers is rib breathing combined with relaxation of your low abdominal muscles during inhalation. Relaxed abdominal muscles allow you take a full breath, and minimize throat and neck tension during exhalation. Your lower abdominal muscles contract slightly as you exhale working in opposition to your diaphragm, which is controlled by keeping your rib cage open. When your rib muscles, diaphragm, and abdominal muscles control the work of breath support, your larynx can function without interference from its surrounding muscles.

BREATHING EXERCISES

■ Breath observation

This exercise is helpful in encouraging proper abdominal action in singing. Simply observe your body's natural movement and don't try to do anything special to influence your breathing.

1. Lay on the floor and place a small book approximately 1 1/2 inches thick under your head to align your body.

2. Focus your attention on your natural breathing process. As you inhale, your abdominal muscles below your rib cage rise, and as you exhale, they move inward. Observe the openness of your ribs around your waistline and memorize this feeling.

3. Rest your hands on your abdomen and breath normally, observing the rise and fall of your belly.

4. Stand up and reproduce this breathing action, expanding as you inhale.

■ Releasing abdominal muscles

This is especially useful for singers who need to become aware of how to release their lower abdominal muscles to take a full breath.

1. Stand with your feet about 18 inches away from a table (or the back of a chair).

2. Lean with your hands on the edge, as if you were looking at something on the table.

3. Take a slow, deep breath, letting your belly feel as if it will fall toward the floor. Don't hold your abdominal muscles in, but rather allow them to drop, assisted by gravity.

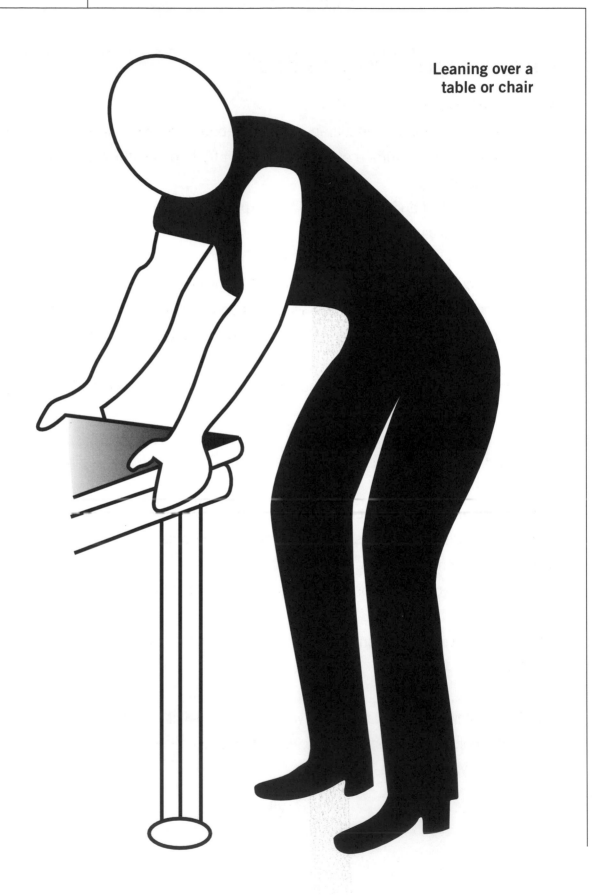

Leaning over a
table or chair

4. Exhale, with firm abdominal muscles.

5. Inhale again, feeling the expansion in your back muscles and the release of your abdominal muscles toward the floor.

6. Try singing a few easy passages of a song, letting your abdominal muscles drop toward the floor when you inhale between phrases.

7. Stand upright and try to get the same released feeling in your abdominal muscles when you inhale (refer to diagram on page 32).

■ Extending your breath

This exercise can help coordinate and energize your breath support. Practice Step One until you can make it through comfortably, then add on Step Two, then Step Three. Take care not to inhale too fast or raise your chest when you inhale. During the exhalation phase of each step, try to maintain the openness in your ribs for the entire count. When all three steps can be performed consecutively without stopping, increase the exhalation count to 25 or 30. Put your metronome on 80 beats per minute.

Step One

1. Inhale to a count of 10, taking in two tiny sips of air per metronome beat, expanding your lower abdominal muscles and ribs.

   Exhale for 20 beats using repeated short hisses, two hisses per metronome beat. After 20 counts, begin the next inhalation.

2. Inhale again to a count of 10, taking in two tiny sips of air per metronome beat.

   Exhale for 20 beats using one long, sustained hiss.

3. Inhale again to a count of 10, taking in two tiny sips of air per metronome beat.

Sing "ah" on a comfortable pitch for 20 beats. Try to maintain the feeling of openness in your ribs for the entire exhalation. (Continue without stopping to Step Two if you successfully complete this with no problem.)

Step Two

1. Inhale to a count to 10, taking in one long, continuous, slow breath.

   Exhale for 20 beats using repeated short hisses, two hisses per metronome beat.

2. Inhale again to a count of 10 in a slow, continuous sip.

   Exhale in a slow continuous hiss to a count of 20.

3. Inhale again to a count of 10 in a slow, continuous sip.

   Sing "ah" on a comfortable pitch for 20 beats. Try to maintain the feeling of openness in your ribs for the entire exhalation. (Continue without stopping to Step Three if you successfully complete the first two steps.)

Step Three

1. Inhale in a quick catch breath in one count.

   Exhale for 20 beats using repeated short hisses, two hisses per metronome beat.

2. Inhale in a quick catch breath in one count.

   Exhale for 20 beats in a continuous hiss.

3. Inhale in a quick catch breath in one count.

   Sing "ah" for 20 beats.

WHEN YOU BREATHE, your vocal cords open and allow air to pass through without resistance. During singing, your closed vocal cords resist the air being expelled, which causes them to vibrate in a fluttering motion. This initiates the process of vocal sound production, or phonation.

To demonstrate the action of your vocal cords during singing, vibrate your lips in a lip trill.[1] Begin by blowing air out and making a bubbling sound with your lips. Then add vocal sound to the lip trill. If your jaw is loose, your lips somewhat moist, and your breath flow constant, you will probably be able to trill your lips consistently. Now, think about the action of your vocal cords. If there is no intruding tension from surrounding muscles, your vocal cords are adequately lubricated, and breath flow is constant, you will probably be able to vocalize throughout your range.

The larynx

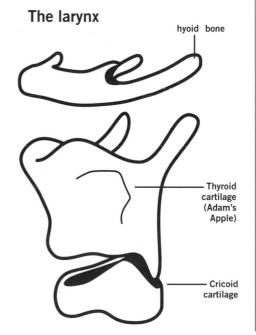

hyoid bone

Thyroid cartilage (Adam's Apple)

Cricoid cartilage

---

[1] *If you have tried repeatedly and cannot make this trilling sound, you can do this demonstration by placing your tongue between your lips and blowing.*

Your vocal cords are located in your larynx (voice box), which is comprised of intrinsic (internal), and extrinsic (external) muscles, cartilage, and bone. Your larynx is located at the top of your trachea (windpipe), a cartilaginous tube through which air passes to and from your lungs

The larynx is suspended in place in the neck by a complex series of muscles commonly referred to as strap muscles. These muscles are capable of influencing sound by elevating or lowering the larynx. Undue tensions in these muscles caused by poor vocal technique can adversely affect the quality of your vocal tone.

The system of nerves that controls all the muscles of the larynx is the most complex in the human body. Your brain controls the action of this complex system automatically. Thinking of speaking or singing coordinates all of the nerves and muscles in the larynx to respond accordingly. Then with adequate air pressure provided by the respiratory system, your vocal cords vibrate, producing sound.

ANATOMY

The outer structure of the larynx is comprised of three major parts: the hyoid bone, the thyroid cartilage, and the cricoid cartilage.

The *hyoid bone*, located at the top of the larynx, is the only actual bone. The protruding bump at the front of the throat (Adam's apple) is the front part of the *thyroid cartilage*. The thyroid cartilage is larger and more prominent in men than in women. The cricoid cartilage, at the bottom of the larynx, connects the voice box to the trachea.

On top of the larynx is a flap-like cartilage called the epiglottis, which prevents food and liquid from going down the trachea into the lungs.

The *arytenoid cartilages* are positioned on top of the back of the cricoid cartilage with a flexible joint that enables complex motion. The arytenoid cartilages open and close during breathing and phonation, and are involved in changing pitches.

The vocal cords are quite small. They stretch across an opening about the size of a nickel in men, a dime in women. This may help you understand more clearly the delicate nature of your instrument, as well as put its size in perspective when looking at illustrations or videos. Vocal cords can look deceptively large in print or on a television screen.

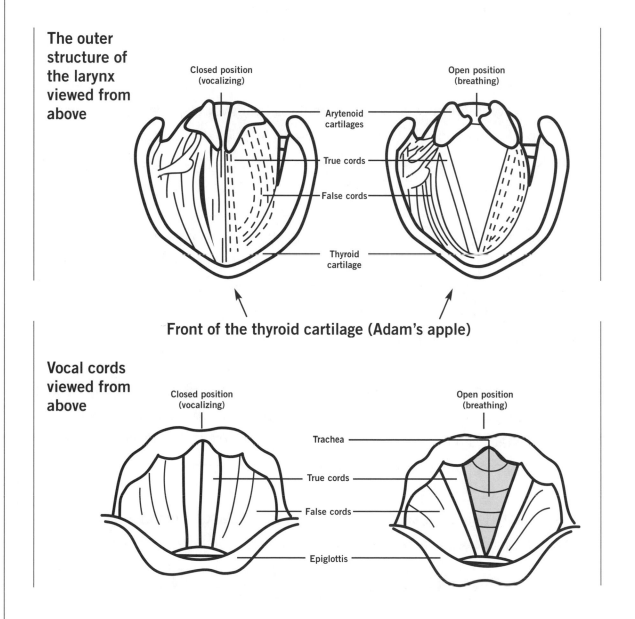

The outer structure of the larynx viewed from above

Closed position (vocalizing)

Open position (breathing)

Arytenoid cartilages

True cords

False cords

Thyroid cartilage

Front of the thyroid cartilage (Adam's apple)

Vocal cords viewed from above

Closed position (vocalizing)

Open position (breathing)

Trachea

True cords

False cords

Epiglottis

INITIATING TONE

There are several ways to initiate a tone, with style, dramatic interpretation, and lyrics all playing a role in how this is accomplished. If a phrase begins with a vowel, or the drama of a song calls for an explosive onset, a singer might begin with a glottal (hard) onset. Other expressions might begin with an aspirate (breathy) onset. But for most singing, the most efficient way to initiate tone is a coordinated (clean) onset.

A *glottal attack* is an explosive onset of tone produced when air pressure is built up under closed vocal cords and suddenly released with a popping sound. In spoken English, this commonly occurs in words that start with vowels. Speak the phrase, "I ate an apple," separating each word with a small, gentle pop. Now, contrast the glottal attack by connecting the end of each word to the beginning of the next, as well as elongating the vowel sounds. This should sound like, "I yea ta napple."

Generally speaking, excessive use of the glottal attack is tiring to your vocal cords and should be avoided unless it's needed for clarity in pronunciation. Singers who tend to use glottal attacks can soften them by adding a very slight H at the beginning of words that start with vowels, and as the attack becomes softer, begin to think the H sound without actually pronouncing it.

Aspirate or *breathy onsets* are characterized by an H sound preceding words that begin with vowels. A breathy attack sounds like "(h)I (h)ate (h)an (h)apple." Although this type of attack is not necessarily hard on your voice, it is not an efficient way to use your breath and can adversely affect the intelligibility of lyrics.

In a coordinated onset, a singer initiates tone in a balanced manner, starting with breath and voice together for a clean beginning without harshness or breathiness. The following exercise can help singers learn to coordinate the starting and stopping of breath and tone. Repeat each exercise moving up by half steps.

Balanced Onset Exercises

Example 3.1

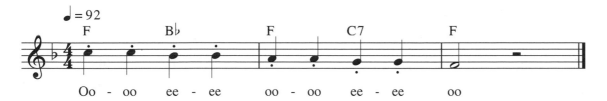

Oo - oo   ee - ee   oo - oo   ee - ee   oo

Example 3.2

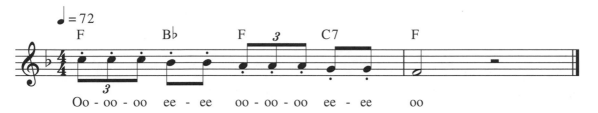

Oo - oo - oo   ee - ee   oo - oo - oo   ee - ee   oo

TIMBRE REFERS TO TONE quality in music. Acoustically, tone quality is comprised of two parts: the fundamental tone (the lowest possible frequency of a tone) and higher frequency harmonic overtones. The vibrator (vocal cords) creates the fundamental tone, and harmonic overtones are produced when this vibration sets air molecules in the resonators in motion. A resonant voice rings because harmonic overtones in the human resonators color and amplify the fundamental tone.

Tone quality can be described in terms of "tone colors," such as bright, dark, warm, clear, or brilliant. *Chiaroscuro* is an Italian word used to describe timbre that has both dark and bright characteristics. Because it has richness and brilliance, this kind of tone is thought of as well balanced.

The resonating system of the human voice contains a complex series of air-containing spaces in the head and neck called the *vocal tract*. The size, shape, and aperture of individual cavities affect tone quality, as does the texture of each resonator. Understanding how your resonating system works will help you broaden your range of vocal colors and sing more expressively. Awareness of how proper resonance feels and sounds will help your voice carry better and flow easier.

Profile of vocal tract

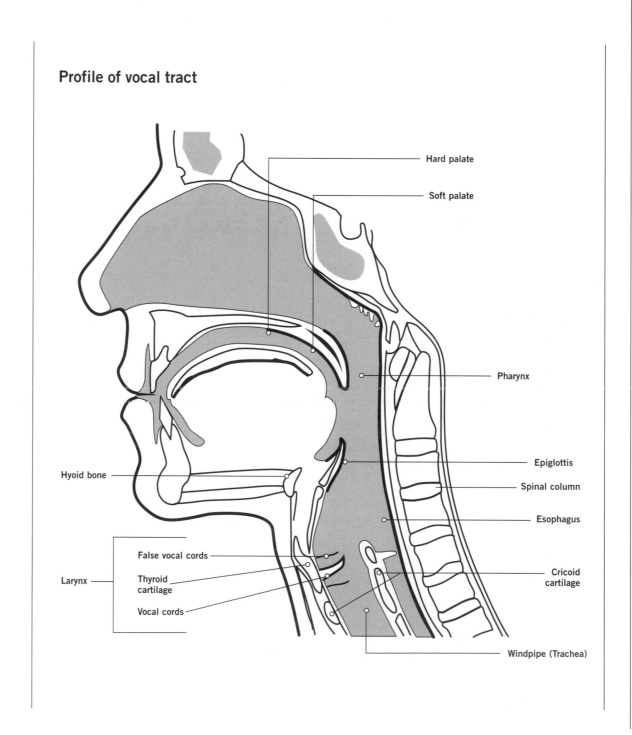

Hard palate

Soft palate

Pharynx

Epiglottis

Spinal column

Esophagus

Hyoid bone

False vocal cords

Larynx

Thyroid cartilage

Vocal cords

Cricoid cartilage

Windpipe (Trachea)

THE RESONATORS

Your vocal sound is a result of many factors, including familial, social, and regional influences, and also the size and shape of your larynx and vocal tract. Because every person's physical makeup and influences are different, your vocal sound is unique to you. The resonators that create your individual vocal sound are discussed below.

■ The pharynx and mouth

The *pharynx*, typically referred to as the "throat," consists of the area behind the nasal cavity (nasopharynx), mouth (oropharynx), and larynx (laryngopharynx). The *nasopharynx* is the passage from the back of your nasal cavity to your throat. The *oropharynx* is the back of your throat that you see when you open your mouth looking in a mirror, while the *laryngopharynx* is the gateway to the *esophagus*, the food tube leading to your stomach. The pharynx and the mouth are flexible and together form your largest resonating cavities. You can affect your sound quality by changing the size and shape of your mouth using your jaw, cheeks, lips, and tongue. The pharynx also affects tone because it is muscular and flexible.

■ The chest

The chest is not an efficient resonator because it contains many organs, and the composition of its tissues makes it absorb sound. The vibrations you feel when singing in a low range or at a high volume are thought to be vibrations that actually originate in the laryngopharynx.

■ The larynx

Just above the vocal cords are two small folds called the false vocal cords. In normal singing and speaking, the false vocal cords do not vibrate to make sound. There is a space between the true and false vocal cords called the ventricle, which is thought to be a small, but an important resonator.

■ The nasal cavity

The nasal cavity produces a very distinct feeling of vibration when your voice is freely produced. It is thought that the vibrations felt in the nasal cavity actually originate in the nasopharynx.

DISCOVERING YOUR RESONANCE

Resonant tone has carrying power and a clear, ringing sound. In popular music you will hear all kinds of vocal colors used, such as brightness, warmth, breathiness, or clarity. It is helpful to be able to sing with different tone colors at times in popular music. Learning to maximize your resonance will help you discover the bright tone colors of your instrument. Once you have the capability to sing with a clear tone, you can always choose to not use it. If you develop a clear, resonant tone first, then using an occasional breathy tone will be easy.

Remember that you do not hear yourself as others hear you. You hear your own voice vibrating inside your head, while others hear your voice conducted through the air. You can develop a resonant tone by increasing your awareness of how resonance feels, and an awareness of how it should sound by using a tape recorder.

■ Feeling your tone resonate

To feel your tone resonating, hum a moderately high note and notice the vibrations behind your eyes, cheeks, forehead, lips, and roof of your mouth (hard palate). These combined areas are sometimes referred to as your mask. You might also feel vibrations in your chest or other parts of your body, depending on the volume, pitch, and vowel sound you are singing.

If your voice is resonating well, it will feel comfortable. Any sensation of tickling in the throat, tightness, or pain indicates there is something wrong. Excess tension will interfere with tone and prevent it from resonating freely. Tone that does not resonate efficiently takes more effort to produce. This extra effort causes tension and makes singing laborious and tiring.

If your voice is resonating well, it will feel flexible. A free tone is more likely to resonate well. The tone should feel as if it could go up or down in pitch, be louder or softer, or change to a darker or brighter color. If you feel "stuck" on a note, or your throat feels closed, tension is probably interfering with good resonance.

If your voice is resonating well, it will feel "*buzzy,*" as sympathetic vibrations of your voice create a feeling of buzzing in your mask. The intensity of vibrations you feel may depend on the part of your range and the vowel you are singing. Voiced consonants such as Z, M, or N, or closed vowels such as ee and eh, are more likely to cause a distinct feeling of vibration in the lips, nose, and mask. Open vowels such as ah and oh may take more practice to discover the correct resonant feeling.

■ Hearing your tone resonate

The best way to hear that your voice is resonating well is to record yourself singing. If you record yourself singing, you may notice a bell-like "ping" or ringing quality in the sound of your voice on certain pitches or vowels. The brilliance of a resonant voice can augment tonal colors and can be used to convey intense emotions.

A resonant voice sounds as if it flows without tightness in the throat and neck muscles. Efficient use of resonance can help you increase volume without force. In other words, if your voice is resonating well, you do not have to use force to create volume.

A resonant voice sounds in tune. Your ability to match pitches accurately is affected by resonance. A tone that does not resonate well can lack overtones, making pitch sound flat.

■ Imagining

"Placing the tone" refers to a mental concept in which you imagine your tone resonating, usually in a more forward position in the mask. Try to avoid actively physical manipulating your voice when you are striving for better resonance; this may cause unnecessary tension that works against the resonance you are trying to increase.

Discovering your resonance means experimenting with imagery that sparks your understanding and leads you to progress. Try this imagery and see what works for you.

1. Imagine that the tone continually vibrates on your front teeth. This may help you to discover a way to create brilliant tone without using physical manipulation.

2. Mentally focus on the lyrics of your song to transmit emotional energy. If you are focusing on expressing the spirit of the song and become committed to that expression, you can clear emotional blocks. Emotional blocks can create physical tension that hinders resonant tone.

3. Imagine that you are smiling inside your mouth. The "inner smile" is an image commonly used to help singers raise their soft palates, which increases the open space in the pharynx where tone resonates.

The following exercises are intended to increase your awareness of resonance. Repeat the patterns moving up by half steps.

Resonance Exercise 1

Glide quickly from the mee to the yah sound to feel your tone vibrating in a forward position in your mouth. It will almost sound as if you are singing, "meow," like a cat.

Example 4.1

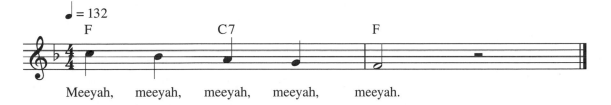

Meeyah,   meeyah,   meeyah,   meeyah,   meeyah.

Resonance Exercise 2

Sing the ng with the back of your tongue close to your soft palate, keeping your mouth open. Feel where the tone vibrates on the ng and open to the ah, imagining that your tone vibrates in the same place.

Example 4.2

(Hu)ng   ah

VOCAL REGISTER is a series of consecutive pitches that have a similar tone quality and are produced using the same muscular actions of the vocal mechanism. Some singers have naturally seamless voices with little or no obvious register changes, while others have extreme tone quality changes in each register.

Registers can be likened to gears in a car transmission, with first gear being your lowest register. As you sing an ascending scale you will probably reach a point where you have to shift gears or registers. This switching of gears in a voice is an adjustment in muscular action, which usually occurs automatically if it is not forced. As you shift registers, you may notice a distinct change in tone quality or that your transitions are not completely smooth even if you aren't forcing. Just as shifting gears smoothly in a manual transmission takes coordination and practice, changing registers smoothly in singing requires muscular coordination and practice.

Blending is a method of coordinating the muscle action used in singing in order to blur the distinction between different registers for seamless transitions. Blending typically works best from the top down; it is easier to extend the higher registers downward to make transitions smooth. Blending from the lower notes upward without introducing muscular tension requires extra care. Try these descending exercises to experiment with blending your registers.

Blending Exercises

In each exercise, move smoothly from note to note. Lighten and become softer as you descend. Repeat the patterns, moving up by half steps.

Example 5.1

Example 5.2

Example 5.3

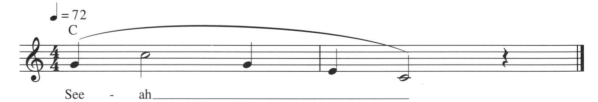

Example 5.4

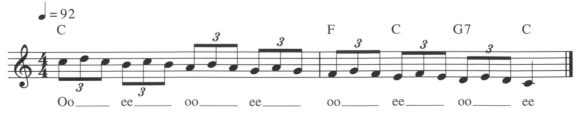

Singing too forcefully in your register transition areas can make shifting more difficult. When your voice is forced, has insufficient breath energy, or lacks coordinated muscle action, your vocal cords can make sudden, uncontrollable adjustments that produce a breaking or cracking sound. To keep your voice from breaking at register changes, it is important to balance energetic breath support with the relaxation of the muscles in your throat, neck, face, and shoulders. Watching yourself in a mirror can help you identify unnecessarily tight muscles.

Singers with well-coordinated voices do not have to think actively about shifting registers when performing. They treat their voices as a unified system, with transitions occurring as the result of practiced muscular coordination.

A coordinated voice also gives the singer the most choices in terms of tone color and sound for a more versatile, expressive instrument. The goal of understanding registers is not to separate them, but to blend them and balance your entire voice.

How many registers?

Because the vocal cords are hidden from view, there are many theories about how registers should be approached and taught. Some believe that a one-register vocal system should be taught in order to support the concept of unified voice with no separation. This theory also holds that discussion of registers tends to confuse students. Others believe that there are two registers, head (high) and chest (low) voice, that identify the distinct physical sensation of vibration that occurs when singing.

The three-register theory seems to be the most widely accepted explanation for how chest and head voice can be integrated and smoothly connected. The three primary registers are chest (low), middle (medium), and head (high) registers.

In addition to chest, middle, and head registers, there is one additional high register in men's voices and one in women's voices. Men's adjunct high register is called *falsetto*. Falsetto is a register above head voice. Some women have an upper register above head voice, commonly referred to as *flute voice*. These are the highest tones Mariah Carey demonstrates on some of her recordings (above high C in pitch and almost whistle-like in quality).

The words we use to describe vocal issues affect the way we approach them when singing. Sometimes the transitional area between registers is referred to as a *break*, implying the voice is broken, or that it breaks off or stops abruptly. Many others prefer to use the term *passaggio*, Italian for "*passage*," because it provides a very effective image for easing the transitions when doing registration work.

REGISTERS, RESONANCE AND RANGE

The terms *register*, *resonance*, and *range* are commonly confused. *Head register* refers to the series of lighter sounding notes produced in the upper range. *Head resonance* is the feeling of sympathetic vibrations in the front of the mouth, face, and head (see chapter 4). *Range* refers to the full scope of pitches, from lowest to highest, either in a song or in a singer's voice.

How large a range should a singer have? By exploring your voice to the fullest, including your head register, you should have at least two octaves of vocal range. Singers with a range of less than an octave probably have not fully explored all parts of their voice, or have transition problems indicative of a weak head register. Even if you do not like the sound of your head register, practice will strengthen and build your voice. It takes time and patience. Accessing your head voice widens your choice of repertoire and gives you more expressive tone colors (see range chart, chapter 9).

Develop your vocal range to its fullest capacity, but remember that expression, and color are more pleasant to most listeners than pyrotechnic displays of high and low notes. This kind of vocal "showing off" can become crass, unmusical, and draw attention away from the music. Riffing with improvised melodic embellishment is exciting, but only if you can do it with taste that adds beauty and expressiveness to the song.

YODELING

Exaggerating the register break when making the switch between chest and head voice is a vocal embellishment called *yodeling,* which has been long popular in country music and is now used in pop music as well. A singer who yodels makes quick, obvious switch from chest voice to head voice (e.g., listen to Leann Rimes' song "Blue" from the same-titled 1996 album).

Smooth register transitions, however, are used for most styles of music including a variety of popular music, jazz, and musical theater. If you have a natural seamless sound to your voice, learning to yodel is not for you. Instead, enjoy your voice's natural advantage of easy register transitions. Many singers find it difficult to both yodel and make smooth transitions. Your muscles can be trained to transition between registers either way, and it is difficult to undo smooth transitions.

Using head voice is commonly regarded as a healthy way to produce tone at higher pitches. Whether or not a singer naturally has obvious changes between registers varies from person to person. However, most singers will eventually need to learn how to transition into head voice without breaking.

Registration work is a long-term project that will require time and practice. Quick-fix solutions for smoothing register transitions are usually temporary and will not establish a reliable technique that holds up in performing situations.

TIPS FOR WORKING ON REGISTERS

1. Use your head voice even if the transition is not smooth. Transitions can be smoothed out with practice. Head voice is a large portion of most women's ranges; for men it is smaller, but equally as important. Accessing and strengthening your head voice makes more range and tone color available to you.

THE CONTEMPORARY SINGER

54

ELEMENTS OF VOCAL TECHNIQUE

2. Exercises with descending pitch patterns can be helpful in blurring the lines between registers. They also make it easier to pass into a lower register.

3. Exercising your head register can help improve the quality of your middle and lower voice by increasing flexibility, and creating a sense of fearlessness about high notes.

4. Sliding exercises can help induce laryngeal relaxation making register transitions easier.

5. High notes: use them or lose them. As with any physical activity, if you don't do it regularly, you will lose muscle tone. The same is true for singing in your upper register. Voices tend to settle lower and become heavier and sluggish if they are not exercised throughout the entire range.

6. Vocalize at least one whole step higher than you plan to sing in public. Psychologically, it produces a sense of empowerment and positive attitude to know you could sing a step higher if you had to. Physically, high notes need over tones to make them sound in tune and not forced or screamed. Your highest notes in performances will vibrate with overtones and sound more relaxed and in tune if you exercise your voice higher than you plan to sing in public.

BELTING

Belting is a singing style, with a sound dominated by the chest voice, which sounds loud, full, and emotional. Belting typically refers to extending the chest voice register higher in pitch beyond the point one might usually switch to head voice. This style of singing is used in musical theater, gospel, rock, blues, and r&b music. The term belting is also used in a generic sense to describe a forceful, energetic way of singing that both men and women use. "He was really belting out that song."

There are two main theories of belting. The first promotes mixing or blending chest resonance into the middle register. The second purports that the chest register is not mixed, but rather gradually stretched in size through exercises. In popular music, belting is considered to be a legitimate method of singing. Healthy belting can be achieved only if singers are careful to maintain their vocal health, avoid overuse, and use common sense when singing.

Why does belting require special attention?

1. Belting involves high, loud singing for extended periods of time.

2. There is a tendency for singers to add unnecessary pressure to the throat and the surrounding vocal mechanism because of the emotional nature of belted songs. Women especially have a tendency to add more weight to their middle voice than is natural, and must be cautioned against pushing.

3. Singers sometimes ignore basic common sense regarding health care and vocal hygiene. This can lead to serious vocal problems when coupled with strenuous singing and poor technique.

4. Many singers lack a sense of the delicate nature of the vocal mechanism and feel they are invulnerable to vocal problems.

Open-chest voice is similar to shouting and can be described as a manner of singing in which the low register is forced up as high as possible. It is potentially damaging to force open-chest voice up to reach high notes. Belting, on the other hand, involves approaching high notes with a singing quality, either by mixing the top notes or gradually extending the chest register. There are different methods for belting. However, do not listen to anyone who tells you to scream or shout in order to approach high pitches.

If you always blend a majority of head resonance throughout your middle register, maintain adequate breath support, and stay in good health, it is unlikely you will injure your vocal cords. But there are no absolute guarantees. Opera, just like popular music, can be sung with too much force. Singers who belt should confer with a teacher to help minimize tension and keep a close watch on vocal health.

GUIDELINES FOR BELTING

Skillful belting feels:

- easy in your throat
- as if there is very little air escaping
- as if you can move to other pitches easily
- resonant in your mask

Skillful belting sounds:

- full, but not strained or screamed
- clear and ringing
- as if the tone is easy to produce

A skilled belter looks:

- relaxed in the mouth, jaw, and throat
- connected to the emotion of the song
- energetic

Singers who can belt are in demand in contemporary music now more than ever. But if you damage your voice, your singing career may end long before you reach your prime. Singers need to exercise their entire vocal range, even if they never plan to sing in their head voice in public. Working in your head voice for a lighter touch on high notes can also provide a balance for belters that improves the quality of the primary performing register, the belt voice.

Belting is very exciting, emotional style of singing, but use caution. If you feel tightness or tickling in your throat when singing, you are probably pushing. While some singers can sing using an easy, unforced belt voice without straining, for others it seems impossible to develop a good sounding belt range without forcing, or sounding as if the tone is swallowed. Forcing your voice not only detracts from the emotion of the music, it can lead to vocal strain and serious vocal problems. *Singers who do not exhibit a healthy inclination for belting should explore other styles of singing.*

OOD DICTION MEANS that consonants are articulated, vowels and syllables are enunciated, and words are pronounced in a manner appropriate to the style of music being sung. Proper diction is important for conveying the mood, emotion, and story of a song in any language you use.

FORMAL AND INFORMAL DICTION

In many languages there are different styles of speaking. Language can be formal if one is addressing dignitaries or at a solemn event. Classical music written by English speaking composers, such as Aaron Copland or Benjamin Britten, is pronounced in a more formal, stylized manner. Formal pronunciation, including flipped Rs and big, exploded consonants, can help singers project without electronic amplification in a large room, even over an orchestra.

Contemporary popular music has an informal, colloquial pronunciation similar to spoken English. Informal pronunciation means there are no flipped Rs, and in some styles, singers can change rhythms to follow the natural accents in words and phrases in normal speech. Of course, the contemporary music singer still needs to communicate with an audience. Awareness of the balance between clarity and the subtleties of spoken pronunciation is essential.

MICROPHONES

Most popular singers use a microphone, which affects diction. Their challenge is to enunciate clearly, without sounding overly formal. Also, consonants can produce a popping sound if sung directly into the mic. To eliminate this, singers hold the microphone at an angle to the mouth, lightly articulating Ps and Ts over the top of the mic rather than directly into it (see chapter 10).

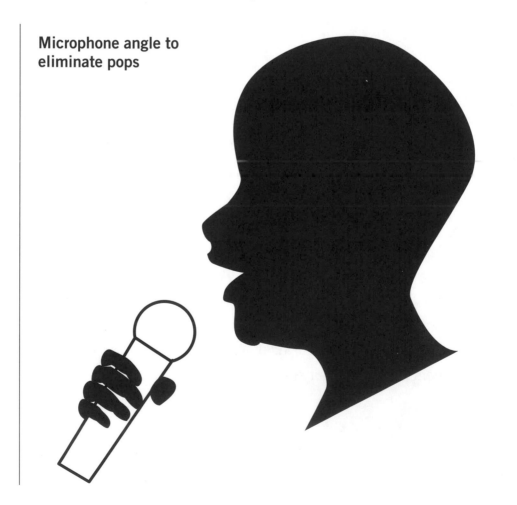

Microphone angle to eliminate pops

SINGING AND NON-SINGING DICTION

Singing with good diction involves a different set of skills than speaking with good diction. First, in singing, vowels are sustained longer than in speech. If a vowel is not clear, sustaining it over a long note makes it even harder to understand.

Second, not all syllables are accented equally. For lyrics to be intelligible, sung words must have the same weak and accented syllables as speech. Your challenge is to avoid emphasizing unaccented syllables, even if the weak syllable is stretched over a long note.

Finally, words are generally sung higher than they are spoken. The slight, natural adjustment to vowel sounds when singing high in your range is called *vowel modification*. This will occur naturally if the tone is resonating efficiently, there is adequate breath support, and the tongue, jaw, and throat are relaxed. Singers should mentally focus on the true vowel, as the mouth and back of the throat open to allow the tone to project freely without sounding pinched (see Vowel Modification below).

Vowels are bright, dark, or neutral in color. These colors occur naturally when vowels are properly pronounced.[2]

FIVE PRIMARY VOWELS

ah	aisle
ay	mate
ee	meet
oh	obey
oo	flute

These five primary vowels are the basis of all English vowels. When you vocalize on these vowels, you can hear your basic vocal sound. Singing scales, arpeggios, and other vocal exercises on primary vowels helps you hear your voice clearly and helps

---

[2] *See Appendix A for a diction guide containing examples of basic American English vowel sounds, including the five basic vowel sounds with variations, and some foreign language equivalents.*

you learn to feel consistent resonance over a wide range of notes. This helps you know when your voice needs increased focus or energy. In standard American English, the five primary vowels are found in related forms, some more open or more closed (ee and eh, oh and aw) and combined to make compound vowels (see below).

COMPOUND VOWELS (DIPHTHONGS AND TRIPHTHONGS)

A compound vowel includes more than one vowel sound in a single syllable, as in (my = mah + ee). They are also called diphthongs or triphthongs (double or triple vowels within a single syllable). For most styles of music, the first, or primary, vowel should be sustained on long notes, with the secondary vowel(s) quickly added at the end of the word. In country music, the secondary vowel of a diphthong may be sustained to give the pronunciation a bit of a twang. If a Southern drawl is not a part of your natural accent, purposely adding this twang usually sounds unnatural.

DIPHTHONGS

ear	*ih uh*
	(R is pronounced as an unaccented, slightly rounded uh)
day	*deh ee*
air	*eh uh*
sigh	*sah ee*
now	*na oo*
oar	*oh uh*
boy	*bo ee*
no	*no oo*

The final R in words such as ear, your, and sure is often just hinted at or eliminated in standard American English. This is true in the following triphthongs as well.

TRIPHTHONGS

fire   *fah ee uh*

our   *ah oo uh*

VOWEL MODIFICATIONS IN YOUR HIGH RANGE

When you sing in the top third of your high range you probably need to modify the vowel you are singing to sound relaxed. The following chart indicates how to modify four of the five primary vowels (ah does not need to be modified).

Vowel Modification

ee modifies by adding *ih* as in the word "hit"

ay modifies by adding *ih* (as above)

oo modifies by adding *ŏŏ* as in the word "put"

oh modifies by adding *aw* as in the word "saw"

THREE KINDS OF ATTACKS

Glottal, breathy, and coordinated attacks (see chapter 3) affect diction in different ways.

The harsh *glottal attack* begins tone with a burst of air pressure sounding like a pop. Because this is tiring to the vocal cords and can create excessive choppiness in musical phrases, it should be avoided by linking to the previous word whenever possible.

Try singing, "I am on an airplane," using a single repeated tone, separating each word so you feel small bursts of air at the vocal cords. Now link the words together to create a smooth flow without separation: "Ahee yeah maw na neh ruhplane." The second way of articulating the phrase feels smoother. Skillful word connection, the mark of natural-sounding diction, makes your singing flow. It helps you sing long, connected melodic lines, and helps make your lyrics intelligible. Occasionally, you might find it necessary to use a glottal separation in order to clarify meaning. A gentle glottal attack can be helpful, as in, "Lend me your (/) ear," which otherwise might sound like "Lend me your rear."

Another weak diction habit is a *breathy attack* at the beginning of words, when air escapes before the vocal cords vibrate. This results in an audible H at the beginning of words that start with vowels. If you sing, "I love you," on a single repeated pitch and allow a bit of air to escape before tone begins, it will sound like, "Hi love you." This usually happens unintentionally. You can work to eliminate the H by practicing onset exercises.

Onset Exercises

Practice these slowly, taking care to coordinate the beginning of a tone to avoid a glottal or breathy attack. Repeat the patterns moving up by half steps.

● *Example 6.1*

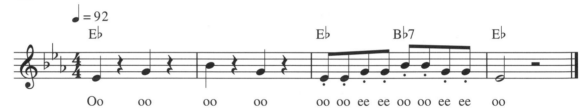

● *Example 6.2*

The third kind of onset is the coordinated attack, in which breath and voice start together. Not only does this make words beginning with vowels clean and easy to understand, it is not harsh on the vocal cords.

CONSONANTS

Consonants can be voiced or unvoiced. Voiced consonants are sounded using the vibrations of the vocal cords. Unvoiced consonants do not involve vocal cord vibrations (see examples below).

There are several voiced/unvoiced consonant pairs that use the same mouth position. To distinguish voiced and unvoiced consonants, lightly touch the front of your throat at your Adam's apple (larynx). You will feel vibration when you articulate a voiced consonant. Notice the identical positions of the mouth for each pair listed below.

Voiced consonant		**Unvoiced consonant**	
v	victory, lover	*f*	feeling, life
th	these, wither	*th*	with, thesis, thing
b	biscuit, robber	*p*	pencil, whimper
z	because, does, zoo	*s*	safe, house, whiskers
d	dog, riddle, load	*t*	toe, root, counter

PRONUNCIATION CHECKLIST

1. Rs in words such as free, river, and very are never flipped or trilled as they are in British English or Italian.

2. Rs found at the ends of words or preceding consonants are minimized or eliminated, and the vowel before them is elongated (e.g., charm, harm, word, earth, girl, heart, apart). Soften and *slightly round* the final R in words such as helper, lover, chair, more, and your.

3. Try to link final consonants to the beginning of the next word unless linking compromises the text's meaning. You can also avoid glottal attacks using skillful linking. Try saying, "Emily and Alan argued every other afternoon."

4. Be careful to not reverse R and L. L is articulated with the tip of the tongue lightly touching the back of the top front teeth (see page 66). When articulating the

American R, however, the tip of the tongue does not touch the teeth. Instead, the sides of the tongue rise to the teeth as in, "Cry rivers and streams." The American L lightly touches the back of the top front teeth as in, "William, will you lift the yel low lamp?"

5. Many words spelled with the unvoiced S are actually pronounced with a voiced Z, as in wings, charms, arms, and roses. Also, in the word "of," the F is pronounced as a voiced V as in "I think of you. Of course I do."

6. Elongate vowels and quickly articulate consonants at the end of words.

7. The TH consonant combination requires a quick movement of the tongue outward almost beyond the top teeth. It may feel as if you are almost going to stick out your tongue. TH can be voiced, as in "the," or unvoiced as in "with" and "thought." Try saying, "The thoughtless old thing withered away all these months."

8. On diphthongs that are sung over long tones, lengthen the first vowel and gently glide to the second vowel, without emphasizing or lengthening it.

> "Goodbye"   is sung *goodbaaa<u>ee</u>*
> "Yesterday"   is sung *yestuhrdaaa<u>ee</u>*

9. Any R that precedes a consonant within a word or in an adjoining word can be minimized and almost eliminated in singing.

> "Heart"   is sung *hahh-rt*
> "Charm"   is sung *chahh-rm*
> "Yesterday"   is sung *ye-stuhr-daa<u>ee</u>*
> "For me"   is sung *fohh-rme*
> "I never saw" is sung *ahee neh-vuhr saw*

10. An R preceding a rest or silence in songs can be slightly muted or completely
dropped.

"Scarborough Fair"

Try to incorporate informal pronunciation into this song, including sustaining vowels
and minimizing the Rs before consonants.

Example 6.3

Independent tongue movement exercise

Use this exercise to develop facile tongue movement for articulating Ls.

Place one finger on your chin and open your mouth (wide enough to insert two fingers). Extend your tongue to your top teeth, without moving your chin or closing your mouth, and lightly articulate "la, la, la, la, la, la, la, la" on a single pitch. Start slowly, making sure to let the tongue relax down to the bottom of your mouth after each articulated consonant. Go up in pitch by half steps, but stay in the middle of your range and sing lightly. Experiment with vowel sounds like lee or loo.

Example 6.4

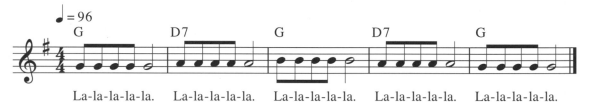

La-la-la-la-la.　　La-la-la-la-la.　　La-la-la-la-la.　　La-la-la-la-la.　　La-la-la-la-la.

Articulation Exercise

This exercise is helpful in developing skillful linked articulation of W, L, and Y. Repeat the pattern moving up by half steps.

Example 6.5

Will　you,　will　you,　will　you,　will　you　　Wil - liam?

ELEMENTS OF VOCAL TECHNIQUE

THE CONTEMPORARY SINGER

Humpty Dumpty Etude

This classic nursery rhyme text is a good articulation exercise. Repeat the pattern moving up by half steps.

 *Example 6.6*

Hump - ty Dump - ty sat on a wall, Hump - ty Dump - ty had a great fall.

All the king's hors-es and all the king's men could-n't put Hump-ty to-geth-er a-gain.

All the king's hors-es and all the king's men could-n't put Hump-ty to-geth-er a-gain.

- Practicing
- Maintaining Vocal Health
- Beyond the Basics
- Performing

2 MASTERING THE SKILLS

PART

PRACTICING HELPS you internalize and perfect techniques. You can use practice sessions to learn new tunes, strengthen your voice, extend your breath support, clarify diction, and fine-tune all aspects of your singing.

Practice sessions should be no more than one hour in length. Other instrumentalists, such as guitarists or pianists, seem to be able to practice for hours without problems. However, vocal cords can tire more easily, especially in young or inexperienced singers. Practicing for long periods of time at random, infrequent intervals can reinforce old bad habits and create new problems. Because of this, singers should practice four to six days a week, for thirty to sixty minutes at a time.

If you miss your practice sessions don't become discouraged and quit. Try to get back in the swing of things and pick up where you can. Improve and freshen your practice routine, to keep yourself from becoming bored. When you are training, it is best to be consistent, so don't become discouraged if you have setbacks. Move ahead with renewed commitment.

Plan to rehearse several times well in advance of a performance. This way you can avoid vocal burn out and become completely comfortable with your music before a performance. It will also give you a comfort level that helps you feel more prepared and less anxious about performances. Feeling well prepared goes a long way toward staving off stage fright and nervousness

PRODUCTIVE PRACTICE

■ Location

If you practice at home, it is important to work where you can relax and not be self-conscious. You need to feel free to make mistakes, and not hold back for fear of disturbing neighbors or family. This might mean scheduling your practice time when others are away. If there is no place at home to practice, inquire at a local school or house of worship to see if there is a room that you could use regularly. Some places charge a small fee to use the facility.

■ Keyboard

Wherever you practice, you will need some kind of keyboard for checking pitches.

■ Mirror

Sometimes singers shy away from the mirror because they are embarrassed to look at themselves, or become distracted and critical of their appearance. Try not to focus on your hair or face, but see your body, posture, and expression in a more detached way, as your instrument. We cannot see the inner workings of our instruments while we are practicing, but we can observe tension in the face, neck, and jaw, which indicates a problem. It is important to use the mirror to help correct awkward or tense looking movements. The muscles of your throat can become tight to compensate for a collapsed chest posture. Align your body in order to allow the muscles of your throat to function freely.

■ Tape Recorder

If you have ever heard your speaking voice on tape, you probably thought, "That's not how I sound!" This is because we hear our own voices through vibrations inside our heads while others hear our sound conducted through the air. To hear a more realistic (though imperfect) representation of your voice, use a cassette recorder in practice and at your voice lessons. You can learn from hearing your own singing as well as your teacher's comments. Try to listen objectively, and don't be distracted from your goals by being overly critical.

■ Metronome

A metronome will help you establish and maintain tempos when working on songs and keep you from rushing when practicing scales.

ESTABLISH A ROUTINE

An organized practice routine helps you achieve more because you stay mentally focused and waste less time. If you follow this routine daily, you will find that you look forward to your practice time and gain the benefits of daily vocal exercise.

PRACTICE ROUTINE

I.   Beginning Warm-up
   a. Physical Stretches (2–3 minutes)
   b. Warm-up Vocalizations (3–5 minutes)
II.   Vocal Technique (10–20 minutes)
III. Song Study (15–20 minutes)
IV. Cool Down (2–5 minutes)

I. BEGINNING WARM-UP

You probably wouldn't run a couple of miles before warming up and stretching. In the same way, it is advisable to warm up vocally before working on vocal technique or songs. The equivalent of stretching your legs before you run, vocal warm-ups increase the blood flow to your muscles and gradually release tension to prepare your body for activity. The few minutes of exercises recommended here are intended to prepare your voice for more activity and are generally not enough to completely warm up your instrument. For a more comprehensive warm-up, complete the beginning warm-up and the vocal technique segment of this recommended practice routine.

A. Physical stretches (2–3 minutes)

It is important to begin singing with physical freedom because we sing and perform with our entire bodies, which need to be prepared for activity.

NOTES ON WARM-UPS

1. If you feel pain, stop immediately.
2. Don't hold your breath while stretching.
3. A stretched muscle is in a weakened position, so don't stress it by forcing or bouncing.
4. Read the directions for each exercise thoroughly before attempting it.
5. Choose a few of the following stretches. Do only what feels right and good to you. Listen to your body and use common sense.
6. Modify stretches to suit your needs or physical limitations.

Gentle Head Rolls

Purpose: to stretch the strong muscles of the neck and to release tension.

Let your jaw hang loose and open throughout this stretch. Go at your own pace, circling your head in both directions. If you become dizzy, keep your eyes open.

1. Gently drop your head so your chin is close to your chest, and let the weight of your head stretch the strong muscles of your neck. Do not push your head down—let it hang.

2. Starting from this position, slowly roll your head around until your right ear is close to your right shoulder.

3. Continue rolling your head until you're looking upward, elongating your spine, letting your mouth and jaw hang open, and taking care to avoid dropping your head all the way back, which stresses your neck muscles.

4. Continue the head roll circle until your left ear is near your left shoulder, pausing to stretch your neck.

In a continuous, slow movement, roll your head through each of these positions: chin to chest, ear to shoulder, eyes upward, and ear to shoulder. If your feel tension in a particular spot, pause and let the weight of your head stretch it out before continuing. Complete two or three full rotations and then reverse direction.

Neck Tension Releaser

Purpose: to release tension in neck muscles that may inhibit free laryngeal function in singing.

Your neck muscles are complex and can be susceptible to injury if you force your head into any position. Be gentle with this exercise and use common sense.

1. Lean your right ear to your right shoulder and feel the weight of your head elongate the muscles on the side of your neck.

2. Reach your right arm over the top of your head and rest your right palm on your left ear, simply letting the weight of your arm increase the stretch in your neck muscles. *Do not pull your head.*

3. After you have stretched sufficiently (10–30 seconds), move your arm from your ear and just let your head hang in this position for a few seconds.

4. Next, support your head with your right hand, using it to bring it back to its upright position. To avoid stressing the stretched muscle, don't use your neck muscles alone to pull up your head. Repeat on your left side.

Shoulder Rolls

Purpose: to release tension in the upper back and shoulders.

Many people carry tension in their shoulders. This stretch will help release shoulder tension that might inhibit free vocal production.

Proceed at a slow, relaxed pace, moving from one position to the next without stopping. Focus on using a full range of motion. Remember to breathe normally.

1. Bring both shoulders up to your ears, then roll them back so your shoulder blades almost touch in back.

2. Bring them down to a relaxed position, and then forward to round your upper back.

3. Reverse directions and roll in a continuous motion.

Rib Stretch

Purpose: to stretch and develop awareness of the rib muscles, and improve fullness of breath.

Rib stretches help release tension and prepare your body for the extended breathing used in singing.

1. Stand with your feet about shoulder-width apart.

2. Reach up with your right arm, palm flat to the ceiling, and stretch it upward and over the top of your head a bit leaning to your left.

3. To increase this stretch, bend your right knee as you stretch your right arm up (your left leg should remain straight). You should feel a good stretch in your right-side rib muscles.

4. Repeat this stretch on your left side.

Full Roll-Down

Purpose: to increase awareness of abdominal and rib expansion during breathing and stretch your back, leg, and postural muscles to release tension.

When you are bent over at the waist, keep your knees loose (not locked) and only bend over as far as it feels comfortable. Do not force your palms to touch the floor.

1. Standing with feet hip-distance apart, slowly drop your chin to your chest. Continue to roll down, leading with your head, proceeding one vertebra at a time until you are bending over at the waist.

2. In this position, take a full breath that expands your belly and ribs (the belly expansion will make you rise from the floor slightly) then exhale. Check the back of your neck to make sure you are not lifting your head, but rather letting the top of your head drop to the floor.

3. Still in this rolled-down position, breathe normally as you slightly bend and straighten your knees a few times, feeling the stretch in the back of your legs.

4. Now shift your weight back slightly, so your hips are over your feet. With slightly bent knees, take one more breath, exhale, and slowly roll up one vertebra at a time, sensing your feet push into the floor. This action will help you use your legs to stand up again, instead of your newly stretched back muscles.

Chewing

Purpose: to induce relaxation in the facial muscles and free your jaw.

Stand or sit in a comfortable, relaxed position and imagine the sensation of your head floating effortlessly toward the ceiling.

1. Pretend you have two large pieces of bubble gum in your mouth, one on each side. Chew with exaggerated movements, with an open mouth, saying "mum-mum-mum."

2. Chew for a few seconds and rest. Do three or four repetitions of these exercises, then rest.

3. Sing or speak a line of text using the chewing action with vigorous movement of the lips, jaw, and cheeks. This exercise can be done in brief intervals throughout the day.[3]

Self-massage

Purpose: to release tension in your neck, facial muscles, and jaw.

You can target your own specific muscle tensions in this self-massage routine.

1. Standing or sitting comfortably and with your head level, massage the back and sides of your neck with the pads of your fingers in a gentle circular motion.

2. Work your fingers up the muscles in front of your ears and along the edge of your jaw.

3. Let your mouth drop open and massage in the soft spot directly under your chin with your thumbs.

4. Gently continue up the back of your neck to your head and place your fingers firmly on your scalp and move your entire scalp around. Imagine air entering between your skull and your scalp.

[3] Miller, R. The Structure of Singing: "Froeschel's chewing." (London, Schirmer Books Collier MacMillan Publishing, 1986), pp. 233–255.

5. End your massage by tracing long, firm strokes with your fingers along your eye brows, one at a time, from the inside corner to the outside corner.

B. Warm-up vocalizations (3–5 minutes)

Sighs, humming, sliding, and lip trills are great for getting the "cobwebs" out and increasing blood flow to your vocal cords. Vocal slides and other nontraditional vocalizations like the ones suggested here allow your voice to function freely and prepare your voice for more vigorous activity.

Slides

Purpose: to begin vocalization exercises; useful especially for singers who are very tense.

During this exercise, check your jaw and neck for tension, and release it as you go. Explore the middle range of your voice, which should flow freely and have a consistent tone quality. Stand in front of a mirror and begin to vocalize by sliding your voice up and down.

1. Start at or slightly above your speaking pitch and gently say, "hoo," letting your voice slide down in pitch in a slow, smooth descent. Imagine that you let the sound fall out of your body without trying to control or manipulate it.

2. Start at a slightly higher pitch and repeat.

3. Continue to a comfortably high level, and then proceed back down again.

Lip Trills

Purpose: to initiate tone production with a steady airflow and relaxed jaw.

Lip trills can be valuable at the start of a warm-up session partly because they sound silly and help free you from inhibitions about singing. Practice to develop evenness in the trilling of your lips and in your tone quality. Don't be discouraged if at first you cannot make your lips bubble consistently. Many singers find that they can vocalize on a lip trill easier than on any other syllable. If this is true for you, take inventory of your vocal production, posture, and the sensations in your throat and neck when trilling. Evaluate how your voice feels and how you might develop the same sense of freedom singing on vowel sounds.

1. First try to make the sound of a motorboat by loosely bubbling your lips without any pitch. Let your jaw hang as if you have no control over the muscles in your mouth and tongue. Start by blowing air over the lips and letting them vibrate.

2. When this becomes consistent, add pitch and slide freely through the middle part of your voice using a descending pattern.

3. If you have tried to make your lips trill without success, place your index fingers gently at each corner of your mouth. If this helps, vocalize lip trills with your fingers in this position. Take care not to slouch if you bring your hands to your mouth. If you still cannot do a lip trill, use the humming exercise instead.

Sliding Warm-up

Combine sliding, which helps induce laryngeal relaxation and lip trills, to maintain a consistent airflow, for an effective beginning warm up. Repeat the pattern moving up by half steps.

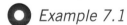 *Example 7.1*

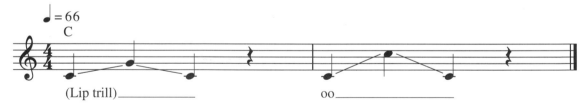

Humming

Purpose: to initiate tone production while increasing your awareness of forward resonance.

Light humming can be an ideal beginning vocalization because the buzzing sensation in your lips, mouth, and nose helps ensure correct natural tone placement.

1. Take a relaxed breath and lightly hum with your lips barely touching. The inside edges of your lips should buzz with vibrations.

2. As you continue to vocalize, first with descending slides, then with descending fifths pitched at the keyboard, try to feel the vibrations in your "mask."

Descending Hum/Slides

Example 7.2

II. VOCAL TECHNIQUE (10–20 MINUTES)

This part of practicing will complete your warming up and help you work out vocally. During technique work, identify what you need to improve in your singing (increasing range, agility, breath control, improving tone quality). Regular vocal technique work will help keep your voice in shape, ready for the demands of singing. The purpose of technical work is to develop new skills and reinforce muscle memory. In singing, we learn by intellectually understanding concepts and by training muscles. It is both an intellectual and a physical process.

If you have skipped the beginning warm-up, I recommend that you back up and complete 2–3 minutes of light vocalizing first. Though many singers start practice by vocalizing scales, preceding vocal technique work with a beginning warm-up that includes physical stretches and easy vocalizing on a descending slide pattern is much more sensible. If you are working on vocal flexibility and agility, for example, you may find that your voice feels sluggish and resistant to quick, light movements, if you have not warmed up. If you complete the recommended beginning warm up, you can work more directly toward free, agile production and avoid the frustration of trying to sing before your voice is agile and your body is relaxed.

Identify your goals for your vocal technique practice. Have a purpose for every exercise or scale you sing. You can adapt exercises you know to suit your needs or make up your own exercises. Repeat the patterns moving up by half steps.

Major/Minor Triplet for Flexibility

Example 7.3

Extended Five-note Pattern for Flexibility and Breath

Example 7.4

Two Fives and a Nine for Flexibility, Range, and Breath

Example 7.5

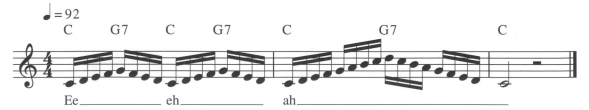

Legato Flexibility Exercise

Example 7.6

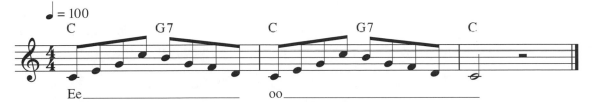

Long Tones for Vowel Equalization and Breath Extension

Example 7.7

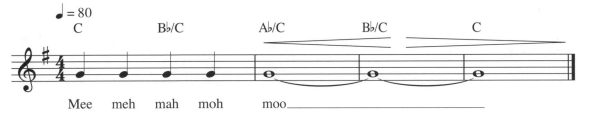

Octave Arpeggio for Range Extension and Flexibility

Example 7.8

III. SONG STUDY (15–20 MINUTES)

It takes more flexibility to sing words and melody together, so after you have warmed up and worked out, your voice should be ready for the more demanding task of singing songs. This part of your practice routine is set aside to perfect notes and rhythms, study lyrics, add stylistic interpretation and combine all these details into a technical and musical whole.

Seven steps to learning a new song

1. Rhythm

It is important to learn the notes and rhythms of your songs first. Take the time to read through the song rhythmically, and clap, or say "tah," on the written rhythms. Use a metronome to maintain a steady beat, and don't skip this step just because you already know the song from a recording. Recording artists take liberties with written notes and rhythms. You need to know the original written notes and rhythms to see what the composer intended—then you can make it your own interpretation. In some styles of music you can take a great deal of liberty with the rhythms, and in other styles it is not appropriate.

2. Melody

After learning the rhythms, plunk out the melody on a keyboard. Learn the shape of the tune and review any tricky intervals, without worrying about keeping a strict rhythm. How does the melody lie in your voice? You should be able to sing through the song without straining.

If the song feels too high or too low, experiment, singing it in different keys. Once you have decided on a key, you need written music or a lead sheet in that key. Do not ask an accompanist to transpose on sight during an audition or performance. Computer programs can transpose tunes and produce charts that are easy to read. *Band-in-a-Box*, for example, includes the accompaniment for many tunes and allows you to transpose them easily. Finale and Overture require more skill, but can produce better, more sophisticated charts.

Jazz standards and pop tunes are often transposed into a key that suits the singer's voice. Some musical theater pieces, such as songs by Cole Porter, have become jazz standards and also can be transposed. Opera arias, however, are usually performed in the key in which they were written. The same goes for classic musical theater repertoire (e.g., Oklahoma, Carousel, The King and I) and other music of this genre, which is generally intended for specific voice types.

3. Rhythm and melody without lyrics

Stand up, away from the piano or keyboard, and sing your song in rhythm on a favorable vowel sound, but without the lyrics. Make the melody flow from note to note, observe dynamic markings, and check tricky rhythms and intervals. Plan where you will breathe, and work out your phrasing by marking (') in your music. This basic groundwork will save you time in the long run. If you've planned your phrasing well, you won't get stuck having to breath in the middle of a word or run out of air at the end of phrases.

4. Add basic accompaniment

Sing the melody in rhythm on a favorable vowel with the accompaniment or basic chord changes—don't skip this step. Never take a song into an audition or performance situation without first working with the accompaniment. It can change your entire concept of the melody and throw you off balance in the pressure of a performance situation. If you are working from a lead sheet, there are many ways a song can be harmonized or played with a different rhythmic feel. It depends on your accompanist and how well you describe the rhythmic feel and tempo you want.

5. Study the lyrics

Look up words you don't understand, and look for underlying meaning in the text. Can you relate to it enough to give a good interpretation? You don't need to have lived the story of a song to sing it, but you should be able to empathize enough with the lyrics to give a meaningful interpretation. Think of yourself as an actor interpreting dramatic text for an audience.

6. Listen to recordings

Listen to recordings by other artists and make observations that help you define your concept of a song. Constantly imitating the sound of other singers is not vocally healthy. However, you can learn a great deal from recordings by observing the phrasing, tempo, rhythmic feel, and interpretation. How does the singer interpret the melody, rhythm, and harmony? Is the key of the song higher or lower than the key you are singing? Notice the singer's voice quality. Do you like it? Is the rhythmic feel or groove in the accompaniment what you imagined it would be like? How is it different from the printed music? What is the style the song (ballad, up-tempo, rock, jazz, Latin, etc.)? Answering these questions when you listen will help you fine-tune your concept of a song.

7. Interpret the song

Interpreting means adding your own personal expression to a song. It can be in the way you deliver the lyrics, or if stylistically appropriate, changes to the melody or rhythm. It also includes changes from specified dynamics, a different harmonization, addition or subtraction of vibrato in your voice, and experimenting with different vocal colors. Interpretation should come after you do the basic groundwork to learn a piece.

The best way to begin is to study the text. If you address the lyrics, the rest will come with practice and experience. Understand what you are singing and try to express the feelings and emotions of the lyrics to your audience. If you watch yourself in a mirror, you will see that subtle expression in your eyes can enhance your communication of a song. Singers can also learn to interpret by studying standard songs and transcribing the actual melodies sung by great singers. Studying what great singers do with a song can spark your own ideas.

IV. COOL DOWN (2–5 MINUTES)

It is as important to cool down vocally after practice as it is to cool down after a physical workout. The purpose is to bring your vocal cords back to a less active state so your speaking voice doesn't feel unstable. By easing the transition of your vocal mechanism from one activity to another, there is less shock to your voice. It is especially important to cool down if you are going out into cold weather, or if you have been singing high notes for a while.

To cool down, repeat the body and voice work of the beginning warm-up from the first part of your practice session. Are your shoulders or other parts of your body sore after practice? Stretch out physically, targeting the tension spots in your body. Lighter stretches can be combined with light humming or sighs, and you should also repeat some of the less intense technical exercises.

Mental practicing

Mental practicing is rehearsing without using your voice. It can be used when you are vocally tired, ill, or when you are healthy but are not mentally focused enough on the tasks at hand. Mental practice not only rests your voice, but also can bring mental alertness back to a practice session and be an effective method of problem solving. It can also be used to take a break from regular vocal practice to conserve your voice.

If you mentally practice a song with intensity, you can learn without actually singing. Athletes know that mental practicing can help solve problems as well as fine-tune performance. As we sit in an armchair mentally practicing, we actually produce muscle contractions (so small they cannot be felt) that are similar to the ones we produce when we perform. Try this guided imagery exercise to improve your mental focus.

Guided imagery exercise

Relax in a comfortable chair and notice your breathing. It should be deep and relaxed. Imagine yourself in the place where you usually practice or perform. Imagine how quiet and peaceful the surroundings are. Now imagine the details: the floor, the height of the ceiling, the smell of the room, the temperature, the sound and feel of the place. Mentally go to the place in this room where you sing. Notice how your muscles feel as you prepare to sing. Take inventory of your body position in this imagined space, and feel the anticipation of the performance. Imagine yourself taking a deep breath and beginning your song, singing through each phrase flawlessly. In your imagery, you will always breathe in the right spots and sing the way you want. Proceed through your performance phrase by phrase, not skipping, but singing the song all the way through in your mind. Sing through the performance feeling you have done your best.

Repeat this exercise, emphasizing your awareness of sound, and feel. It is important to see yourself succeed. Imagine your sense of pride in your accomplishment at the end of your mental practice. Sense the feel, sounds, and energy of a live audience. Imagine a positive audience reaction and your feeling of accomplishment.

Strong emotions are involved in the mental practice of correct vocal skills. During your guided imagery, if negative thoughts or mistakes creep into your thinking, stop the imagery, rewind it like a videotape in your mind, and proceed forward again in slow motion, frame by frame, seeing yourself execute the trouble spots easily, without any catches. Work through any negative thoughts and turn them into positive images.

Breathing for relaxation.
Breath is essential to making sound for singing. Concentrating on deep breathing before practice and performance will help relax your muscles and focus your mind. With a focused mind and relaxed body, you will be ready for singing. If you don't take the time to relax, you will find singing is much harder work. You may be fighting with residual tension and negative thoughts that prevent efficient muscle coordination.

Take a deep breath, imagining you fill up the bottom of your lungs first. Let your abdomen relax and ribs open. Breathe in through your nose and mouth. Your throat should feel relaxed. Your diaphragm will stretch downward and your abdomen should relax outward allowing your lungs to expand. Let your ribs relax and exhale all of your air. Draw your abdominal muscles in to completely empty your lungs. Remember to inhale and think of relaxation, exhale and release any tension. Repeat this exercise several times over the course of the day to release tension and invigorate your body and mind. This exercise is specifically for releasing tension and improving mental focus. It is similar to the breath action used in singing, but in relaxation exercises, your rib muscles don't resist the action of your diaphragm during exhalation.

IF SINGERS WERE to sing only when they feel completely healthy and stress free, many of us would never be able to make a living performing. That is why it is important to prevent problems by knowing yourself, your voice, your limits, and how to take care of yourself.

VOCAL HEALTH GUIDELINES

If singing hurts, don't sing.

As simple as this sounds many singers get caught up in the moment and don't listen to their bodies when they are tired and should rest vocally. Disregard for your own vocal health, combined with pressure from a music director or bandleader to rehearse songs repeatedly, can tire or strain your voice.

Pain in your larynx can be a sign of a problem. Singers experiencing pain, huskiness, or hoarseness and loss of high range should see a throat specialist (laryngologist) experienced in working with singers. Performing arts venues, music colleges, conservatories, and other singers can usually refer you to such a doctor. Often, general "ear, nose, and throat" doctors (otolaryngologists) do not have the specialized expertise in performing-arts medicine to optimally help vocalists.

Singers should watch for signs of vocal cord swelling, characterized by slight hoarseness or raspiness, a speaking voice that feels higher and huskier than normal, and a vocal quality that sounds coarse and less than clean. Frequently, there is a loss of high range, the upper passaggio (chapter 5) feels unstable, and you need more breath support than normal because of inefficient vocal cord vibrations due to swelling. A virus can cause this type of problem, as can overuse of your voice.

If you have what seems to be more than a simple cold, consult a qualified specialist for advice and treatment.

Sometimes, when singers suspect a problem beyond a cold, they delay going to a doctor because they don't want a serious vocal problem to be confirmed. Don't delay! Go to a laryngologist who works with singers. A skilled specialist will be more sensitive to your personal feelings about your singing. They can offer advice regarding any upcoming singing engagements.

Singing over a cold.

There are times when you can sing with a cold and times when you should absolutely rest your voice. When an occasional cold comes on, you can rely on breath support and body awareness to get through rehearsals and concerts without exacerbating fatigue or doing permanent damage.

You can usually sing over a cold if you have nasal congestion but no throat symptoms. You might have a bit of nasality to your tone, but in general, congestion can be sung over (or through). The first line of treatment for your singing voice is moisture. Drink a lot of water to keep your vocal tract mucus thin. Inhaling steam seems to be helpful for the same reason. Cough drops can keep you from coughing to the point of hoarseness, but the sugar and menthol in them can dry you out. Caffeine, alcohol, and smoking should be avoided because these are all drying to your voice and body. Herbal teas (caffeine-free) can be soothing and add moisture back to your system as well.

Sprays that numb throat pain are usually not recommended for singers. Throat pain indicates that you should not be singing. Singing while you are numbing your throat pain with sprays, aspirin, ibuprofen, acetaminophen, or anything else, can be a recipe for problems. Consult your doctor for advice about the use of any medication.

When you have a cold, focus on your breath support, and pay close attention to your voice for any signs of fatigue.

Choose your repertoire carefully, and avoid music that is unusually taxing in range or intensity.

If you need to change the key of a song, do it. It is not an artistic compromise to transpose pop songs into a comfortable range. Many contemporary singers are men with unusually high ranges, such as Stevie Wonder and Sting, or women with high belt voices, such as Whitney Houston and Celine Dion. Work to extend your range with scale patterns and exercises. But remember that some songs may not be right for your voice, no matter how much you like them.

Develop your own unique voice.

You should listen to great singers, study them, transcribe and sing great solos, listen to phrasing, and try to figure out what makes these singers unique. But remember that it is not vocally healthy to continually imitate others to the exclusion of developing your own voice. Voices often don't fully mature until singers are in their mid-twenties or even into their thirties, so be patient and don't force your voice.

Pay attention to the way you speak.

Over the course of a day, most of us speak far more than we sing, and as singers, we need to be aware of how we use our voices in speech. Beyond being a means of communication, your voice is a vital part of your personality and psyche, and you should treat it with care.

Singers can be gregarious, outgoing, and emotional people. Because your instrument produces both your speaking and singing voice, it follows that your singing can be negatively affected by poor speaking habits. To prevent this, employ touch-distance talking.[4] Only speak to those who are within an arm's length, or touching distance, away. This will help you control the urge to shout and prevent unnecessary strain on your voice.

In American culture, people tend to speak in lower pitched, less resonant voices, perhaps because they are associated with strength, seriousness, and intelligence. While this characterization of a low or husky voice especially affects the way women speak, many men also speak in a lower voice than is comfortable in order to command respect or convey a businesslike seriousness. This can be detrimental to singing, dragging down your voice and making your muscles work harder than necessary to produce sound.

Singers who habitually speak too low can adversely affect their tone production. The tendency to speak too low can make a singer timid about singing high notes. You can benefit from observing yourself and your speech habits for patterns that may be wearing to your voice.

Check where you tend to pitch your voice by speaking a phrase and finding its approximate pitch on the piano. Try to elongate a syllable and find a range where your speaking voice lies. If you speak much lower than you sing, imagine that you are elevating the focus of your speaking voice from chest resonance to more nasal resonance rather than raising your pitch. You may find that this results in a slight pitch change, but that it feels and sounds more natural than actually trying to speak at a higher pitch. Make sure you are phonating clearly. In addition, support your speaking voice as if you were singing, using a steady flow of breath. Avoid making unusual sounds.

Whispering is tiring to your vocal cords, so don't make the mistake of thinking it con-

4 Burk, K. *"Reducing Vocal Abuse: 'I've Got to Be Me.'" Language, Speech and Hearing Services in Schools, vol. 22* (Rockville, MD: American Speech-Language-Hearing Association), pp. 173–178.

serves your voice. You can actually strain your voice by whispering when you should be resting vocally.

Avoid prolonged talking around noise, dust and smoke.

Performing

Performing environments such as theaters, clubs, and bars are often dusty, smoky, and noisy—all things to be avoided by singers. While this is often out of your control, you can do some things to help prevent vocal burnout.

1. Avoid smoky areas.

Do your best to avoid smoke filled rooms and don't hang around smoky areas on your breaks.

2. Keep quiet on breaks.

Talking over background music and other noise makes you talk louder than normal and can lead to vocal strain.

3. Avoid alcohol and caffeine while performing.

Your vocal cords should be well lubricated for your voice to function best. Alcohol and caffeine dry your body and vocal mechanism, so it is best to avoid them when you are performing. Alcohol can also limit your judgment about how loud you are singing, impair your ability to sing in tune, and lead to unnecessary strain. Drinks containing alcohol and caffeine can also lead to reflux laryngitis (see page 96).

Travelling

In cars, airplanes, trains, and other vehicles, background noise forces you to speak louder than normal, which can be detrimental to your voice.

1. Airplanes

The air on planes is typically very dry and recycled throughout the plane—conditions that dehydrate the vocal mechanism and body. Responding to a talkative seatmate on a long flight can wear out your voice. Drinking alcohol can compound this wear and tear.

Before travelling, prepare your body by super-hydrating, drinking eight to ten glasses of water a day for several days beforehand.

2. Cars

It is one thing to sing along to the radio as you drive in a car, and quite another to practice there. Background noise makes you have to sing louder to hear yourself. Your posture is compromised by the car seat, so you are not as likely to support your voice adequately. It is more productive to practice in a place where you can really hear yourself and concentrate on what you are doing.

Avoid throat clearing.

Throat clearing is hard to avoid when you have a stubborn spot of thick mucus rattling around and you're trying to sing. But when you clear your throat, you not only remove the bothersome mucus, you can irritate the leading edges of your vocal cords. This makes your body produce more mucus to protect them. It becomes a circular problem, so coughing and throat clearing should be avoided. When practicing, try to sing the mucus off. If you must clear your throat, do it gently, and avoid habitual throat clearing.

If you have severe coughing spasms caused by bronchial irritation, see a doctor. You might benefit from medication that controls coughing, thereby minimizing irritation to your vocal cords. A doctor's treatment may also involve antibiotics, reflux treatment, or mucus-thinning medications, such as guaifenesin. Be aware that many over-the-counter decongestants have the tendency to dry out your vocal cords.

Develop good rehearsal habits.

Warming up before rehearsals will help you avoid straining your voice. During a long rehearsal, be sure to take breaks, drink plenty of water, use a well-positioned monitor that lets you hear yourself sing with an amplified band, and conserve your voice by marking (see page 102) when necessary. Do not schedule a long rehearsal the evening before or the day of a performance; this can take the freshness out of your voice.

Stay physically fit.

Your body is your instrument. Whatever you do to improve the health of your body and mind eventually shows up in your voice as increased vitality and energy. Singing is physically demanding, and maintaining good health is essential to career success. Physical exercise can help you stay physically and mentally alert, as well as have more energy.

Drink water.

Make sure to drink six to eight 8 oz. glasses of water per day. Drinking plenty of water can help your voice function better because your vocal cords must be well lubricated to vibrate without too much friction. The water you drink does not go immediately to your vocal cords. Although you feel the immediate relief of water in your throat, water goes to your stomach and passes through your entire system before hydrating your vocal cords. It takes time for this to happen, so be sure to drink water before you feel thirsty.

The two best ways to increase water intake are:

1. Carry a 16 oz. water bottle with you to sip on frequently, and refill it three or four times a day.

2. Drink two 8 oz. glasses of water before each meal and before you go to sleep.

You will have to urinate frequently when you begin to increase your water intake. However, once your body becomes accustomed to it, the urge to urinate often diminishes. Drinks with alcohol and caffeine may contain water but should not be counted toward your daily water intake because of their drying effect on your body.

Eat well-balanced meals.

Eat lightly and well in advance of a performance. Large amounts of food and liquid take up space in your body and may interfere with breath management. Milk products can cause excessive mucus production and should be avoided before singing, if it affects you adversely.

Reflux occurs when the contents of your stomach migrate back into the esophagus and throat causing inflammation. Singers sensitive to reflux react to a number of foods and drinks that can impact their vocal condition and singing by causing *reflux laryngitis*. Singers are particularly prone to reflux due to the high abdominal pressure that is used in breath support.

Dr. Steven Zeitels, director of the Division of Laryngology at the Massachusetts Eye and Ear Infirmary in Boston, notes that most individuals with laryngeal reflux do not have heartburn, as is commonly thought. Reflux increases the mucus production often associated with throat clearing, produces an ill-defined feeling of fullness in the throat, and can cause hoarseness, chronic coughing, and difficulty in swallowing. Consuming soda, citrus, spicy foods, caffeine, and alcohol can precipitate and aggravate reflux. Singers should consult with a laryngologist if this is suspected to be a problem.

Eating disorders such as bulimia and anorexia plague many people, especially women, and can ruin your voice and health. In a music career, appearance can be considered very important and singers sometimes take desperate measures to be thin. Laxative abuse, bingeing and purging, starving, and abusing weight-loss drugs can sap your vitality and strength. Repeated vomiting erodes the lining of your throat and mouth and irritates your throat. Because these urges can become uncontrollable and seriously affect your health, if you think you have an eating disorder, get professional help.

Get plenty of rest.
Everyone has different needs for sleep. Know how much sleep you need to function best and maintain a regular sleep schedule as much as you can. Rest your voice whenever possible. Schedule time to unwind during your day. This will help you have renewed energy when you need to sing. Don't wait until you burn out before you schedule down-time away from stressful activities.

If you sing with an amplified band, always use a microphone.

Singers who cannot hear themselves tend to compensate by over-singing. This is a sure way to wear out your voice. Use a microphone when singing with an amplified band. Position yourself so you can hear your voice from an amp or monitor.

Keep your microphone in a separate bag that's easy to locate in your living space. This will be your gig bag, ready to go at a moment's notice. All you have to do is grab it and go. In addition to your microphone, it should contain a mic cord and XLR-to-1/4 inch transformer for connecting to a guitar or keyboard amp. Find out about the sound system, monitor, and other equipment in the performance space so you will know what to bring.

Pay attention to common medications, including contraceptive pills.

Only a trained doctor or voice specialist can evaluate your need for medications. Ask your doctor about prescription and nonprescription medications and their effects on your voice. Antihistamines, aspirin, and other common medicines can affect your vocal health.

In some women, birth control pills affect the mass of the vocal cords, resulting in less flexibility and loss of high range. The levels of hormones in these drugs vary according to brand and dosage, as does their effect on individual women's voices. If you are already taking birth control pills and experience changes in your voice, consult your doctor. However, it is best to consult a laryngologist before beginning these medications.

Do not smoke.

Any singer who is serious about having a career in music should not smoke.

Smoking has long been known to cause emphysema and cancer of the mouth and vocal tract. It irritates vocal tract membranes and your vocal cords. When these membranes are dry and irritated from the chemicals in smoke, your body tries to compensate with secretions. These make you need to clear your throat, which causes further irritation.

Take care of yourself.

Many singers complain of being sick with various colds and illnesses all year long. But if they examine their daily voice use, practice habits, and vocal hygiene, the most basic elements of maintaining good health are being slighted or ignored.

TIPS FOR HEALTHY LIVING

- Eat a variety of healthful foods including whole grains, fruits, and vegetables.
- Get enough sleep at regular hours.
- Stick to a moderate exercise routine.
- Wash your hands with soap and warm water frequently.
- Drink six to eight 8 oz. glasses of water each day.

You only have one voice.

Some singers seem to be able to scream constantly and still sustain a successful career in rock music. Others can have a single incident of voice abuse and end up with vocal cord nodules. The limits of safe vocal use vary greatly from person to person. How you take care of yourself, and your overall health, vitality, and attitude, have a major affect on your singing.

Learn what it takes for your voice to be in peak shape and ready to sing. Learn what triggers stress for you; it can sap your energy and make you susceptible to illness. Know your tendencies for talking too much, drinking, and other excesses. Self-knowledge is one of the keys to maintaining your voice.

Some singers purposely try to add huskiness to their voices by screaming, smoking, or drinking because they see this sound as desirable for singing rock music. Such singers can end up with no voice at all. Tearing down your voice is not the way to add character. Instead, build it by learning how to sing and exploring all the possibilities of your instrument. Gain performance experience and interpret your songs with sincere emotion, rather than manipulating your voice in a way that can permanently damage and limit your vocal possibilities.

Voices and bodies that are abused eventually will show the wear and tear. Not everyone recovers or can continue singing once they develop problems.

Possible causes of nodules, polyps, and chronic laryngitis

Many factors can contribute to the development of vocal cord nodules, polyps, and chronic laryngitis. The list below is intended to show some of the possible causes and contributing factors to these serious vocal maladies.

NON-SINGING FACTORS

- Shouting, screaming, and yelling, including cheerleading.
- Poor speaking habits.
- Repeated straining as when lifting heavy objects.
- Talking over background noise at concerts and clubs, or in airplanes and cars.
- Making odd noises with your voice.
- Reflux.
- Smoking.
- Excessive coughing and habitual throat clearing.
- Excessive dryness of the vocal mechanism caused by your environment, lack of adequate hydration, medications, or over-consumption of alcohol and/or caffeine.

SINGING FACTORS

- Not warming up.
- Singing at the extremes of your range for long periods.

- Imitating other singers to the exclusion of developing your own voice.
- Singing without adequate amplification.
- Insufficient breath support.
- Pushing your voice when overtired or sick.
- Overusing your voice.

MARKING FOR VOICE CONSERVATION

Marking is a way of singing that helps you save your voice during rehearsals. To mark a melody, sing just the first few notes of a phrase, and mentally sing the other notes. Raise the lowest and lower the highest notes in your song by an octave (octave displacement) to avoid the extremes of your range. Men can use falsetto to approach high notes. All singing should be light when you are marking.

Marking saves your voice by minimizing its use. It should be used when you are not feeling well, or during rehearsals scheduled just before a performance. Too much practicing before a performance can take the freshness out of your voice. In theater music, singers mark during lighting and technical rehearsals, when it is not important for them to sing at full volume.

Singers often have strong emotions when performing and become carried away by the moment, losing self-control and singing full voice when they should be resting, so listen to your body.

The marking examples are intended to give singers an idea of how to conserve their voices. Notice how the examples eliminate high notes, condensing the melody to a smaller range and omitting every other phrase.

The altered melodies suggested for marking might be too low for tenors and high sopranos. Adjust markings and song keys to suit your voice. There are no set rules. Marking is successful if you benefit from rehearsal while conserving your voice.

TIPS FOR MARKING

What to do when marking

1. Warm up lightly first.
2. Maintain energetic breath support.
3. Sing only the first few words of a phrase, singing the rest mentally.
4. Displace notes at the high and low extremes of your range by an octave to avoid straining. Plan this in advance.
5. Men can sing high notes in falsetto when marking.
6. Always sing lightly when marking.

What to avoid when marking

1. Don't sing everything down an octave.
2. Don't whisper or withhold breath support.
3. Don't lose concentration.
4. Don't succumb to pressure from peers or directors and sing full voice against the advice of your doctor.
5. Don't mark all of the time. You should sing a concert, recital, or other long performance using your full voice several times over a period of several weeks or longer to make sure you are familiar with phrasing and breath pacing, and to help you develop stamina.

Marking example: "Shenandoah"

The melody of "Shenandoah" has a range of an octave and a fourth and marking reduces it to a sixth. Van Morrison's recording of "Shenandoah" from The Long Road Home is a pop version of this traditional song.

Example 8.1

"Shenandoah"

Example 8.2

American Folksong

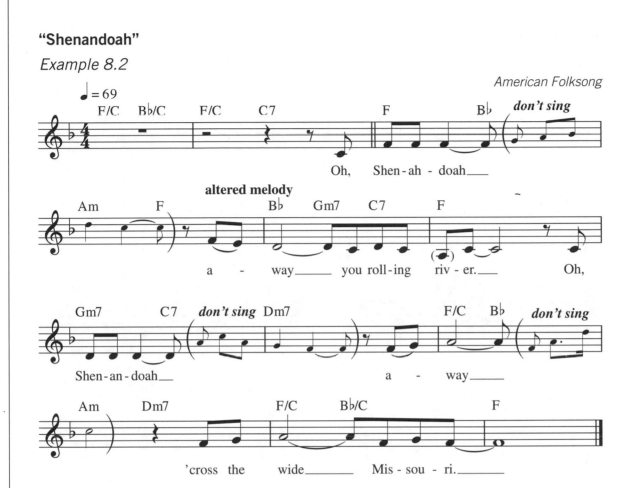

Marking example: "The Water is Wide"

"The Water is Wide" has a range of an octave while marking reduces it to a sixth. James Taylor's recording of "The Water is Wide" from New Moon Shine may be of interest to you. Pay special attention to the way he rhythmically embellishes this song. This recording is a good study in vocal embellishments in a pop style.

Example 8.3

English Folk Song

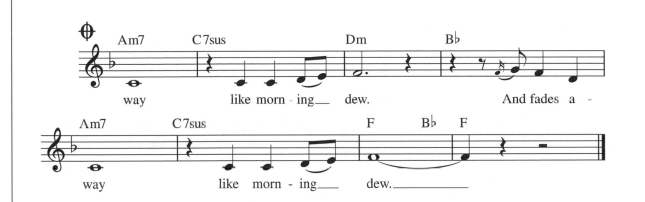

ELEMENTS OF VOCAL TECHNIQUE

THE CONTEMPORARY SINGER

"The Water is Wide"

Example 8.4

Learning to keep your voice healthy is an important part of your studies. If you take care of your instrument and follow common sense, you will stay healthy and sing well.

BREATH MANAGEMENT, resonant tone, registration, and articulation are interconnected parts of the overall process of singing. A great performance is an integration of these actions, where they occur almost simultaneously. Working to make them automatic should be the goal of aspiring singers.

ELEMENTS OF GOOD SINGING

1. Intake and management of air
2. Tone production
3. Articulation
4. Expression of ideas and emotions

Vibrato

Vibrato is the regular pulsing or oscillation of a single pitch produced by an alternating current of nerve impulses transmitted to the muscles of the larynx. Combined with efficient breath management and a feeling of relaxation in the neck, jaw, and tongue muscles, these nerve impulses allow vibrato to occur.

Certain variations in speed and width of vibrato are considered to be normal. Normal speeds range from six to eight pulses per second, with much faster oscillation (bleat or tremolo) caused by excessive tension or manipulation of the laryngeal muscles. Slower, wide oscillations of a semitone or more in pitch, result in a wobble that can be caused by a lack of adequate breath support or by pulsing the abdominal muscles. Irregular vibrato pulsation can be caused by fatigue, poor breath support, unnecessary pressure added to singing, or vocal cord injury.

Straight tone, tone without any vibrato, is used in many different styles of music. While vibrato can add dimension and color and is considered to be a sign of free vocal production, being able to add and subtract vibrato can be a great asset in singing popular music.

If you lack vibrato and want to develop it, be sure not to force it. Most singers will develop vibrato if the other aspects of their singing are functioning well. Pleasant vibrato is dependent upon the balance of energy and relaxation in the breath management process. It will develop when your voice is ready, sometimes before adolescence, sometimes after, and should not be forced.

If you are curious about what vibrato feels like, work on exercises that induce light, flexible movement. You can also try to experiment by saying with a dramatic flair at a moderately high pitch level, "I'm a ghost!" Draw out the word ghost and let your voice shake a bit, making a ghostly sound. Try to remember the feeling of letting your voice go and see if that relaxed feeling can be transferred to singing the same words on single pitch. You might also try a trill, a rapid alternation between two pitches a half-step apart. Repeat the following pattern moving up by half steps.

Example 9.1

Ah _____

Sustaining power

Being able to sustain a musical line gives you more interpretation and phrasing choic-es. In other words, you should be able to choose phrasing that fits the lyrics and shape of the musical line, rather than have it be dictated by lack of breath. Work to keep ener-gized until the end of a musical line, and don't let your energy flag on descending phrases. In the following exercise, repeat the pattern moving up by half steps.

Flexibility and Sustaining Exercise

Example 9.2

Ah _____

Dynamics

You can use volume to vary the intensity of a song and add to its interpretation. In order to be able to sing well at loud and soft levels, you must have good breath sup-port. Sing lightly in the middle of your range on the next exercise, repeating the pat-tern moving up by half steps.

112

Dynamic Flexibility and Control

Example 9.3

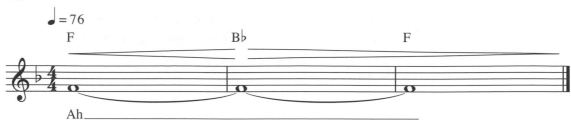

Intonation

The ability to sing in tune is very important. Pitch problems are often related to excessive tension and/or breath control problems. For example, a singer who is singing flat might be lacking adequate breath energy or they might be using too much air pressure and over-blowing. Sharp singing can be caused by too much muscular tension or pushing. Vowels that are not clear can also affect intonation. When the singing process is coordinated—with adequate breath, proper registration, clearly pronounced vowels, and good emotional energy—it is more likely to be in tune.

Agility

Agility is important in singing melodic embellishments in gospel and much other popular music. Think of performances by Aretha Franklin, Stevie Wonder, and other popular artists. Agility requires freedom from muscular tension and reliance on steady air pressure. Working on a variety of melodic patterns can help you develop the ability to articulate fast runs of notes. Repeat the patterns moving up by half steps in the following exercises.

Minor Pattern 1

Example 9.4

Minor Pattern 2

Example 9.5

Minor Pentatonic Pattern

Example 9.6

Pentatonic Triplets

Example 9.7a

Alternate Rhythm Pentatonic Triplets

Example 9.7b

Pentatonic Sixteenths

● *Example 9.8*

Descending Minor Pentatonic Pattern

● *Example 9.9a*

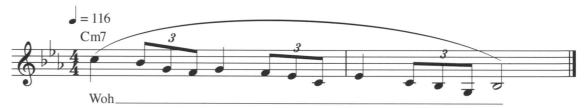

Ascending Minor Pentatonic Pattern

● *Example 9.9b*

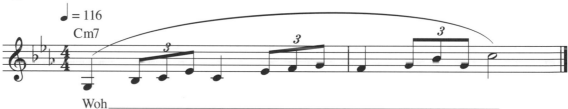

Voice Classification

Your voice can be classified according to several factors. These include your tone quality, where register transitions exist, your total range, and the part of your range that is most comfortable.

There are six basic voice types: soprano, mezzo-soprano, alto, tenor, baritone, and bass. Most young singers fit into one of these classifications, with the most prevalent voice types being soprano and baritone. It is important to note that the ranges in the voice classification chart are approximate and will vary depending on each individual's instrument and skill level.

The lowest female voice type is contralto, also referred to as "alto." The term "alto" is most commonly used in choral singing, describing the voice part below soprano and above tenor. In mixed choirs (men and women), lower-voiced women sing alto. In men's and boy's choirs, the alto part is sung by either adult male countertenors (the highest sub-classification for tenor voices) or by boys. Contralto is a voice classification used in classical singing to identify the lowest female voice type.

Belting is not a voice type, but rather a style of singing for women whose primary performing register is chest voice. Belters are often classified as either sopranos or mezzo-sopranos, but they sing in a chest-voice dominant style. The belter's range is included on the voice classification chart for your information.

Voice classifications

Bass

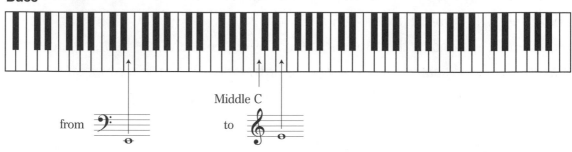

Baritone

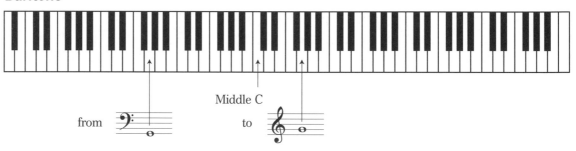

Tenor

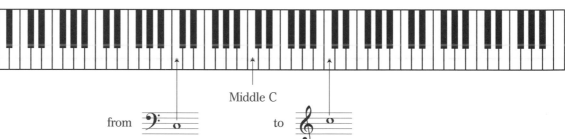

Alto (Contralto)

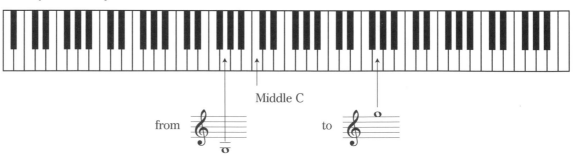

Mezzo - Soprano

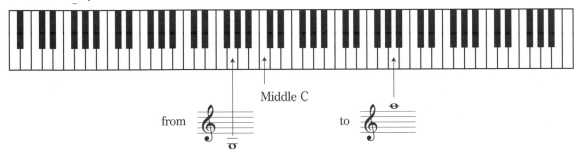

Middle C

from   to

Soprano

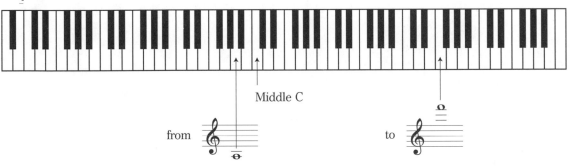

Middle C

from   to

Belter Range

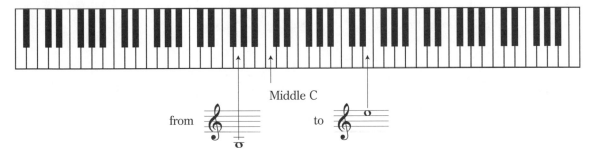

Middle C

from   to

ow to develop performing skills

It is valuable to practice performing for friends, family, and classmates to get a sense of how to direct your energy. You will gain experience and develop self-confidence by performing for an audience.

The size of your performing venue and the style of music you sing will dictate the size of your gestures and expressions. In a large auditorium, you can make larger gestures, move more, and fill the room with your energy. In a smaller venue, you can tone down the activity of your body, hands, and face, but keep the emotional energy level high.

In terms of style and depending on the venue, musical theater songs often require the performer to sing in character to portray the song. Jazz songs can have dramatic content too, but the style requires more subtle interpretation. You can learn a lot about performance technique by watching performers in a variety of styles. This will help you get a sense of what will work for you.

Understand a song's lyrics and find a way to empathize with its message or story. Tell the story. If you have trouble connecting with an audience, the following tips can help you begin to turn your focus away from self-consciousness and toward your music.

FOCUSING YOUR PERFORMANCE

Eyes

Many singers find it easier to sing for a large, anonymous audience in a concert hall than for a small audience in an intimate space. Discomfort seems to increase when singers are confronted with smaller performance space, and closer, watchful eyes. Although you might want to close your eyes to aid concentration and ward off self-consciousness, this can keep you from communicating with your audience. Try to keep your eyes open and focus outward to relate your song.

In a small space, try looking at your audience's foreheads or earlobes to give the sense you are directly looking at them without having to make eye contact. Don't look too high toward the back of the room. This may help you communicate your song.

Another technique is to find three focal points in the room. Looking straight out from center stage, envision 12 o'clock as directly behind the audience. For the other two

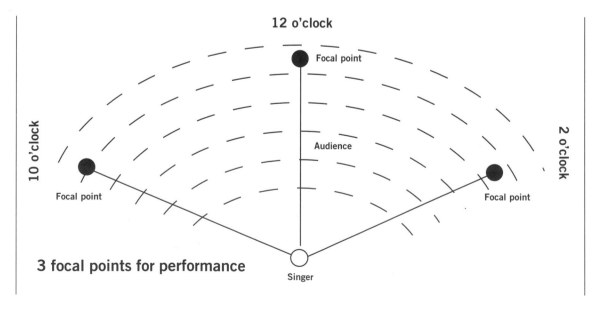

3 focal points for performance

points, look toward 10 o'clock to your left and 2 o'clock to your right. Avoid constantly scanning the room while performing. Instead, shift your focal point based on the songs' lyrics, or at changes in the form of the tune.

Hands

Gesture with your hands if you feel the urge. Some singers suddenly freeze and drop hand movement mid-stream when they become self-conscious. Try to follow through if you begin a gesture. Notice how you use your hands when you are speaking. Hand movement should be a natural offshoot of expressing yourself. Videotaping yourself will help you see what looks right for you.

Microphone technique is important in helping you get your best sound. It also gives you something to occupy your hands; however, don't fidget with the mic cord or wave it around in front of your mouth. Poor microphone technique detracts from your performance.

If you are accompanying yourself, don't let your playing detract from your singing. You should probably be more skilled on your accompanying instrument than you are as a singer. After all, you have to do two things at once, so you should be very proficient at both. Self-accompanied singers should be aware of posture to minimize tension and to maximize breath capacity.

CLASSICAL TO POP TRANSITION

Here are some ways classically-trained singers can get a better pop sound in their singing.

Vibrato

Singers often use less vibrato in popular music than in classical music, although some gospel and blues singers use a lot. Listen to singers in the style of popular music you like best, noting how much, how little, and when vibrato is used. Be aware of your vibrato and experiment with a straighter tone.

Diction

Modify formal diction to a more informal style of pronunciation. Depending on the style of popular music, you may need to pronounce lyrics more like everyday spoken language, in some cases even changing rhythms and phrasing to follow the natural accents in words.

Tone quality

Individuality is prized in popular music. The best tone for singing pop music is your natural voice enhanced by the skillful use of breath support and good diction. Be sure not to artificially darken your tone and that there is enough resonance in your tone to yield a balanced sound.

Volume

Most popular singers use microphones to amplify their voices to achieve balance with amplified instruments. Microphones make it possible for a singer with a small voice to be heard clearly. They have also made it possible to establish a more intimate style of singing ballads. Classical singers may need to scale back their volume to achieve a pop sound. Gain experience using a microphone so you can feel comfortable.

MICROPHONE TECHNIQUE

Microphones can be a great asset to singers. They also create fear in those who do not know how to use them, so some singers choose to avoid microphones and sound reinforcement altogether.

In contemporary music, however, you need to learn how to get a good sound with a microphone. How to achieve this can vary with performing venues, and it is an ongoing challenge for singers. Amplified sound is a part of many styles, and singers of popular music need to own a microphone and know how to set up to use it to their best advantage. It is also important for your vocal health when trying to project over an amplified band or even with a piano in a club. If you can't hear yourself due to a lack of amplification, you can over-sing and strain your voice.

A microphone can make you sound fuller and louder than you do naturally; however, it is not a substitute for vocal technique. By learning to sing you improve tone quality, flexibility, projection, expression, and more. Mics pick up and transmit everything, both good sound and bad. It is important to develop your voice to its fullest capacity so that the microphone serves as a tool, not a crutch.

In choosing which mic to purchase, consider your performing venue. Will you be singing in clubs where there is already a sound system you can plug in to? Are you joining a band that owns a sound system? Are you going to be in a recording studio where everything is set up? In all of these venues, you will need these basics.

- low-impedance microphone
- mic cable
- XLR-to-1/4 inch transformer

More elaborate set ups might also include:

- small amplifier with a 10" to 12" speaker
- digital reverb unit

Consider a basic model like the Shure SM58 for your first microphone purchase. It costs around $100 and will work in all kinds of live performance situations. Recording studios will have microphones for you to use, but you should have your own mic for performing anywhere else.

You will also need a heavy-duty microphone cable to connect your mic into the sound system. Most soundboards are set up to accept low-impedance mics (these have three small prongs in the mic base), but you should also purchase an XLR-to-1/4 inch transformer. This adapter makes it possible to connect a low-impedance mic into a guitar or keyboard amplifier that has a 1/4 inch plug.

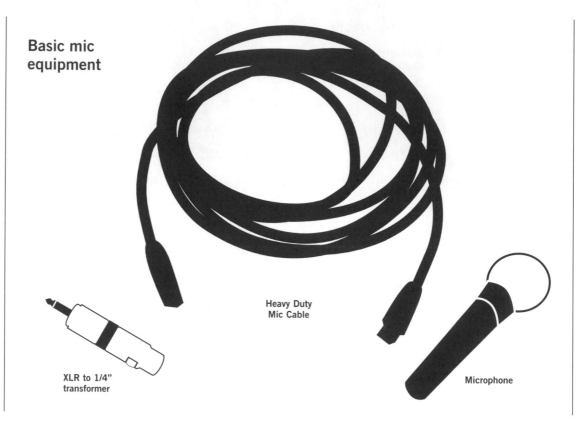

Basic mic equipment

XLR to 1/4"
transformer

Heavy Duty
Mic Cable

Microphone

After hooking up your microphone, position yourself so you can hear. Depending on the performance situation, you will probably need to hear your voice from a monitor, which is often angled up from the floor and pointed toward you. It will help you to know how loud you are singing, and keep you from blowing out your voice.

A problem with amplification is feedback, that all-too-familiar screeching sound you get sometimes when using a mic. Feedback results when the pickup range of your mic intersects with the amplified sound pattern of your speaker. To avoid this, don't point your mic at the speaker, and watch out for the feedback zone.

In rooms with a lot of hard surfaces such as concrete walls, linoleum, or hardwood floors, your voice may seem to bounce around the room, or reverberate, making it easy to hear yourself. This kind of a room is described as "live." Singers generally prefer them because it is easy to project and hear. You sound good singing in the shower because it is a good reverberation chamber. Rooms with upholstered furniture, carpet, and heavy curtains, on the other hand, absorb sound. If you sing in a "dead" room like this you might feel your voice is being swallowed up, that you can't hear yourself, or that your voice has no carrying power.

You can also add effects to your sound electronically. The most basic effect is reverb, which makes an amplifier emulate the sound of a live room, making your voice sound fuller. This can keep you from pushing too hard for volume. The next best thing to singing in a live room is adding reverb from an amp or digital reverb unit. Too much reverb can make you sound like you're lost in a cave, so use it with discretion.

Most performing venues with a sound system will be able to add reverb to your vocal sound. If you want your own amp, a small one with a 10" to 12" speaker and built-in reverb can be purchased for around $250. There are many brands and prices, and a small practice amp can be useful for singers who regularly work with a rhythm section or band. You should be hooked into the main sound system with the band and also into your own amp so you can hear yourself. Even better than reverb built into your amp is connecting to an external digital reverb unit. It offers more control over the amount and quality of the sound you want and costs around $100.

ADVICE FROM AN EXPERT

DONNA MCELROY, associate professor in the Voice Department at Berklee College of Music in Boston, is a professional singer with years of performing experience covering many styles of music. She offers the following advice:

How loud should you sing when using a microphone?

For ballads and sacred songs, treat the mic as if it were the ear of a dear loved one; a wonderful old person who'd given you some great advice. This evokes a different sound than if you were talking to a kid who's acting up in the supermarket. You would still be the same relative distance from the mic, but the intensity of volume and breath propulsion would be radically different, ranging from soft and very tender to the big voice of an angry or desperate cry. The well-adjusted, well-chosen mic will pick up the inflection or the intensity that is projected from the singer.

Can microphones enhance a weak voice?

Mics have been mischaracterized as a tool to provide body and presence for the vocalist. In my opinion, the mic should not be used as a crutch to provide these qualities. They should already be there and the mic should augment what the singer is already doing with his or her instrument. The projection a voice teacher drills into a singer's technique should be at its peak every time they sing so that sound personnel can get used to how this voice should be EQ'd.

How close and at what angle should a mic be held?

It depends on the mic, the song, the stage volume, the brand of mic, how close you want the mic to be—so many factors contribute to the efficiency of mic use. This takes time, so there should never be any one answer to this question.

Flexibility and the ability to give maximum options to sound people is the key. It never hurts to ask these questions of the sound personnel testing your mic levels. The sound person might even change to a different mic, or set up two or three different brands of mics. If you get the sound you like, ask the sound person for the brand and model number of the mic.

In your opinion, what basic equipment should a singer have?

Until you have a record to sell or a known sound to re-emulate over and over, the singer only needs to have a mic, a cord, and an XLR adapter for plugging into the guitar or keyboard amp. It is nice to bring your own amp, but lots of times, there's an amp available at the gig. Before the gig, ask what you're expected to have. If you're just going to sit in, bring a mic-cord-XLR package.

PERFORMANCE ANXIETY

Many singers suffer nervousness or fear when performing. This anxiety manifests itself in many ways, including sweaty palms, dry mouth, too much saliva, and shaky knees. The interference and self-doubt that performance anxiety creates is very real for many singers. Here are some ideas to help you combat debilitating nervousness or even the lesser symptoms that keep you from singing your best.

Be prepared

Adequate preparation can go a long way toward offsetting the nervousness singers experience. If you know that you have not spent enough time studying the lyrics or memorizing the song, you can sabotage your own performance. It can take several weeks or months to get a song into your voice, mind, and body to the point you do not have to constantly focus on the next line or phrase. To reduce self-consciousness and self-doubt, allow enough time to thoroughly absorb the music before you perform.

Avoid using alcohol to relax

Alcohol can help you lose your inhibitions, but it is much better to deal with your nervousness in a proactive way. Address your anxieties. Many vocalists find they are less nervous after they gain experience performing. Some need help from professionals who work with musicians in performance anxiety workshops. If you can't perform without alcohol, you should seek professional help.

Mental practice

Combat performance anxiety by eliminating negative thinking about your performance. Singers can mentally practice an entire performance to develop a sense of assurance, knowing what is going to happen and setting events moving in a positive direction. This can help control or eliminate negative thinking in performance. If you mentally practice one time for every three times you actually sing through your concert, you will be able to conserve vocal energy, correct errors, and sing with less anxiety (see Visualization in chapter 7).

Build a base of positive performing experiences

Plan to perform several times, over a period of months, for a friendly audience, with well-prepared music in a comfortable setting. Give yourself the opportunity to feel positive about your performances. If you do this repeatedly, and have a good experience, you may find that your confidence grows and you will be ready to branch out to other venues.

Breathing for relaxation

Since our voices are wind instruments, we need air to make them sound. The act of breathing also helps us get more oxygen to our brains and muscles to induce relaxation. Nervousness can make breathing shallow, and shallow breaths can create panic. This leads to more high breathing and the problem becomes circular.

Taking a few deep, relaxing breaths in preparation for performing can help. Don't hold your breath during instrumental introductions or during interludes. Include deep, relaxing breaths during your mental practice as well.

Sounding "good"

Sometimes the overwhelming desire to sound good can get in a singer's way. This focus pulls our thinking inward too much, making it difficult or even impossible to be expressive. Wanting to sound good can make you start to focus on every little muscle movement or note. This kind of micromanaging is the death of spontaneous expression and lyrical singing. The bigger picture is lost to inward thinking and selfish control. If positive thinking is balanced with dedicated practice, you can relinquish conscious control and perform freely. As jazz pianist Kenny Werner writes in his book *Effortless Mastery*, "Technical mastery creates freedom."

It is very important to practice regularly with good focus. Stick with the task at hand, perhaps over a series of weeks or longer, until you have mastered it. It may take longer than one school semester. Vary your practice routine and find different ways to approach your challenges. Give yourself time to learn and grow.

Think when you practice. Then allow yourself time to turn off your mind and just sing. Repetition will teach your muscles to remember how to do the things you've been practicing. Then let go.

THERE ARE MANY different kinds of auditions, each with its own requirements. This text cannot address them all, but there are some universal guidelines that can help you to have a successful experience.

AUDITION GUIDELINES

Follow instructions

If the audition literature lists specific song requirements, be sure your material meets them. Many auditions require you to choose at least two songs in contrasting tempos, but always check. If there are no specific requirements, perform songs that show what you do best and display your uniqueness as a singer. This will set you apart from the crowd and may give you the edge you need to succeed.

Prepare

Auditions are not the time to try out new, untested material. Give yourself plenty of time to do a mock audition to test your material out a few times. Ask a friend to videotape you so you can self-correct before the actual audition. The more you know about what to expect, the more likely you will feel in control and not surprised, nervous, or flustered.

Memorize

Make sure that everything you plan to sing for an audition is memorized. In this regard, there are no exceptions. You must perform from memory.

Warm up

Always warm up before an audition. Your job is to present yourself at your best. Your best voice reveals itself after you have gotten the morning cobwebs out and your vocal engine is running smoothly. For an early morning audition, get a good night's sleep, wake up early, and warm up enough that you can sing freely right from the start of your audition. Warming up takes time. If you have an audition at 8 a.m., you should be up and humming gently or singing lightly by 6 a.m.

If you cannot warm up before you arrive because of travel time, or if you are unfamiliar with the audition site, call in advance and ask where you can warm up before your audition.

Arrive early

Arrive early to give yourself time to find the audition room, get settled, and focus on your music. A late arrival to an audition is very poor form. Always plan extra time to get where you need to be.

Accompaniment

Don't assume that there will be an accompanist provided. Find out if you should bring an accompaniment tape or CD, and bring a portable player in case the audition room doesn't have one.

If an accompanist is provided, be courteous to them—it reflects badly on you if you treat them poorly. Tape separate pages of music together. This makes it easier for the accompanist to read and keeps them from getting out of order or falling off the piano.

Be prepared to count off the tempo for the accompanist. Practice this. If when you begin, something sounds different than you expect, don't look accusingly at the pianist. Keep going unless everything is falling apart. If it is, stop, take a deep breath, count off the tempo, and begin again. Lead confidently and the accompanist will follow, even if you are wrong. If something doesn't go as expected, count it as a learning experience. Take responsibility for everything that happens in an audition.

Make sure your music is in the right key for you. Although some audition pianists are capable of transposing on sight, there is always the chance that they will make an error and compromise your audition. Your job is to present yourself at your best. Don't take the chance that someone else will jeopardize your audition.

Never ask an accompanist to transpose your audition song to a different key in an audition or any other performance situation.

Good preparation of materials gives an accompanist a better shot at supporting you and making your audition successful. Also, ask if you will need to bring sheet music with written-out accompaniment, or a lead sheet with chord changes.

Musical selection

Choose music that meets the audition requirements, sheet music or a legible chord chart, displays the best qualities of your singing, is not overly long, and is reasonably easy to play.

A cappella pieces are not recommended unless you have perfect pitch. Even then, they may not be the best choice for an audition, as the audition team can benefit from hearing you interact with accompaniment. If it is appropriate for the style of music you are singing, edit out long instrumental interludes in your audition pieces.

Some auditions call for a 16-bar-long excerpt of your music. This is often used at large open auditions or "cattle calls" where hundreds of singers audition for one or two jobs, and need to be heard in a short time. Your 16-bar cut should include your best singing, perhaps displaying your high range. Work this out in advance of the audition.

What to wear

Dress for the occasion. If you have a formal audition, dress accordingly but be comfortable enough to breathe. It is important to be comfortable for less formal auditions too, but it helps to look like you put some effort into your appearance. Many singers perform better if they are well dressed because they feel better about the way they look. Practice your audition in the clothes you plan to wear so the feeling of new or unfamiliar clothes and shoes doesn't distract you.

Performing skills

Your movement and gestures should be appropriate for the size of the audition space and style of music. Smaller rooms require less movement, larger rooms may need a bit more. Always be sincere and be yourself. Focus your eyes on the auditioners' foreheads or earlobes so you don't corner them into looking directly into your eyes. This can be uncomfortable for you and for the audition team.

After you sing

After you are finished singing, you may ask when you can expect to hear the results if you don't know. But other than that, keep your exit simple. Say "thank you," smile, pick up your music, and leave. Asking auditioners how you did as soon as you are finished is not recommended. People who audition usually have a full day of continuous listening scheduled. They will be better able to evaluate your audition given the time to discuss their impressions and put their thoughts into writing.

I HAVE SELECTED THREE CLASSIC songs for you to practice singing: a pop ballad, a medium-swing jazz tune, and a medium- to up-tempo Motown song.

"YESTERDAY"

Many singers, including Ray Charles, En Vogue, Boyz II Men, and Michael Bolton, have recorded this classic pop ballad first sung by Paul McCartney. The original key would be appropriate for high-voiced male singers. Men who sing this song in the original key should have an easy high F in order to sing the middle section freely and without tension. Women and lower voiced men who sing Yesterday may prefer to use the lower key of C to get a nice pop sound. The high E and F in the higher key can be difficult for some women to sing lightly and without too much vibrato. If you have trouble singing them with a straighter tone, choose the lower key.

This song has a wide range of ten notes and can be challenging in terms of range and expression. When performing pop songs, work to strike a balance between singing expressively and being subtle. A lot of hand movement or melodramatic facial expressions do not enhance this song. Strive to be sincere and draw upon your own emotional experience to make the song appropriately genuine and heartfelt.

Yesterday (key of F)

Words and Music by John Lennon
and Paul McCartney

THE CONTEMPORARY SINGER

ELEMENTS OF VOCAL TECHNIQUE

138

Yesterday (key of C)

Words and Music by John Lennon and Paul McCartney

"I'M BEGINNING TO SEE THE LIGHT"

My favorite recording of this song is by Ella Fitzgerald on her Duke Ellington Songbook recording. Ella sings it in the key of C, which is fairly low for most women. But after she sings the song once through as written, she masterfully embellishes to create her own variation of the song, which extends up quite high. If singers start with the melody too high, there is no room for embellishment above the melody.

Women who sing this song in the key of C should sing an octave lower than the melody is written. If the melody were written where it is sung, all the notes would need ledger lines. It is much more practical to notate it on the staff. Singers who feel more comfortable singing higher can use the key of G, singing the notes on the staff as written.

I'm Beginning to See the Light (key of C)

Words and Music by Don George, Johnny Hodges, Duke Ellington and Harry James

THE CONTEMPORARY SINGER

140

ELEMENTS OF VOCAL TECHNIQUE

I'm Beginning to See the Light (key of G)

Words and Music by Don George, Johnny Hodges, Duke Ellington and Harry James

Medium Swing

nev - er cared much for moon-lit skies__ I nev - er wink back at
nev - er went in for af - ter - glow__ Or can - dle light on the

fi - re - flies__ But now that the stars are in your eyes__ I'm be -
mis - tle - toe__ But now when you turn the lamp down low__ I'm be -

gin - ning to see the light.____ I ____
gin - ning to see the light.__

Used to ram - ble through the park__ Sha - dow box - ing

in the dark__ Then you came and caused a spark_ That's a

four a - larm fi - re now.____ I nev - er made love by

lan - tern shine_ I nev - er saw rain - bows in my wine__ But

now that your lips are burn-ing mine_ I'm be - gin-ning to see the light.__

"I HEARD IT THROUGH THE GRAPEVINE"

Marvin Gaye sings the most famous version of this song, although Gladys Knight and the Pips and many others have also recorded it. The Gladys Knight and the Pips version features a different melody and it is interesting to observe the lyric changes she makes. Marvin Gaye's version is used here, with alternate lyrics included for a female singer.

Men should observe the use of falsetto in Marvin Gaye's recording and experiment with this in their singing. This falsetto effect can be achieved with practice, and by making your voice lighter.

I Heard It Through the Grapevine (key of E♭m)

*Words and Music by Norman J. Whitfield
and Barrett Strong*

THE CONTEMPORARY SINGER ELEMENTS OF VOCAL TECHNIQUE

D.S. al Coda

2. I know a man ain't supposed to cry,
(Take a good look at these tears in my eyes)
Baby, but these tears I can't hold inside.
Losin' you would end my life, you see,
'Cause you mean that much to me.
You could have told me yourself
That you loved someone else.
Instead, I heard it through the grapevine *(etc.)*

3. People say believe half of what you see,
Son, and none of what you hear,
But I can't help bein' confused.
If it's true please tell me, dear.
Do you plan to let me go
For the other guy (girl) you loved before?
Don't you know,
I heard it through the grapevine *(etc.)*

THE CONTEMPORARY SINGER | ELEMENTS OF VOCAL TECHNIQUE

146

I Heard It Through the Grapevine (key of Cm)

Words and Music by Norman J. Whitfield and Barrett Strong

C Interlude

D.S. al Coda

3. Peo-ple say be-lieve half__

__ it through the grape-vine, not much long-er would you be my ba-

Hon-ey, hon-ey I know__

(etc. to end)

by, Yeah,__ yeah, yeah,__ yeah, Heard__

that you're let-tin' me go,__ Said I heard__ it through the grape-vine,

fade and repeat

Ooh,__ I heard__ it through the grape-vine, Ooh, noo, I heard__

2. I know a man ain't supposed to cry,
   Take a good look at these tears in my eyes
   Baby, but these tears I can't hold inside.
   Losin' you would end my life, you see,
   'Cause you mean that much to me.
   You could have told me yourself
   That you loved someone else.
   Instead, I heard it through the grapevine *(etc.)*

3. People say believe half of what you see,
   Son, and none of what you hear,
   But I can't help bein' confused.
   If it's true please tell me, dear.
   Do you plan to let me go
   For the other guy (girl) you loved before?
   Don't you know,
      I heard it through the grapevine *(etc.)*

THE BASIC VOWEL sounds are represented here in several languages. Two of the word examples in English are not pure vowels, but rather, diphthongs. They are indicated as diphthongs by symbol (d) next to the word.

BASIC ENGLISH WITH FOREIGN LANGUAGE VOWELS

Vowel	English	Italian	German	French	Japanese
ee	weak	si	sie	hiver	<u>いい</u>じま
ih	hit		immer		（イとエの中間 - エの口でイを言う）
ay	day (d)	vero	leben	été	<u>えい</u>
eh	met	belle	denn	clair	<u>エ</u>プロン
ah	father	casa	Mann	ras	スカ<u>ー</u>ト
aw	crawl	gloria	kommt	folie	（アとオの中間 - アの口でオを言う）
oh	tone (d)	dove	so	hôtel	に<u>おう</u> （匂う）
oo	clue	piu	Du		<u>ゆうう</u>つ

There are several specific vowel sounds not listed above that are characteristic of English. They are found with many different spellings, some of which are listed below. Nonnative English speakers may need to concentrate on these in order to be understood when singing and speaking English.

VOWEL SOUND	ENGLISH WORD
er	earth, girl, world
	(minimize Rs before consonants)
uh	much, but, young, love, does, flood
short u	put, full, good, woman, would
short a	mash, flat, cat, grab
short i	hit, rely, women, busy, bitter

PRONUNCIATION PRACTICE

Here is a list of words and phrases that can be challenging to nonnative speakers of English. Many of these words focus on the pronunciation of R and L as well as difficult links between words. Try creating phrases with these ordinary words and practice them daily.

Usually	Remembering	Industrial	Experience
Unusually	Literate	Published	Admiration
River	Lovely	Lyrics	Friendly
Would	Little	Material	Freely
Reality	Illiterate	Recording	Dreams
Severity	Literacy	Criminally	Dreamily
Deliberate	Probably	Ceremonially	Thrilling
Million	Release	Miraculous	Thrills
Trillion	Believable	Miraculously	
Really	Absolutely	Marvelous	
Rarely	Industry	Illusion	

Will you still love me?

I've wanted it desperately.

These are tough wounds to heal.

The very thought of you thrills me.

I've been running through the wilderness.

Red leather, yellow leather.

I would freely urge the fellow to apply.

You drive me crazy.

You went through with it.

I believe that you would be unfaithful.

The night was like a thousand others.

The toothless old thing filled her mouth with moss.

A trillion stars illuminate Riley's miraculous flight.

The yellow thread creates an illusion that runs through the material.

The circumference of the remaining area will provide ample room for the

caterers to construct their forty-layer tiramisu!

Abdomen: The portion of the body lying between the pelvis and chest (not including the back) that houses the majority of the digestive organs.

Adam's apple: The protruding aspect of the thyroid cartilage in the front of the neck, which is more prominently visible in males.

Alto: The lowest female voice type, also known as "contralto." The term alto is also commonly used in choral singing to refer to the voice part below soprano and above tenor.

Articulation: The process of producing consonants in speech and singing.

Articulators: The parts of the mouth involved in the creation of sounds for speech and singing.

Arytenoid cartilages: The two

pyramid shaped cartilages to which the vocal cords are attached. Primarily, they control the position and tension of the vocal cords during phonation and breathing.

Aspirate: A speech sound characterized by air preceding the onset of tone, sounds like the letter H.

Aspiration: In speech, the sound of air preceding or following vocal cord vibration; in medicine, when a foreign object, or the contents of the stomach (as in reflux) is sucked into the lungs. Aspiration can lead to lung infection.

Attack: The beginning of vocal cord vibration in response to airflow. See Onset.

Belting: A style of singing where the chest voice register is either extended or mixed upward to make a loud, emotional, full sound. Belting is sometimes used in musical theater, blues, rock, and pop singing.

Breath management: The efficient process of breathing used in singing.

Bass: The lowest of male voice types.

Baritone: The most common male voice type, higher than bass and lower than tenor.

Bulimia: An illness involving self-induced vomiting to control weight.

Cartilage: The connective tissue characterized by firm consistency. It is softer and more flexible than bone and relatively nonvascular in nature.

Catch breath: A quick breath taken to renew air supply, not indicated by a rest in music.

Chest resonance: The sensation of vibration felt in the lower throat and upper chest areas of the body when singing or speaking. Chest resonance is thought to originate in the lower pharynx rather than the chest. It can be felt more easily when singing at a lower pitch level, or at a high volume.

Chest voice/register: The lower register of a voice with sensations of vibrations in the chest. Also referred to as heavy mechanism, and low register.

Cricoid cartilage: The lower circular cartilage of the larynx attaching the larynx to the trachea (windpipe).

Consonant: A speech sound created by interrupting the flow of air with articulating organs.

Contralto: The lowest female voice type, also called alto. The term contralto is most commonly used in operatic voice typing. Alto is commonly used in choral singing to refer to the voice part below soprano and above tenor.

Diaphragm: The large double-dome shaped muscle that separates the chest from the abdominal cavity, and which facilitates the breathing process.

Diphthong: A double vowel occurring in a single syllable (e.g., my = mah + ee).

Diction: The formation and delivery of words according to established principles of pronunciation.

Dynamics: The aspect of music referring to relative loudness or softness in musical performance.

Edema: The excessive accumulation of fluid in tissues; swelling.

Embellishment: The ornamentation of a melody, adding notes above and below it or changing the existing rhythm of a song to enhance interpretation.

Epiglottis: The leaf-shaped cartilage flap that covers the glottal opening, which helps keep food out of the larynx.

Exhalation: The part of the breathing cycle when the air is expelled from the lungs.

Expression: The interpretation of mood, feeling, and intent in music. It also refers to the physical aspect and involvement of interpretation (e.g., facial expression).

Falsetto: The highest, lightest register of the male voice.

Flexibility: The ability of the voice to make rapid adjustments in pitch, dynamics, and to move with agility over a series of pitches.

Flute voice/register: The highest register of a female voice marked by a whistle-like quality. It is also referred to as an upper extension, whistle tone, fla-geolet. Flute voice is lighter and thinner than the head voice register.

Forward resonance: A desirable sensation of the voice vibrating in the mask

Fundamental tone: The basic sound produced by the vibrating vocal cords.

Focus: A sense of concentrated vocal energy resulting in a clear, efficient tone quality.

Glottal attack: The onset of tone occurring on words beginning with

vowels. Breath pressure is built up under closed vocal cords, then quickly released either harshly or gently.

Glottis: The space between the vocal cords.

Groove: A continuous rhythmic pattern used in songs to establish style and feel.

Hard attack: See Glottal attack.

Hard palate: The bony portion of the roof of the mouth.

Head resonance: A sensation of vibration in the area of the forehead when singing in a higher register. Head resonance os thought to originates in the upper pharynx and mouth rather than the head. It can be more easily felt when singing at a higher pitch level.

Head voice/register: A higher register of a voice, with sensations of vibrations in the head.

Hyoid bone: A U-shaped bone located at the top of the larynx.

Hum: A vocal sound made with closed lips.

Inhalation: The part of the breathing cycle when air is taken into the lungs.

Intonation: Singing or playing in tune.

Improvisation: Spontaneous melodic and rhythmic invention.

Intercostals: The muscles between the ribs.

Imagery: The use of words to create mental pictures or images that illustrate vocal concepts.

Laryngitis: An inflammatory condition of the larynx. Can be caused by illness, smoking, or vocal misuse.

Larynx (Voice box): An organ at the top of the trachea composed of bone, cartilage, ligaments, and muscles and membranes. It contains the vocal cords, which are closed during phonation and swallowing and open during breathing.

Legato: Smooth and connected.

Mask: The area of the eyes, nose, cheeks, upper lip, and teeth, which has a sensation of vibration while singing.

Middle voice/register: The middle register of a voice with sensations of vibrations in the mask, and head. Also referred to as medium register, middle voice, blended, or mixed register.

Mezzo-soprano: A female voice type with a range just slightly lower than a soprano.

Nodules (Nodes): Callous-like growths on the vocal cords, usually resulting from vocal misuse.

Onset: The beginning of vocal cord vibration in response to airflow. See Attack.

Oscillation: Repeated movement back and forth.

Open chest voice: Loud, forceful singing in the lowest vocal register for women. If open chest voice is overused and/or pushed up high in range, vocal strain or damage may occur.

Otolaryngologist: An ear, nose and throat doctor.

Overtones: The upper harmonics that result from the fundamental tone setting air in the human resonating system in motion.

Palate: The roof of the mouth in two parts, hard and soft.

Passaggio: The transitional passage or bridge between vocal registers.

Pharynx: The region above the larynx and behind the mouth generally referred to as the throat.

Phonation: In singing, the vibration of the vocal cords, which produces sound.

Polyp: A mass that can grow on the vocal cords as a result of various kinds of abuse, including smoking and screaming; typically the result of recurrent vocal hemorrhage (bleeding).

Reflux: A backflow of stomach contents into the esophagus and throat that causes inflammation, hoarseness, chronic coughing, a feeling of fullness, a lump in the throat, and increased mucus production.

Register: The term used to designate a portion of the vocal range in which the notes have a similar tone quality and are produced by the same muscle action.

Resonance: The intensification of a fundamental tone through sympathetic vibration.

Resonator: The surfaces or air containing cavities that vibrate in response to a fundamental tone.

Riffing: Improvised melodic embellishment.

Scatting: Melodic and rhythmic vocal improvisation using nonsense syllables (scat syllables), which are imitative of musical instruments.

Soft palate: The roof of the mouth behind the hard palate; it is flexible and muscular.

Staccato: Short, separate articulation of notes.

Sternum: The breastbone, in the center of the chest, to which the ribs attach.

Straight tone: A tone without vibrato.

Timbre: Tone color.

Thyroid cartilage (Adam's apple): The largest cartilage of the larynx.

Trachea (Windpipe): A cartilaginous tube through which air passes to the lungs.

Trill: The rapid alternation of two adjacent pitches.

Triphthong: A triple vowel in a single syllable (e.g., air, your, fire, our).

Unvoiced consonant: A consonant articulated without vocal cord vibration (e.g., P, H, F, S, K).

V

Vamp: An accompaniment pattern repeated until the soloist begins to sing or play.

Vibrato: An oscillation of tone above and below a pitch center produced by alternating nerve impulses.

Vocal coach: A professional who works with singers, teaching repertoire, language pronunciation, style, and performance (as opposed to a "voice teacher," who teaches vocal technique.)

Vocal cords: Two muscular folds formed by the thyroarytenoid muscles, capable of closing over the windpipe and vibrating in response to air pressure from the lungs, resulting in vocal tone. They open during breathing and close during phonation and swallowing.

Vocal fry: A vocal sound sometimes referred to as "glottal fry" because of the grating sound made when insufficient air pressure is used for vocalization.

Vocal tract: The resonating system comprised of the larynx, pharynx, and the mouth cavity.

Vocalise: A vocal exercise designed to achieve specific objective(s).

Vocalize: To sing a melody or scale pattern on a vowel sound, sometimes for the purpose of warming up.

Voice teacher: A professional who teaches singing technique. May also act as a Vocal coach. (see Vocal coach)

Voiced consonant: A consonant articulated with vocal cord vibration (e.g., Z, V, G, B).

Vowel: A speech sound produced when breath is not interrupted (e.g., ee, ay, oo, oh, ah).

Vowel modification: The vowel adjustments made to allow for tone equalization when singing at higher pitch levels.

WEB SITES

■ **Center for Voice Disorder** of Wake Forest University
www.bgsm.edu/voice

An interesting, user-friendly Web site with pages on warming up, preventing vocal cord nodules, the ten most common problems of singers, survival tips for the choral singer, and more.

■ **Johns Hopkins Medical Center**
www.med.jhu.edu

An interesting site with information on voice disorders.

■ **National Center for Voice and Speech**
www.ncvs.org

Check out the pages at this site found through the "General Public" link entitled "Tips to keep you talkin'" and "Rx and Voice and Speech."

■ **Mark Baxter Vocal Studios**
www.voicelesson.com

Voice teacher Mark Baxter explores topics of interest to singers, with an emphasis on pop and rock singing.

■ **CD Now**

www.cdnow.com

A good source for locating all kinds of recordings by song title, artist, etc.

BOOKS

Alderson, Richard. **Complete Handbook of Voice Training.** West Nyack, NY: *Parker Publishing, 1979.*

Balk, Wesley. **The Complete Singer-Actor.** Minneapolis: *University of Minnesota Press, 1977.*

Green, B. with W.T. Galway. **The Inner Game of Music.** Garden City, NY: *Doubleday, Anchor Press, 1986.*

Lessac, **A. The Use and Training of the Human Voice** (revised). Mountain View, CA: Mayfield Publishing Company, *1967.*

Linklater, Kristen. **Freeing the Natural Voice.** New York: *Drama Book Specialists, 1976.*

McClosky, D.B. **Your Voice at Its Best.** Plymouth, MA: *Memorial Press, 1972.*

McKinney, J. **The Diagnosis and Correction of Vocal Faults.** Nashville, TN: *Genovex Music Group, 1994.*

Miller, Richard **The Structure of Singing. London**: Schirmer Books, *Collier MacMillan Publishing, 1986.*

Sataloff, R.T. **Vocal Health and Pedagogy.** San Diego, London: *Singular Publishing Group, Inc., 1998.*

Ungerleider, S. **Mental Training for Peak Performance.** Emmaus, PA: *Rodale Press, Inc., 1996.*

Werner, K. **Effortless Mastery.** New Albany, IN: *Jamey Aebersold Publishing, 1996.*

MUSIC

American Folk Songs and Spirituals. Milwaukee, WI: *Hal Leonard Publishing, 1996.*

The Beatles Fake Book. Milwaukee, WI: *Hal Leonard Publishing, 1987.*

Classic Rock Fake Book (revised). Milwaukee, WI: *Hal Leonard Publishing, 1996.*

The Definitive Country Collection. Milwaukee, WI: *Hal Leonard Publishing, 1992.*

Mantooth, F. **The Best Chord Changes for the World's Greatest Standards.** Milwaukee, WI: *Hal Leonard Publishing, 1989.*

Mantooth, F. **The Best Chord Changes for the Most Requested Standards.** Milwaukee, WI: *Hal Leonard Publishing, 1990.*

Sher, Chuck. **Latin Real Book (vocal).** Petaluma, CA: *Chuck Sher Publishing, 1997.*

Sher, Chuck. **The New Real Book, Vols. 1, 2, and 3 (vocal).** Petaluma, CA: *Chuck Sher Publishing, 1984 and 1995.*

Walters, R., ed. **The Singers Musical Theater Anthology.** (2 vols. each for soprano, mezzo soprano/belter, tenor, baritone/bass, and duets). Milwaukee, WI: *Hal Leonard Publishing, 1987.*

The Ultimate Pop/Rock Fake Book. Milwaukee, WI: *Hal Leonard Publishing, April, 1997.*

Ultimate Gospel (revised). Milwaukee, WI: *Hal Leonard Publishing, August, 1983.*

THE CONTEMPORARY SINGER

ELEMENTS OF VOCAL TECHNIQUE

ANNE PECKHAM is a singer, voice teacher, clinician, and choral conductor. An associate professor in the Voice Department at Berklee College of Music since 1987, Anne teaches private voice lessons and vocal labs, directs the Berklee Concert Choir, and develops curriculum for the "Elements of Vocal Technique" lab required of all vocal students. She also co-founded Berklee's Musical Theater Workshop. Anne serves on the executive board of the National Association of Teachers of Singing, Boston Chapter.

Score Compose Arrange

with Berklee Press

berklee press

AS SERIOUS ABOUT MUSIC AS YOU ARE

Berklee Press DVDs: Just Press PLAY

Kenwood Dennard: The Studio/ Touring Drummer

| ISBN: 0-87639-022-X | HL: 50448034 | DVD $19.95 |

The Ultimate Practice Guide for Vocalists

| ISBN: 0-87639-035-1 | HL: 50448017 | DVD $19.95 |

Featuring Donna McElroy

Real-Life Career Guide for the Professional Musician

| ISBN: 0-87639-031-9 | HL: 50448013 | DVD $19.95 |

Featuring David Rosenthal

Essential Rock Grooves for Bass

| ISBN: 0-87639-037-8 | HL: 50448019 | DVD $19.95 |

Featuring Danny Morris

Jazz Guitar Techniques: Modal Voicings

| ISBN: 0-87639-034-3 | HL: 50448016 | DVD $19.95 |

Featuring Rick Peckham

Jim Kelly's Guitar Workshop

| ISBN: 0-634-00865-X | HL: 00320168 | DVD $19.95 |

Latin Jazz Grooves Featuring Victor Mendoza

| ISBN: 0-87639-002-5 | HL: 50448003 | DVD $19.95 |

Jazz Expression: A Toolbox for Improvisation

| ISBN: 0-87639-024-6 | HL: 50448036 | DVD $19.95 |

Basic Afro-Cuban Rhythms for Drum Set and Hand Percussion

| ISBN: 0-87639-030-0 | HL: 50448012 | DVD $19.95 |

Featuring Ricardo Monzón

Vocal Technique: Developing Your Voice for Performance

| ISBN: 0-87639-026-2 | HL: 50448038 | DVD $19.95 |

Featuring Anne Peckham

Preparing for Your Concert

| ISBN: 0-87639-036-X | HL: 50448018 | DVD $19.95 |

Featuring JoAnne Brackeen

Jazz Improvisation: Starting Out with Motivic Development

| ISBN: 0-87639-032-7 | HL: 50448014 | DVD $19.95 |

Featuring Ed Tomassi

Chop Builder for Rock Guitar

| ISBN: 0-87639-033-5 | HL: 50448015 | DVD $19.95 |

Featuring "Shred Lord" Joe Stump

Turntable Technique: The Art of the DJ

| ISBN: 0-87639-038-6 | HL: 50448025 | DVD $24.95 |

Featuring Stephen Webber

Jazz Improvisation: A Personal Approach with Joe Lovano

| ISBN: 0-87639-021-1 | HL: 50448033 | DVD $19.95 |

Harmonic Ear Training

| ISBN: 0-87639-027-0 | HL: 50448039 | DVD $19.95 |

Featuring Roberta Radley

Feed the fire
Career Fuel for working musicians

Berkleemusic.com

Berkleemusic is the new anytime, anywhere online destination where musicians can find jobs and gigs, study with Berklee professors and network with other music industry professionals.

Online music school

Choose from 5 learning streams: **Production, Music Business, Writing, Education** and **Performance.** Designed for musicians, educators and working professionals, courses run from 3 to12 weeks on a six-semester annual calendar.

Music career center

This online crossroads is a 24 by 7 home for monitoring industry buzz, managing personal and professional contacts, finding jobs and gigs, accessing career development tools and networking with like-minded individuals worldwide.

Berklee|*music.com*

Learn more at www.Berkleemusic.com

English and Welsh Infantry Regiments
An Illustrated Record of Service

by
Ray Westlake

SPELLMOUNT

Staplehurst

British Library Cataloguing in Publication Data:
A catalogue record for this book is available
from the British Library

Copyright © Ray Westlake 1995, 2002

ISBN 1-86227-147-X

First published by Spellmount Ltd in the UK in 1995

This paperback edition published in the UK in 2002 by
Spellmount Limited
The Old Rectory
Staplehurst
Kent TN12 0AZ

Tel: 01580 893730
Fax: 01580 893731
E-mail: enquiries@spellmount.com
Website: www.spellmount.com

3 5 7 9 8 6 4 2

Printed in China

To the memory of John `Larry` Lowe
who loved books.

Acknowledgements

The kind help and advice given by regimental secretaries and museum staff of the following has been invaluable - The Queen`s Regiment; The Buffs, Royal East Kent Regiment; The King`s Own Royal Regiment (Lancaster); The Royal Warwickshire Regiment; The Devonshire Regiment; The Somerset Light Infantry; The Prince of Wales`s Own Regiment of Yorkshire; The Green Howards; The Lancashire Fusiliers; The Cheshire Regiment; The Royal Welch Fusiliers; The South Wales Borderers; The Royal Gloucestershire, Berkshire and Wiltshire Regiment; The Worcestershire and Sherwood Foresters Regiment; The East Lancashire Regiment; The Duke of Wellington`s Regiment; The Border Regiment; The Royal Hampshire Regiment; The Staffordshire Regiment; The South Lancashire Regiment; The Welch Regiment; The Essex Regiment; The Loyal North Lancashire Regiment; The Northamptonshire Regiment; The King`s Own Yorkshire Light Infantry; The Durham Light Infantry; National Museums and Galleries on Merseyside; Museum of Lincolnshire Life; Newarke Houses Museum; Blackburn Museums and Art Galleries; Sussex United Services Museum; Derby Museum and Art Gallery and Rotherham Metropolitan Borough Council. Also the following - Geoffrey J. Crump; Norman Holme; Jim Kelleher; G. Archer Parfitt; Ernie Platt; Lieutenant-Colonel J.D. Sainsbury, TD, FSA; Dave Seeney, Graham Stewart; Professor Charles Thomas and John Woodroff who's dedication to, and often life-long study of, their own particular regiments has once again been an important source of information to this writer.

Contents

Introduction

The publishers of this book have in recent years produced two fine `Pictorial Histories` - `The Scottish Regiments` by Patrick Mileham and from R.G. Harris - `The Irish Regiments.` Therefore it is the intention of this volume to fill the gap, at least as far as the Regular Army battalions of the several English and Welch infantry regiments are concerned. My own books `The Territorial Battalions` and `Kitchener's Army` (both by the same publisher and in the Pictorial History series) hopefully have covered those aspects of each regiment.

The regiments dealt with in this book are those formed as a result of the army re-organisation of 1881. In this year some sixty-nine infantry regiments were created which appeared in the Army List under the heading of `Territorial Regiments.` It must be pointed out here that this definition should not be confused with `The Territorial Force`, an organisation introduced in 1908 and comprising non-regular formations. Of the sixty-nine regiments, ten would be Scottish and eight Irish. The remaining fifty-one were composed of three Welch and forty-eight English. A complete list can be seen in Appendix `B`.

It will be appreciated that a history of each regiment can often run to several volumes. Consequently in the amount of space available here only a brief summery of service can be offered. Therefore background history to each campaign and battle has been left out and the information provided restricted to a simple digest of events and record of stations outside England, Scotland and Wales. The several campaigns and battles that appear in the records of each regiment can be described as `principle` - minor skirmishes and operations that occurred during the many years that regiments garrisoned areas have been left out.

Under the heading `Titles`, those held by each regiment at various times in its history have been listed. Although the name of a regiment (as in the case of a person) is important and correct designations should be used for the relevant period, it is not unusual to see several versions in use at any one time. These discrepancies, however, are usually minor. In most cases the titles listed are based upon those shown in the Official Army List or as preferred by the regiment. Regiments were at first known by the names of their colonels e.g. Colonel Sir William Clifton's Regiment of Foot. Although this systems was in the main efficient, a certain amount of confusion did occur when colonels of regiments had the same name. Therefore, in 1751, all regiments were numbered according to their seniority and thereafter known as e.g. the 10th Regiment of Foot. The next overall change in the titles of infantry regiments took place in 1782. This year seeing introduction of geographical affiliations eg. 10th (North Lincoln) Regiment of Foot. Numbers finally gave way to titles in 1881.

The histories of badges and uniform indisputably would qualify for a life-time's research in their own right. Once again I have offered only the briefest in sight into these intricate matters. Under the heading 'Badges' I have not attempted to record every badge worn, but simply the devices used on various forms of insignia. In the vast majority of cases items that form part of a badge such as crowns, wreaths and stars have no particular historic significance. The origins of many badges have been lost in time and these are generally referred to officially as a regiment's 'Ancient' badge. Other and more obvious devices represent campaigns and battles fought, royal patronage and other important events in history. Uniform has also been dealt with in the simplest of forms - just the colour of facings (collar and cuffs) being provided. All regiments, with the exception of The King's Royal Rifle Corps and The Rifle Brigade who had dark green uniforms, would wear scarlet (or red) jackets.

In cases such as 'The Buffs' and 'Green Howards', what originated as a nickname has evolved into part of an official title. Every regiment has acquired at least one nickname throughout the years of its existence, many being short-lived and often in use by just a few individuals. Some names would stand the test of time, however, and what was at first relevant to just one battalion later became that by which the whole regiment became affectionately know. I remember one old veteran of the Great War who was proud to refer to himself as one of the 'Diehards'. He had served with the 11th Battalion of the Middlesex Regiment which had been formed in 1914 and recalled how he and other recruits were made aware of the heroic stand of the 57th Regiment (later 1st Battalion, Middlesex Regiment) at Albuhera. Fought just over one hundred years before, the battle brought about what was to become one of the best known nicknames of the British Army. It is such nicknames that have been included in this book.

Each regiment appears under the title held at the present, or at the time of its amalgamation or disbandment. The order used is according to seniority (see Appendix 'B'). The period covered runs from the formation of each regiment through until its merger with another.

As an 'illustrated' reference to service this book should naturally include a generous helping of photographs. I believe Spellmount have not let us down and hopefully the reader will from this combination of interesting photographs and good basic regimental history be encouraged to find out more about the history and traditions of some of the finest regiments in the world. There is always good reason to record the doings of brave men and their regiments, especially now where the most recent of post-war army reorganisations has left us with just four from the fifty-one that we started with in 1881.

The Queen's Royal Regiment (West Surrey)

Titles

1661-1684 The Tangier Regiment.
1684-1686 The Queen's Regiment.
1686-1703 The Queen Dowager's Regiment of Foot.
1703-1715 The Queen's Royal Regiment of Foot.
1715-1727 The Princess of Wales's Own Regiment of Foot.
1727-1751 The Queen's Own Regiment of Foot.
1751-1881 2nd (The Queen's Royal) Regiment of Foot
1881-1921 The Queen's (Royal West Surrey Regiment),
1921-1959 The Queen's Royal Regiment (West Surrey).

1st Battalion

Raised by Henry, Earl of Peterborough for garrison service in Tangier, 1661. Mustered at Putney Heath and sailed January, 1662. Served in Tangier against the Moors until evacuation to England, 1684. First battle honour "Tangier 1662-80" (the oldest in the British Army) not awarded until 1909. Fought at Sedgemoor, 1685. During the campaign in Ireland took part in siege of Londonderry, 1689; battle of the Boyne, 1690, the assault on

Below - Drummer, 2nd (The Queen`s, Royal) Regiment, 1850. The headdress is the "Albert" pattern shako and was in use 1844-1855. Note special drummers` shoulder wings and lace. Illustration by P.W. Reynolds.

Right - Artist`s impression (J. Finnemore) of 2nd Battalion, The Queen`s (Royal West Surrey Regiment) at the battle of Colenso 15th December, 1899. The battalion`s casualties at this action were almost one hundred.

Facing Page: Above - First World War post card from an illustration by Lawrence Colborne. One of a series of similar cards that turn up with the caption amended to suit other regiments.

Below - Shooting Team - Depot, The Queen`s Royal Regiment (West Surrey), 1937. Seated centre is Major G.A. Pilleau who was wounded at Loos with the 2nd Battalion on 25th September, 1915 and fought on the Somme with the 1st Battalion in 1916. He was awarded the Military Cross.

Athlone and the fall of Limerick, 1691. To England then Flanders, 1692. Fought at Landen, 1693 and was present at siege of Namur, 1695. To England, 1696. Independent company sent to Bermuda in 1701 and served there until disbanded in 1763. Took part in operations along Spanish coast, 1702 including attack on Cadiz and capture of Vigo. To Flanders, 1703 and with one other regiment (Dutch) held out against forty thousand French at Tongres for twenty-eight hours before being taken prisoner. Served in Spain and Portugal, 1704-08 - siege of Valencia, attack on Albuquerque and action at Badajos, 1705; capture of Alcantara, Ciudad Rodrigo, Salamanca and Madrid, 1706; battle of Almanza, 1707. To Canada then England, 1711; Gibraltar, 1730; Ireland; 1749; Gibraltar, 1768; England, 1775. Assisted in quelling the Gordon Riots of June, 1780. To Gibraltar, 1783; England, 1792. Formed into detachments for service as marines, 1793. Detachment went to West Indies and saw action at Martinique, others served in Lord Howe`s fleet during "The Glorious 1st of June, 1794". Regiment to the West Indies and saw action at Martinique and Guadeloupe. Newly raised 2nd Battalion sent out from Guernsey to replace 1st Battalion losses due to disease, 1795. Strength reduced to one hundred and sixty-two (originally six hundred and sixty-one). Took part in capture of Trinidad, 1797. To England, 1797. Total strength recorded as just seventy out of an original complement of over one thousand. Served in Ireland during Rebellion, 1798-99, being engaged at Foulkes Mill, Wexford, Kilconney Hill and Ballinamuck. To Holland and took part in Helder campaign, 1799. Present at Egmont-op-Zee and Bergen. Took part in series of raids upon the French coast during 1800 including assault on Quiberon. Fought in Egypt, 1801 - attack on Aboukir Castle, battles of Alexandria, Rosetta and Rahmanieh. To Gibraltar, 1802; England, 1805; Guernsey, 1807; Portugal, 1808. Fought at Vimiera and Corunna. Returned to England, 1809 (detachment remained in the Peninsular and fought at Talavera). Took part in Walcheren expedition of 1809 and present at Flushing. Returned to the Peninsular, 1811 and engaged at Redmha, Fuentes d` Onoro, Ciudad Rodrigo, 1811; Salamanca, Burgos, 1812. To England, 1813, detachments remaining and fighting at Vittoria, the Pyrenees, Nivelle and Toulouse. To the West Indies, 1816; England, 1821; Ireland, 1822; England, 1824; India, 1825. Took part in Baluchistan and Afghanistan campaigns, 1838-40 and present at battles of Ghuznee and Khelat. Saw action at Fort Punella during operations in Kolapore District of Southern Mahratta, 1844. To England, 1845; Ireland, 1847; South Africa, 1851 and engaged in Kaffir uprising, 1851-52. To China, 1860. Took part in action at Sinho and capture of Teng Ku, Taku Forts and Pekin. To England, 1861; Ireland, 1865; Aden, 1866; India, 1868; England, 1879; Ireland, 1883; England, 1890; Malta, 1892; India, 1895; Took part in North West Frontier campaign, 1895-98 serving with Malakand Field Force at Nawagai and Tirah Field Force at Sempagha Pass and Bazar Valley. To Aden, 1908; England, 1910. During the First World War took part in retreat from Mons and battles of the Aisne and Ypres, 1914. Engaged during Somme operations, 1916; battles of Arras and Ypres, 1917 and the Lys, 1918. To England, 1919; Ireland, 1920; England, 1923; China, 1927; Malta, 1928; China, 1930; India, 1934. Present during earthquake at Quetta May, 1935. Moved from North West Frontier to the Arakan, 1943. Later took part in defence of Kohima and operations in Burma. Served in Germany, 1948-53; Malaya, 1954-57; Germany, 1957-59. Amalgamated with 1st Battalion, The East Surrey Regiment to form 1st Battalion, The Queen's Royal Surrey Regiment, 1959.

We'd never have kom if we'd known der QUEEN'S were here

2nd Battalion

Formed, 1795 at Portsmouth and moved to Guernsey. Ordered to join 1st Battalion in the West Indies in November. Heavy losses from hurricane in the English Channel - just three hundred and seventy men reaching Martinique. Amalgamated with 1st Battalion, 1796. New 2nd Battalion formed at Colchester, 1857. To Malta then the Ionian Islands, 1858; Gibraltar, 1862; Bermuda, 1864; Ireland, 1865; England, 1868; Ireland, 1873; England, 1876; Malta, 1877; India, 1878. Took part in Burma War, 1886-88 then returned to India. To England, 1894; South Africa, 1899. Fought at Colenso, Spion Kop, Vaal Krantz, Pieter's Hill and Laing's Nek. Gained battle honour "Relief of Ladysmith." To England, 1904; Gibraltar, 1910; Bermuda, 1912; South Africa then England, 1914. During First World War fought at Ypres, 1914; Neuve Chapelle, Aubers Ridge, Festubert and Loos, 1915; on the Somme, 1916; at Ypres, 1917. Moved to Italy end of 1917 and engaged at Vittorio Veneto November, 1918. To England then India, 1919. Took part in Waziristan operations, 1921. To the Sudan, 1926; England, 1927; Palestine, 1939. During Second World War served in North Africa, Syria, Ceylon, Chindit operations in Burma and Malaya. Disbanded in Germany, 1948.

Badges

The Paschal Lamb - was confirmed as the Ancient badge of the regiment in 1751 but its origins are not clear. It is thought that it formed part of the arms of the House of Braganza and was certainly displayed by 1684. The Sphinx superscribed "Egypt" commemorates service in Egypt, 1801. The Cypher of Queen Catherine within the Garter. A Naval Crown superscribed "1st June, 1794" - awarded for service in the fleet under Lord Howe.

Uniform

Blue facings replaced sea-green by 1768.

Nicknames

`The Tangerines` - from service in Tangier. `Kirke's Lambs` - after Lieutenant-Colonel Piercy Kirke, commanding officer 1682-91 and later his son, 1701-63. `The Pork and Beans` - which is Cockney rhyming slang for Queen's and from the badge - `The Mutton Lancers.`

Left - Colour-belt - 2nd Battalion, The Queen's Royal Regiment (West Surrey). This richly decorated item bears all the regiment's badges and mottos together with a selection of battle honours gained during the First World War.

The Buffs
(Royal East Kent Regiment)

Titles

1665-1689 The Holland Regiment.
1689-1708 Prince George of Denmark's Regiment.
1708-1751 Known by name of Colonel.
1751-1782 3rd (or the Buffs) Regiment of Foot.
1782-1881 3rd (East Kent) Regiment of Foot (The Buffs).
1881-1935 The Buffs (East Kent Regiment).
1935-1961 The Buffs (Royal East Kent Regiment).

1st Battalion

One company raised from the Trained Bands of London at Greenwich, 1572 and under command of Thomas Morgan embarked for war in Holland. Later expanded to four regiments in pay of the Dutch. Majority of personnel returned to England, 1665 and became the Holland Regiment. Served at sea during Second Dutch War, 1665-67 and Third Dutch War, 1672-73. To Flanders, 1678, England, 1679; Flanders, 1689 and present at Walcourt. To England, 1690; Flanders, 1692. Present at Steinkirk and

Right - The Buffs - London October, 1846. On the 13th October, 1846, the 3rd Regiment while passing though London exercised its right to march through the city with drums beating, Colours flying and bayonets fixed. While crossing Blackfriars Bridge a drove of bullocks became disturbed and one of the animals charged into the men and crowd killing a small girl. Report and engraving from the Illustrated London News - 17th October, 1846.

Below - Officer - 2nd Battalion, 3rd Regiment, Dublin, 1874. Note cap insignia - a Dragon with 3 below.

Facing Page: Above - Lieutenant G.R.J. Evelyn - 2nd Battalion, 3rd Regiment who died of fever at Ekowe during the Zulu War, 1879. Engraving from Illustrated London News.

Facing Page: Bottom Left - Quarter-guard.

Facing Page: Bottom Right - 2nd Battalion, The Buffs - Brighton, 1899.
(1) Left to right Major J.B. Backhouse; Lieutenant-Colonel R.A. Hickson who was severely wounded during an action on 10th March, 1900 at Driefontein (succeeded by Major Backhouse) and Captain A.D. Geddes (also wounded).

Landen, 1693. To England, 1698. Took part in expedition to Cadiz and attack on Vigo, 1702. To Flanders, 1703. Present at Schellenburg and Blenheim, 1704; Helixhem, 1705; Ramillies, 1706; Oudenarde, 1708; Malplaquet and siege of Tournai, 1709. To England then Ireland, 1714; Scotland, 1715 and fought at Sheriffmuir. To England, 1716. Took part in raid on Vigo, 1719. To Flanders and War of the Austrian Succession, 1742. Engaged at Dettingen, 1743; Fontenoy, 1745. Returned to England, 1745 and sent to Scotland. Fought at Falkirk and Culloden, 1746. Returned to Flanders, 1747 and took part in battle of Lauffeld. Returned to England in November. To the West Indies, 1758. Took part in capture of Guadeloupe, 1759. To England, 1759; Belle Isle, 1761; Portugal, 1762; Minorca, 1763; England, 1771; Ireland, 1775; North America, 1781. Fought at Eutaw Springs. To Jamaica, 1782; England, 1790. Served on board ship, 1793-94. To Jersey then Flanders, 1794. Present at Nimeguen in November. To England then the West Indies, 1795. Took part in operations in Grenada and St. Vincent. To Jersey, 1802; Ireland, 1803; Germany, 1805; England, 1806; Madeira, 1807; Portugal, 1808. Fought at Douro and Talavera, 1809; Albuhera, 1811; Vittoria, Pyrenees operations, Nivelle and the Nive, 1813; Orthes and Toulouse, 1814. To Canada, 1814; France, 1815; Ireland, 1818. Escorted prisoners to Australia, regiment moving in stages between 1821-23. Left Australia for India, 1827. Took part in Gwalior campaign, 1843 and present at battle of Punniar. To England, 1844; Ireland, 1845; Malta, 1851; Greece, 1854; the Crimea, 1855. Took part in attack on The Redan 9th September, 1855. Major F.F. Maude and Private J. Connors awarded Victoria Cross. To the Ionian Islands, 1856; India, 1858; China, 1859. Took part in attack on Taku Forts August, 1860. To England, 1861; Ireland, 1865; India, 1866; Malaya and Perak expedition, 1874-75. Returned to India March, 1875. To England, 1879; Ireland, 1882; Malta then Singapore, 1885; India, 1887. Engaged during relief of Chitral, 1895; Mohmund campaign and Malakand operations, 1897-98. Victoria Cross awarded to Corporal J. Smith for action at Bilot 16th/17th September, 1897. To Aden, 1903; England, 1904; Ireland, 1910. Crossed to France, 1914 and engaged during battles of the Aisne and Armentières. At Hooge in August, 1915; on the Somme, 1916; Cambrai, 1917; the Somme, Lys and Hindenburg Line battles, 1918. Stationed in Ireland, 1919-21. To Turkey, 1922; Gibraltar, 1923; Egypt, 1924; Gibraltar, 1925; India, 1927; Burma, 1930;

India, 1935; Palestine, 1938; Egypt then Palestine, 1939. Fought in Egypt 1941-42; Tunisia, 1943; Italy, 1944-45. To Greece, 1946; England, 1947. Amalgamated with 2nd Battalion in Hong Kong, 1948. Stationed in Khartoum, 1950 then to England. Served in Egypt, 1951-52; Kenya, 1953-54; Germany, 1955-57; Aden, 1958; Germany, 1959-60. Amalgamated with 1st Battalion, The Queen's Own Royal West Kent Regiment to form 1st Battalion, The Queen's Own Buffs, The Royal Kent Regiment, 1961.

2nd Battalion

Formed, 1678 at Ipswich. Served in Flanders and disbanded same year. Another formed, 1756 which became 61st Regiment (see 2nd Battalion, The Gloucestershire Regiment), 1758. Another formed, 1803. To Alderney, 1804; England, 1807. Disbanded, 1815. Re-formed in Ireland, 1857 and to Malta, 1858; Gibraltar, 1862; West Indies, 1863; Ireland, 1866; England, 1867; Ireland, 1873; South Africa, 1876. Took part in Zulu War, 1879 and then to Singapore. To Hong Kong, 1882; Egypt, 1885; England, 1886; Ireland, 1892; England then South Africa, 1899. Took part in Paardeberg and Bloemfontein operations, 1900. To England, 1902; South Africa, 1905; Hong Kong, 1908; Singapore, 1910; India, 1913; England, 1914. Crossed to France January, 1915 and fought at Ypres. Transferred to Macedonian Front in October. To Turkey, 1918; England then India, 1919; Iraq, 1920; Aden, 1922; England, 1923. Stationed in Palestine, 1936 during Arab rebellion. Fought in France, 1940. To Egypt, 1942 and then into Palestine. Served in Iraq and Persia, 1943 then to India, 1944. Fought in Burma, 1944-45 and then to India. To Malaya, 1945 and stationed in Java, 1946. To Hong Kong, 1947. Amalgamated with 1st Battalion, 1948.

Badges

A Green Dragon - origins of this badge are not certain. Thought to have been a royal award around 1707, a Dragon featuring in the Royal Arms during the reign of Queen Elizabeth I. The Rose and Crown, a Sun in Splendour and Cypher of the Royal House of Denmark - all Ancient badges. The White Horse of Kent with motto `Invicta` - an old badge of The East Kent Militia.

Below - Boy drummer and musicians.

Uniform

Buff facings. Regulation white for English regiments was worn between 1881-90.

Nicknames

`The Buffs` - the buff-coloured jerkins and breeches as worn by the City of London Trained Bands soon lead to nickname. Later officially recognised as part of the regiment`s title. `The Buff Howards` - from the facing colour and Colonel from 1737-49 - Thomas Howard. `The Old Buffs` - also used and probably originated after King George II referred to the 31st Regiment (see East Surrey Regiment) after the battle of Dettingen as `The Young Buffs.` `The Nutcrackers` - from their fighting ability, and `The Resurrectionists` are both from the Peninsular War. The latter as a result of the regiment`s quick reappearance on the field after heavy casualties at Albuhera.

Left - Drum-Major Griggs with drummer boy and boy musicians - 2nd Battalion, 4th Regiment, Malta, 1865. (King`s Own Royal Regiment Museum).

Below - Cap badge.

Bottom - Other ranks glengarry badge - 4th Regiment, 1874-1881.

The King`s Own Royal Regiment (Lancaster)

Titles

1680-1684 2nd Tangier Regiment.
1684-1685 The Duchess of York and Albany`s Regiment of Foot.
1685-1703 The Queen`s Regiment of Foot.
1703-1710 The Queen`s Regiment of Marines or Royal Regiment of Marines.
1710-1715 The Queen`s Own Regiment of Foot.
1715-1751 The King`s Own Regiment of Foot.
1751-1865 4th (The King`s Own) Regiment of Foot.
1865-1881 4th (The King`s Own Royal) Regiment of Foot.
1881-1920 The King`s Own (Royal Lancaster Regiment).
1921-1959 The King`s Own Royal Regiment (Lancaster).

Right - Sergeant-Major and sentry - The King's Own (Royal Lancaster Regiment) c 1897.

Below - Lieutenant-General O.C. Borrett, KCB, CMG, CBE, DSO (Colonel of the Regiment) with Lieutenant-Colonel N.M. Ritchie, DSO, MC (Commanding Officer) inspecting 2nd Battalion, The King's Own Royal Regiment (Lancaster) at Aldershot prior to its departure for Palestine, September 1938. (King's Own Royal Regiment Museum).

1st Battalion

Raised by the Earl of Plymouth and to Tangier, 1680. To England, 1684. Fought at Sedgemoor, 1685. To Ireland, 1690 and present at battle of the Boyne, sieges of Cork, Kinsale and Limerick. To England, 1691; Flanders and fought at Steinkirk, 1692; Landen, 1693 and Namur, 1695. To England, 1696. Served again in Flanders, 1697. Took part in attack on Cadiz and Vigo, 1702. Served as marines, 1703-10 taking part in operations in the Mediterranean including capture and defence of Gibraltar, battle of Malaga, 1704; capture of Barcelona and Carthagena, 1705; Alicante, Iveca and Majorca, 1706; Lerida, 1707; Sardinia and Minorca, 1708. Took part in expedition to Canada, 1711. Returned same year after high casualties during shipwreck in the St. Lawrence. To the Channel Islands, 1713; England, 1715; Channel Islands, 1717; England, 1719; Flanders, 1744. Returned to England for rebellion in Scotland, 1745 and present at Falkirk and Culloden, 1746. Left Scotland for England, 1751. To Minorca, 1753. Present during siege of Fort Philip, 1756. To England, 1756; West Indies, 1758. Took part in attack on Martinique and capture of Guadeloupe, 1759;

capture of Dominica, 1761; Martinique and Havana, 1762. To England, 1764; America, 1774. During American War of Independence present at Lexington, Bunker Hill and Concord, 1775; Danbury, Brandywine and Germantown, 1777. To the West Indies, 1778 and took part in capture of St. Lucia. To England, 1780; Ireland, 1781; Canada, 1787; England, 1797. Took part in Helder campaign of 1799 and fought at Egmont-op-Zee and Alkmaar. Took part in expeditions to Hanover, 1805-06, Copenhagen, 1807, Gothenberg, 1808. To Spain, 1808 and fought at Corunna. Returned to England, 1809 and then took part in Walcheren expedition. Returned to the Peninsular, 1810. Fought at Fuentes d' Onoro, 1811, Badajoz and Salamanca, 1812; Vittoria, San Sebastian, the Bidassoa, Nivelle and the Nive, 1813. To America and fought at Bladensburg and Godley Wood, 1814. Later took part in operations on the Mississippi, battle of New Orleans and attack on Mobile, 1815. To England then Belgium, 1815. Fought at Waterloo then with Army of Occupation in France. To England, 1818; West Indies, 1819; England then Portugal, 1826; Scotland, 1828; Ireland, 1829; England, 1830. Began to move in detachments (guarding convicts) to Australia, 1831. To India, 1837; England, 1848; Malta then the Crimea, 1854. Fought at the Alma, Inkerman and Sevastopol. Private Thomas Grady awarded Victoria Cross and Distinguished Conduct Medal. To England then Ireland, 1856; Mauritius then India, 1857. Took part in attack on Fort Beyt, 1858. To Abyssinia, 1867. Took part in battle of Arogi Ravine, 1868. To England, 1868; Gibraltar, 1874; West Indies, 1879; England, 1881; Ireland, 1886; England, 1891; Malta, 1894; Hong Kong, 1897; Singapore, 1899; England, 1900; (mounted infantry detachments served in South Africa); Malta, 1901; India, 1903; England, 1912. Crossed to France and took part in retreat from Mons, battles of Le Cateau, the Marne, Aisne and Armentières, 1914; Ypres, 1915; the Somme, 1916; Arras and Ypres, 1917 (Private Albert Halton awarded Victoria Cross); the Somme, Lys, Arras, Hindenburg Line and the Selle, 1918. To Ireland, 1919; England, 1922; Palestine, 1930; Egypt, 1932; India, 1934. During Second World War moved to Iraq, 1941 then served in Egypt, 1942; Cyprus and

Above - Private Harry Christian, 2nd Battalion, The King's Own (Royal Lancaster Regiment) who won the Victoria Cross in France October, 1915. (Mike Davies).

Left - Lewis gun team - 1st Battalion, The King's Own Regiment (Lancaster), India, October 1938. (King's Own Royal Regiment Museum).

Below - Private - 1st Battalion, The King's Own (Royal Lancaster Regiment), marching order. Photo taken in Malta c1896.

Leros, 1942-43; Palestine, 1943; Syria, 1943-44; Italy, 1944-45. To Trieste, 1946; England, 1950; Germany, 1951; Korea, 1953; Hong Kong, 1954; England, 1956. Served in Aden and Kenya, 1958-59. Amalgamated with 1st Battalion, The Border Regiment to form 1st Battalion, The King's Own Royal Border Regiment, 1959.

2nd Battalion

Formed in Exeter, 1756. Became 62nd Regiment (see Wiltshire Regiment), 1758. Another formed, 1799 and took part in Helder campaign. Fought at Egmont-op-Zee and Alkmaar. Disbanded, 1802. Re-formed, 1804. To Jersey, 1807. Took part in Walcheren expedition of 1809 then returned to England. To Ceuta, Morocco, 1810; Portugal, 1812. After heavy casualties at Salamanca returned to England. Disbanded, 1815. Re-formed, 1857. To the Ionian Islands, 1859; Malta, 1864; Canada, 1866; Ireland, 1868; England, 1869; Ireland, 1874; England, 1877; South Africa, 1878. Present at battles of Inholobane Hill, Kambula and Ulundi, 1879. To India, 1880; England, 1895; South Africa, 1899. Took part in Tugela Heights operations, relief of Ladysmith and present at Spion Kop, Botha's Pass and Alleman's Nek. To England, 1903; Jersey, 1908; England, 1911; India, 1912; England, 1914. Crossed to France and took part in battles of Ypres and Loos, 1915. Private Harry Christian awarded Victoria Cross. Moved to Egypt then Macedonian Front in October. To England then Burma, 1919; India, 1924; the Sudan, 1929; England, 1930; Palestine, 1938. During Second World War served in Egypt, Syria and Libya, 1940-42; Ceylon, 1942-43; India and Burma, 1944-45. To Egypt, 1947. Moved to the Sudan and from there amalgamated with 1st Battalion at Trieste, 1949.

3rd Battalion

Formed, 1799 and took part in Helder campaign. Fought at Egmont-op-Zee and Alkmaar. Disbanded, 1802.

Badges

The Lion of England - the Ancient badge of the regiment. The Royal Cypher. The Red Rose of Lancaster - taken into use in 1881.

Uniform

Yellow facings changing to blue in 1715.

Nicknames

'The Lions' - from the badge. 'Barrell's Blues' - from the colour of the facings and colonel's name - William Barrell (1734-49).

The Royal Northumberland Fusiliers

Titles

1674-1675 The Irish Regiment.
1675-1751 Known by name of Colonel.
1751-1782 5th Regiment of Foot.
1782-1836 5th (Northumberland) Regiment of Foot.
1836-1881 5th (Northumberland Fusiliers) Regiment of Foot.
1881-1935 The Northumberland Fusiliers.
1935-1968 The Royal Northumberland Fusiliers.

1st Battalion

Raised at Bois le Duc in Holland by Daniel O'Brien, Viscount Clare, 1674. Known as the Irish Regiment until command passed to Sir John Fenwick, 1675. As part of the `English Brigade` fought in the army of the Prince of Orange at Maastricht, 1676 and St. Dennis, 1677. Called to England by King James II, 1685 and placed on British establishment. Took part in the Great Review and returned to Holland. To England, 1688; Ireland, 1690 and took part in battle of the Boyne. Present during attack on Athlone and siege and capture of Limerick, 1691. To England, 1691. After sea service sent to Flanders, 1693. To England, 1697; Ireland, 1698; Portugal, 1707. Fought at the Caya, 1709. To Gibraltar, 1712. Present during siege of 1727. To Ireland, 1728; England, 1755. Took part in operations along French coast, 1757 and again, 1758. Saw action at St. Malo, Cherbourg and St. Cas. Fought in Germany, 1760-63. Present at Warburg, Zierenberg and Kloster Kampen, 1760; Kirchdunkern, 1761. Gained first battle honour at Wilhelmstahl in June, 1762. To England, 1763 then to Ireland. To America, 1774. fought at Lexington and Bunker Hill, 1775; Brooklyn and White Plains, 1776; Bradywine and Germantown, 1777. To the West Indies, 1778 and fought at La Vigie, St. Lucia in December. Saw action in Grenada, 1779. To England, 1780; Ireland, 1781; Canada, 1787; England,1797; Holland, 1799. Took part in Helder expedition and present at Schoorldam, Warmenhuizen, Egmont-op-Zee and Winkel. To Gibraltar, 1800; England then Guernsey, 1802; England, 1804. Took part in expedition to Hanover, 1805. Half of battalion involved in shipwreck off Dutch coast and taken prisoner. Later rejoined remainder of battalion in England. To South America, 1806. Took part in attack on Buenos Ayres, 1807. To Ireland, 1807; Portugal, 1808 and present at Rolica, Vimiero and Corunna. Returned to England February, 1809 leaving detachment that later fought at Talavera in July. Took part in Walcheren expedition, 1809 and present at siege of Flushing. Returned to England in December and to Ireland, 1810.

Above - Hugh, Lord Percy, later 2nd Duke of Northumberland - Colonel of the 5th Regiment, 1768-84.

Below - Drums, 2nd Battalion, The Northumberland Fusiliers St. Georges Day, possibly Strensall Camp, York, 1932. Note red and white roses and Third Colour. Formal approval for Third Colour not given until January, 1933.

To Lisbon, 1812 and fought at Salamanca in July. Present at battles of Vittoria, Nivelle and the Nive, 1813; Orthes and Toulouse, 1814. Left France for Canada May, 1814. To Flanders via England, 1815, then to France. To England, 1818; West Indies, 1819; England, 1826; Ireland, 1827; Gibraltar, 1832; Malta, 1834; Ionian Islands, 1837; Gibraltar, 1842; Ireland, 1843; Mauritius, 1847; India, 1857. During Indian Mutiny took part in relief of Arrah and fought at Lucknow. Three Victoria Crosses awarded. To England via St. Helena, 1860; India, 1866. Served with Peshawar Valley Field Force during Afghan War, 1879-80. To England, 1880; Ireland, 1882; England, 1887; Gibraltar, 1896; Egypt, 1897. Took part in Sudan operations, 1898 and present at Omdurman. To Crete, 1898; England then South Africa, 1899. Fought at Belmont, Graspan, Modder River and Magersfontein, 1899. Engaged at Lichtenburg, 1901 and Tweebosch, 1902. To Mauritius, 1903; India, 1905; England, 1913. Crossed to France and fought at Mons and battles of the Marne, Aisne, Messines, Armentières and Ypres, 1914; Bellewaarde and Hooge, 1915; the Somme, 1916; Arras and Ypres, 1917; the Somme, Lys and Hindenburg Line, 1918. Left Germany for England, 1919. To Germany, 1922; Ireland, 1926; England, 1928; West Indies, 1931; Egypt, 1934. Fought in North African campaign and in Italy, 1944-45. Stationed in Gibraltar, 1947-49. Served in Korea, 1950-51 and gained battle honours `Seoul`, `Imjin` and `Kowang-San.` Fusilier D. Kinne awarded George Cross. Stationed in Hong Kong, 1951-52. Served in Kenya, 1953-55; Northern Ireland, 1956-57; Germany, 1958-59; Hong Kong, 1960-62; Aden, 1966-67. Became 1st Battalion, The Royal Regiment of Fusiliers, 1968.

2nd Battalion

Formed, 1799 and with 1st Battalion to Holland. Stationed in Gibraltar, 1800-02 then disbanded at Winchester. Re-formed at Horsham, Sussex, 1804. To the Channel Islands, 1806; Ireland, 1807; Portugal, 1809. Fought at Busaco, 1810; Sabugal, Fuentes de Onoro and El Bodon, 1811; Ciudad Rodrigo, Badajoz and Salamanca, 1812. Returned to England in November, 1812 and disbanded, 1816. Re-formed at Newcastle-upon-Tyne, 1857. To Mauritius, 1858; South Africa, 1862; England, 1867; Ireland, 1871; Channel Islands, 1874; England, 1875; India, 1880. Took part in Black Mountain expedition, 1888. To Singapore, 1895; England via Gibraltar, 1896; South Africa, 1899. Fought at Stormberg; Reddersburg and Nooitgedacht, 1900. To England, 1903; India, 1913; England, 1914. Crossed to France and engaged during Ypres battles and at Loos, 1915. Transferred to Macedonian Front in October, 1915. Returned to France in June, 1918 and took part in battles of the Hindenburg Line. To England, 1919 then to Mesopotamia. To India, 1921; Shanghai, 1930; England, 1931. Served in Palestine, 1936. Fought in France and Belgium, 1939-40; Italy, 1944; Greece, 1944-45. Disbanded, 1948.

Above - Philip Fitzroy, Northumberland Fusiliers. Served with 1st Battalion during Indian Mutiny and was present at relief of Lucknow. Commanded battalion 1886-88.

Left - `D` Company, 1st Battalion, The Northumberland Fusiliers on manoeuvres in Wiltshire, 1893.

Below Left - Officers - 1st Battalion, The Northumberland Fusiliers - Portsmouth September, 1896. Of this group Captain E.W. Dashwood (fifth from left - back row) would be severely wounded at Belmont on 23rd November, 1899 and Captain E.B. Eagar (first on left - back row) and Second Lieutenant R.W.M. Brine (forth from left, front row) killed. Captain G.L. Ray (first on left, middle row) was killed at Magersfontein on 11th December. All four men had served in the Sudan campaign of 1898 and were present at Omdurman.

Above - The Bandmasters of The Northumberland Fusiliers c1900. Left to right - Mr Shepherd (3rd Battalion), Mr Smith (4th Battalion), Mr Ivermee (1st Battalion) and Mr Wallace (2nd Battalion).

Right - 1st Battalion, The Northumberland Fusiliers at St. Eloi 26th March, 1916. Illustration by Caton Woodville.

Below - Drums, 1st Battalion, The Northumberland Fusiliers - Mullingar, Ireland 1882.

Facing Page: Above - Other ranks` glengarry badge - 5th Fusiliers, pre 1881.

Facing Page: Below - 2nd Battalion, The Royal Northumberland Fusiliers, England 1940. The side-car bears the markings of Southern Command.

3rd Battalion

Formed at York, 1900. To South Africa via Antiqua, 1902. Returned to England and disbanded, 1907.

4th Battalion

Formed at York, 1900. To Ireland, 1901. Disbanded, 1906.

Badges

St. George and the Dragon - the Ancient badge of the regiment also - The King's Crest, Red and White Rose and Rose and Crown.

Uniform

Early records shown the facings as yellow. Green was mentioned in 1742 and by 1751 gosling-green was officially listed. Regulation white for English regiments was ordered in 1881, the old gosling-green being restored in1899.

Nicknames

`The Shiners` - originated in Ireland in 1769 and recognised the regiment's reputation for smartness. `The Old and Bold`, `Fighting Fifth" and `Wellington's Bodyguard` all from the Peninsular War. What ever its official title, the regiment was always referred to as `The Fifth Fusiliers."

The Royal Warwickshire Fusiliers

Titles

1674-1751 Known by name of Colonel.
1751-1782 6th Regiment of Foot.
1782-1832 6th (1st Warwickshire) Regiment of Foot.
1832-1881 6th (Royal 1st Warwickshire) Regiment of Foot.
1881-1963 The Royal Warwickshire Regiment.
1963-1968 The Royal Warwickshire Fusiliers.

1st Battalion

Formed in Holland for Dutch service, 1674 and known as one of The Holland Regiments. Present at siege of Maastricht, 1676 and battle of Mons, 1678. To England, 1685, returning to Holland same year. To England and joined British establishment, 1688. To Ireland, 1690 and present during siege of Charlemont and battle of the Boyne. Fought at Athlone

18

and Aughrim, 1691. To England then Flanders, 1691. Present at Steenkirk, 1692. To England, 1693. Returned to Flanders and Present at siege of Namur, 1695. To England, 1696; Flanders then England, 1697; Ireland, 1698; England, 1702. Took part in expedition to Cadiz and attack on Vigo, 1702 and 1703 expedition to Newfoundland. To Spain and present at siege of Barcelona and capture of Montjuic, 1705 and battle of Almanza, 1707. Took part in capture of Minorca, 1708. Returned to Spain and fought at Almenara, Saragossa and Brihuega, 1710. To Ireland, 1712; England, 1739; Jamaica, 1742; England, 1743; Scotland, 1744. Engaged during Young Pretender's Rebellion and annihilated at Prestonpans, 1745. To England, 1751; Gibraltar, 1753; England, 1763; St. Vincent, 1772. Took part in war with the Caribs. To New York, 1776; England, 1777; Jersey, 1781; Ireland, 1783; Nova Scotia, 1786; New Brunswick, 1791; West Indies, 1793. Took part in capture of Martinique, St. Lucia and Guadeloupe, 1794. To England, 1795; Ireland, 1796; Canada, 1799; England, 1806; Gibraltar, 1807; Spain, 1808. Fought at Rolica, Vimiero and Corunna. To England, 1809 and took part in expedition to Walcheren same year. To Ireland, 1810, Portugal, 1812. Took part in battles of Vittoria, the Pyrenees and Nivelle, 1813; Orthes, 1814. Left France for Canada, 1814 and fought at Niagara. To Belgium then France, 1815; England, 1818; South Africa, 1821; India, 1825; England, 1841 (half of battalion to Aden, 1840 then to England, 1842). To Ireland, 1844; South Africa, 1846. Took part in Kaffir Wars of 1846-47 and 1850-53. (A Reserve Battalion, 6th Regiment formed in Ireland, 1846. Half of battalion stationed in Canada, 1846-48. Disbanded, 1850). To India, 1857; England, 1862; Jersey, 1865; Ireland, 1866; India, 1867. Took part in Hazara expedition, 1868. To Aden, 1879; England, 1880; Ireland, 1885; England, 1890; Malta, 1895; Egypt, 1897. Took part in Second Sudan War of 1898 and present at Atbara and Khartoum. To India, 1898. Took part in Bazar Valley and Mohmand expeditions of 1908. To England, 1912. During First World War took part in retreat from Mons

Below - Colours and Antelope - 2nd Battalion, The Royal Warwickshire Regiment c1897.

Right - Machine gunners - The Royal Warwickshire Regiment c1914.

and battles of Le Cateau, the Marne, Aisne and Armentières, 1914; Ypres, 1915; the Somme, 1916; Arras and Ypres, 1917; the Somme, Lys, Arras, Hindenburg Line and the Selle, 1918. To England, 1919; Ireland, 1920; England, 1923; Palestine, 1931; Egypt, 1932; India, 1933. During Second World War served on North West Frontier in India and Burma, 1945. Left India for England, 1947. Disbanded and 2nd Battalion re-numbered as 1st, 1948. Served in Austria, 1951-53; Korea, 1953-54 then to Egypt. To Cyprus then U.K. 1956. Served in Aden, 1959-60; Hong Kong, 1960-61; Germany, 1961-66; Hong Kong, Borneo and Singapore, 1966; Gibraltar, 1968. Became 2nd Battalion, The Royal Regiment of Fusiliers, 1968.

2nd Battalion

Formed in Liverpool, 1804. To Ireland then Jersey, 1811, England and disbanded, 1815. Re-formed in Preston, 1857. To Gibraltar, 1858; Corfu, 1862; Jamaica, 1864; Scotland, 1867; England, 1868; Ireland, 1870; Guernsey, 1874; England, 1875; India, 1878; Ceylon, 1891; England, 1896; South Africa, 1899. Took part in capture of Pretoria, fought at Diamond Hill and Belfast. To Bermuda, 1901; England, 1902; Malta, 1912; England, 1914. During First World War took part in Antwerp operation and battles of Ypres, 1914; Festubert and Loos, 1915; the Somme, 1916; Ypres, 1917. Moved to Italian Front in November, 1917. Took part in battle of Vittorio Veneto, 1918. One company formed in England and served in North Russia, 1919. Battalion to England then India, 1919; the Sudan, 1930; England, 1931. During Second World War fought in France and Belgium, 1939-40. Took part in D-Day assault landings, 6th June, 1944 then throughout North West Europe. Served in Palestine and Egypt, 1945-47. To England, 1948 and re-numbered as 1st Battalion (see above).

3rd Battalion

Formed, 1898 and to Malta. To Bermuda, 1902; Gibraltar, 1904; South Africa, 1905; England and disbanded, 1907.

4th Battalion

Formed at Colchester, 1900. To Ireland, 1901; England, 1906. Disbanded, 1907.

Badges

An Antelope and The Rose and Crown - Ancient badges. The Bear and Ragged Staff - introduced after 1881 and from the Warwick Militia.

Uniform

Deep yellow facings. Blue after Royal title was conferred in 1832.

Nicknames

'The Dutch Guards' - from Dutch service 1674-88. 'Guise's Geese' - from John Guise - Colonel of the 6th Regiment, 1738-65. The Saucy Sixth' - from the high standards set for recruiting in Warwickshire in 1796.

Below - 1st Battalion, The Royal Warwickshire Regiment - Band, India 1906. Lieutenant-Colonel F.G.F. Browne (right) and Captain L.W. Johnson, Adjutant (left) seated behind bass drum.

The Royal Fusiliers
(City of London Regiment)

Titles

1685-1751 Our Royal Regiment of Fusiliers, also Our Ordnance
Regiment. Known also by name of Colonel.
1751-1881 7th (Royal Fusiliers).
1881-1968 The Royal Fusiliers (City of London Regiment).

1st Battalion

Raised at the Tower of London in 1685 as a regiment to guard artillery
under the command of Lord Dartmouth, Master-General of Ordnance. To
Holland, 1689 and fought at Walcourt in August. To England then Ireland,

1690. Took part in capture of Cork and Kinsale. To Flanders, 1691 and present during siege of Namur. Fought at Steenkirk, 1692; Landen, 1693 and capture of Namur, 1695. To England, 1697; Channel Islands, 1698; England, 1702 and took part in expedition to Cadiz. To Spain, 1706 and engaged at Barcelona. Present during siege of Lerida, 1707. To England, 1708; Spain, 1709; Minorca, 1713. Took part in expedition to Sicily, 1718. To England then Ireland, 1719; England, 1721; Gibraltar, 1732; Ireland, 1749; England, 1755. Served on board ship during expedition to Minorca then to Gibraltar, 1756. To England, 1763; Canada, 1773. Fought at Quebec, 1775. Took part in New York and Philadelphia opeations. Present at capture of Charleston, 1780 and action at Cowpens, 1781. To England, 1783; Gibraltar, 1790; Canada, 1791; West Indies, 1802; England then Ireland, 1806. Took part in expedition to Copenhagen, 1807. To Canada then the West Indies, 1808. Took part in capture of Martinique, 1809 then returned to Canada. To Portugal, 1810 and fought at Busaco in September. Present at Albuhera, 1811; siege of Ciudad Rodrigo, Badajoz and Salamanca, 1812; Vittoria and Pyrenees operations, 1813; Nivelle, the Nive, Orthes and Toulouse, 1814. Returned to England and then to America. Took part in New Orleans campaign, 1815. Returned to England then to Belgium and France. To England then Ireland, 1818; Ionian Islands, 1825; Malta, 1828; England, 1836; Ireland, 1837; Gibraltar, 1839; West Indies, 1844; Canada, 1848; England, 1850; Crimea, 1854. Gained battle honours `Alma`, `Inkerman` and `Sevastopol.` Five Victoria Crosses awarded. To England, 1856; India, 1857. Took part in North West Frontier campaign of 1863 and present at Umbeyla. To Aden then England, 1870; Ireland, 1876; England, 1880; Gibraltar, 1884; Egypt, 1885; India, 1888; Burma, 1900; India, 1903. Took part in 1904 expedition to Tibet and present at Gyantse-jong and entry into Lhasa. To England, 1904; Ireland, 1909. During First World War fought at battles of the Aisne and Armentières, 1914; Hooge and Loos, 1915; the Somme, 1916; Arras, Messines, Ypres and Cambrai, 1917; the Somme, Hindenburg Line and the Selle, 1918. Served in Ireland, 1920-22 then to India. To Egypt, 1939. During Second World War served in the Sudan, 1940-41; Egypt and Syria, 1941; Iraq, 1942-43; Palestine and Syria, 1943; Italy, 1943-45. Served in Germany and Egypt then Korea, 1952-53; Egypt and the Sudan, 1953-54; the Persian Gulf, 1958-59; Kenya and Malta, 1959-61; Germany, 1963-67. Became 3rd Battalion, The Royal Regiment of Fusiliers, 1968.

Above - Uniforms - 7th (Royal Fusiliers) 1785-92. Note fur caps and gloves bearing regimental badge. Illustration by J.P. Groves.

Left - Painting by R. Simkin showing various uniforms of The Royal Fusiliers.

2nd Battalion

Formed in Canada, 1795. Disbanded, 1796. Re-formed at Wakefield, Yorkshire, 1803. To Ireland, 1808; Portugal, 1809 and present at Talavera in July. Fought at Busaco, 1810 and Albuhera, 1811. Sent home after heavy casualties. Recruited up to strength then to Jersey. To England, 1814. Disbanded, 1815. Re-formed, 1857. To Gibraltar, 1858; Malta, 1863; Canada, 1865. Engaged during Fenian Raids, 1866-67. To England, 1867; Ireland, 1872; India, 1874. Served in Afghanistan, 1880 and present at Kandahar. Victoria Cross awarded to Private T. Ashford. To England, 1889; Channel Islands, 1893; Ireland, 1895; South Africa, 1899. Took part in Relief of Ladysmith and present at Rooidam. Captain C. FitzClarence awarded Victoria Cross. To England, 1902; India, 1904; England, 1914. During First World War fought at Gallipoli then to France. Took part in operations on the Somme, 1916; Arras, Ypres and Cambrai, 1917; the Lys, Ypres and Courtrai, 1918. To India, 1919; Aden, 1920; England, 1922; Germany, 1926; England, 1929. Fought in France and Belgium, 1939-40. To North Africa, 1943. in Egypt and Italy, 1944; Greece, 1944-45. Disbanded, 1948.

3rd Battalion

Formed and to Malta, 1898. To Gibraltar, 1899; Egypt, 1901; the Sudan, 1902; Bermuda, 1903; South Africa, 1905; Mauritius, 1909; India, 1911; England, 1914. Crossed to France and fought at Ypres and Loos, 1915. Transferred to Macedonian Front October, 1915. Returned to France June, 1918 and fought at battles of the Hindenbugh Line, Selle and Sambre. Stationed in Ireland, 1919-22 then disbanded.

Above - Members of `B` Company, 1st Battalion, The Royal Fusiliers - India 1936. Note white hackle and foreign service dress.

Right - Drums - 1st Battalion, The Royal Fusiliers c1905.

Facing Page: Above - N.C.Os - 3rd Battalion, The Royal Fusiliers, Gibraltar, 1900. (Army Ordnance Corps - centre, back row).

Facing Page: Below - 3rd Battalion, The Royal Fusiliers. Note cloth shoulder title - RF over 3, white letters and number on red.

4th Battalion

Formed at Dover, 1900. To Ireland, 1904; England, 1909. Crossed to France and present at battles of Mons (two Victoria Crosses awarded), Le Cateau, the Marne, the Aisne, Messines, Armentières and Ypres, 1914; Hooge, 1915; the Somme, 1916; Arras and Ypres, 1917; the Somme, Lys, Hindenburg Line and the Selle, 1918. To Mesopotamia, 1919; India, 1920. Returned to England and disbanded, 1922.

Badges

A Rose within a crowned Garter - the Ancient badge of the regiment possible adopted from the markings on early cannon. The White Horse of Hanover. A Flaming Grenade.

Uniform

Originally yellow facings, changing to blue by 1702.

Nickname

`The Elegant Extracts` - officers for many years were selected from other regiments.

Above - Regimental Sergeant Major - 1st Battalion, The Royal Fusiliers with presentation Kukri, Perugia, 1945.
The gift from 1/5th Royal Gurkha Rifles commemorates the two regiments service together during the fighting in Italy. The R.S.M. wears the formation sign for the 8th Indian Division. (Royal Fusiliers Museum).

Right - Tibet, 1904 - Sergeant Christer, 1st Battalion, The Royal Fusiliers on right. (Royal Fusiliers Museum).

The King`s Regiment (Liverpool)

Titles

1685-1702 The Princess Anne of Denmark`s Regiment of Foot.
1702-1716 The Queen`s Regiment of Foot.
1716-1751 The King`s Regiment of Foot.
1751-1881 8th (The King`s) Regiment of Foot.
1881-1920 The King`s (Liverpool Regiment)
1921-1958 The King`s Regiment (Liverpool).

1st Battalion

Raised, 1685. To Ireland, 1689. Took part in siege of Carrickfergus, 1689; battle of the Boyne and sieges of Limerick, Cork and Kinsale, 1690. To England then Flanders, 1692; England, 1693; Flanders, 1696; England, 1697; Ireland, 1698; Flanders, 1701. Fought at Venloo, Fort St. Michael, Ruremonde and Liége, 1702; Huy and Limburg, 1703; Shellenburg and Blenheim, 1704; Huy and Helixem, 1705; Ramillies and Menin, 1706; Oudenarde and Wynandael, 1708; Tournay and Malplaquet, 1709; Pony a Vendin, Douai, Béthune, Aire and St. Venant, 1710; Arleux and Bouchain, 1711. To England, 1714; Ireland then Scotland, 1715. Fought at Dunblane in November. To Ireland, 1717; England, 1721; Ireland, 1722; England, 1739; Flanders, 1742. Present at Dettingen, 1743; Fontenoy, 1745. To England then Scotland, 1745. Present at Falkirk and Culloden, 1746. To Flanders and fought at Roucoux, 1746 and Lauffeld, 1747. To England, 1748; Gibraltar, 1750; England, 1752. Took part in capture of Aix, 1757. To Germany, 1760. Fought at Warburg, Zirenberg and Campen, 1760; Kirch-Denkern, 1761; Groebenstein and Cassel, 1762. To England, 1763; Canada, 1768; England, 1785; Jersey, 1790; Ireland, 1793. Flank companies to the West Indies, 1793 and fought at Martinique and Guadeloupe, 1794. Rest of regiment to Holland and present at Nimeguen, 1794. To England then the West Indies, 1795. Only four companies arrived (remainder driven back by storm) which took part in capture of Port Royal, Grenada, 1796 then returned to England. To Minorca, 1799; Gibraltar, 1800; Egypt, 1801. Fought at Roman Camp and Rahmanieh. To Gibraltar, 1802; England, 1803; Germany, 1805; England then Ireland, 1806; England, 1807. Took part in 1807 expedition to Copenhagen. To Nova Scotia then the West Indies, 1808. Took part in capture of Martinique, 1809. To Nova Scotia, 1809; Canada, 1810. During war in America present at Ogdenberg, York, Fort George, Sackett`s Harbour, Stony Creek and Buffalo, 1813; Street`s Creek, Lundy`s Lane, Fort Erie and Niagara, 1814. To England, 1815; Ireland, 1816; Malta, 1818; Ionian Islands, 1819; England,

27

1824; Ireland, 1827; Nova Scotia, 1830; West Indies, 1833; Nova Scotia, 1839; Ireland, 1841; England, 1843; India, 1846. During Indian Mutiny fought at Delhi, Agra, Lucknow and Cawnpore, 1857. Present at capture of Sandee, 1858. To England, 1860; Ireland, 1865; Malta, 1866; India, 1868; Aden then England, 1878; Ireland, 1882; England, 1889; Bermuda, 1891; Nova Scotia, 1893; West Indies, 1895; Cape Town, 1897. During Boer War fought at Rietfontein, Lombard`s Kop, Ladysmith, Laing`s Nek and Helvetia. Io Burma, 1902; India, 1905; Ireland, 1908; England, 1912. During First World War took part in retreat from Mons, battles of the Marne, Aisne and Ypres, 1914; Festubert, Loos and Hohenzollern Redoubt, 1915; the Somme, 1916; Arras and Cambrai, 1917; the Somme, Hindenburg Line and the Selle, 1918. To England then Jersey, 1919; Ireland, 1920; Jersey, 1923; England, 1924; Malta; 1926; the Sudan, 1927; Egypt and Cyprus, 1928; India, 1932. During Second World War remained in India, serving in Burma, 1944. To England, 1947; Germany, 1948; England, Hong Kong then Korea, 1952. To Hong Kong, 1953; England, 1955; Germany, 1958. Amalgamated with 1st Battalion, The Manchester Regiment to form 1st Battalion, The King`s Regiment (Manchester and Liverpool), 1958.

2nd Battalion

Formed, 1756. Took part in capture of Aix, 1757. Became 63rd Regiment (see The Manchester Regiment), 1758. Another formed, 1804. Flank companies took part in 1809 expedition to Walcheren. To Jersey, 1809; England then Nova Scotia and New Brunswick, 1810; Canada, 1814. Took part in siege of Plattsburg, 1814. To England, 1815 and merged with 1st Battalion. Re-formed in Ireland, 1857. To Gibraltar, 1858; Malta, 1863; England, 1868; Ireland, 1873; England, 1876; India, 1877. Took part in Afghan War, 1878-80 and present at capture of the Peiwar Kotal, 1878. Took part in Burma War, 1885-87.To Aden, 1891; England, 1892; Ireland,

1st Battalion, The King's Regiment (Liverpool), India, 1930s.

Facing Page: Above - Captain Andrew Moynihan's Company, 2nd Battalion, 8th Regiment - Malta c1865. Captain Moynihan won the Victoria Cross while serving with the 90th Regiment at Sebastopol, September, 1855.

Facing Page: Below - Collar badges - The King's (Liverpool Regiment), 1882-95 - other ranks (top), officers (bottom).

1897; England, 1904; India, 1908. Remained in India during First World War, serving on North West Frontier. To the Sudan, 1920; Hong Kong, 1921; India, 1924; Iraq, 1925; England, 1927; Gibraltar, 1938. During Second World War served in Gibraltar then to Egypt, 1943; Italy and Greece, 1944-45. To Cyprus, 1946; Palestine, Cyprus then England, 1948. Amalgamated with 1st Battalion, 1948.

3rd Battalion

Formed in Ireland, 1900. Disbanded, 1901.

4th Battalion

Formed in Ireland, 1900. Disbanded, 1901.

Badges

The White Horse of Hanover - authorized in 1716. The Sphinx superscribed `Egypt` for campaign of 1801. The Red Rose - adopted in 1881. The Royal Cypher.

Uniform

Blue facings replaced yellow in 1716.

Nicknames

`The Leather Hats` - acquired during war in America, 1812-15.

Above - Bandsman - The King`s (Liverpool Regiment). He wears the pattern of collar badge introduced in 1895.

Right - 1st Battalion, The King`s Regiment (Liverpool), Korea, 1953.

Below - Cap badge - The Norfolk Regiment. The wreath and title scroll were removed after 1935.

Bottom - Ensign and Colour Sergeant with Regimental Colour - 9th Regiment c1813. Illustration by Hamilton Smith.

The Royal Norfolk Regiment

Titles

1685-1751 Known by name of Colonel.
1751-1782 9th Regiment of Foot.
1782-1881 9th (East Norfolk) Regiment of Foot.
1881-1935 The Norfolk Regiment.
1935-1959 The Royal Norfolk Regiment.

1st Battalion

Raised by Colonel Henry Cornwall at Gloucester, 1685. To Ireland, 1689. Took part in battle of the Boyne, 1690, sieges of Limerick and Athlone, battle of Aughrim, 1691. To England, 1694 and took part in expedition to Breast and operations on French coast. Took part in expedition to Cadiz, 1695. To Ireland, 1698; England, 1701; Flanders, 1702. Present at Venloo and Liége, 1702. To England then Portugal, 1704. Besieged and surrendered at Castello de Vide then sent to France. Returned to Portugal and present at Valenza, Albuquerque and Badajoz, 1705; Alcantara and Madrid, 1706; Almanza, 1707. Left Spain for England, 1708. To Ireland, 1709; Minorca, 1718; Gibraltar, 1746; Ireland, 1750; England, 1755; Ireland, 1757; England, 1759. Took part in expedition to Bell Isle, 1761. To England then the West Indies, 1762. Fought in Cuba and gained battle honour `Havannah.` To St Augustine of East Florida, 1763; Ireland, 1769; Canada, 1776. During American War of Independence present at Three Rivers, 1776 and in Saratoga campaign - South Bay and Fort St. Anne. Taken prisoner and returned to England during 1781. To Ireland, 1785; West Indies, 1788. Fought on Tabago, 1793; Martinique, St. Lucia and Guadeloupe, 1794; Grenada, 1795. To England, 1796. Took part in Helder campaign of 1799 and present at Schorel. Took part in expedition to Spain, 1801. To Ireland, 1803. Took part in 1805-06 expedition to the Elbe - part of regiment shipwrecked on French coast and taken prisoner. To Portugal, 1808. Fought at Rolica, Vimiera and during retreat to Corunna. Returned to England and took part in Walcheren expedition of 1809. To Portugal and fought at Busaco, 1810; Fuentes d' Onoro, 1811; Badajoz and Salamanca, 1812; Vittoria, San Sebastian, the Bidassoa, Nivelle and the Nive, 1813. Left France for Canada, 1814. To England then France, 1815; England, 1818; West Indies, 1819; England, 1826; Ireland, 1828; England, 1832; Mauritius, 1833; India, 1835. During First Afghan War took part in storming of the Khyber Pass and gained battle honour `Cabool 1842.` Fought in First Sikh War and present at Moodkee and Ferozeshah, 1845 and Sobraon, 1846. To England, 1847; Ireland, 1848; Malta, 1854; the

31

Crimea, 1854. Fought at the Redan and Sevastopol, 1855. To Canada, 1856; England, 1857; Ionian Islands, 1860; Malta then Gibraltar, 1864; South Africa, 1865; Ireland, 1870; Channel Islands, 1872; England, 1873; Ireland, 1877; England, 1882; Gibraltar, 1885; England, 1886; Gibraltar, 1887; India, 1889; Burma, 1890. Took part in Chin Hills operations, 1892. To India, 1893; South Africa, 1904; England, 1907; Ireland, 1912. Crossed to France and took part in battles of Mons, the Marne, Aisne and Ypres, 1914; Ypres, 1915; the Somme, 1916; Arras and Ypres, 1917. Transferred to Italian Front November, 1917. Returned to France and at battles of the Lys, Somme, Hindenburg Line and the Selle, 1918. Served in Ireland, 1919-22 then to the West Indies, 1923. To Egypt, 1925; Shanghai, 1928; India, 1929. Served on North West Frontier, 1936-37. To England, 1940. Took part in D-Day landings June, 1944 and fought in North West Europe, 1944-45. Left Germany for England, 1950. Served in Korea, 1951-52; Hong Kong, 1952-53; Cyprus, 1955-56; Germany, 1957-59. Amalgamated with 1st Battalion, The Suffolk Regiment to form 1st East Anglian Regiment (Royal Norfolk and Suffolk), 1959.

Above - Officers` shako badge - 9th Regiment, 1816-29. (H.L. King).

Right - Officer - 9th Regiment. Photograph taken in Norwich.

2nd Battalion

Formed, 1799 and to Holland on Helder campaign. Present at Schorel. Took part in expedition to Spain, 1800. Disbanded, 1802.   Re-formed at Sherborne in Dorset, 1804. To Portugal, 1808; Gibraltar, 1809. Two companies fought in Spain and present at Barrosa, 1811. To England, 1813. Disbanded, 1815. Re-formed at Great Yarmouth, 1857. To the Ionian Islands, 1858; Gibraltar then Hong Kong, 1864; Japan, 1866; Ireland, 1868; England, 1869; India, 1874. Took part in Second Afghan War of 1878-80 gaining battle honour `Kabul 1879.` To Burma, 1888. Took part in Chin Hills operations, 1888-89. To India then England, 1890; Ireland, 1897; England, 1899; South Africa, 1900. Took part in Paardeberg operations and present at Karee Sidings, Brandfort and Coetzee`s Drift. To England, 1903; South Africa, 1905; Gibraltar, 1908; India, 1911, Mesopotamia, 1914. Captured at Kut al Amara, 1916. Left India for Mesopotamia, 1921. Later served in Iraq and then to Aden, 1923. To England, 1924; Gibraltar, 1937; England, 1939. Fought in France and Belgium, 1939-40 then to India, 1942. To Burma, 1944; India, 1945. Disbanded, 1948.

3rd Battalion

Formed, 1799. Took part in expedition to Spain, 1800. Disbanded, 1802.

Below - The Fifes - 1st Battalion, The Norfolk Regiment entertaining the camp at brigade training, 1910.

Badges

The Figure of Britannia - origins uncertain. The Castle of Norwich - introduced in 1881.

Uniform

Yellow facings replaced by white in 1881. Yellow was restored in 1925.

Nicknames

`The Holy Boys` - the Britannia badge was mistaken for the Virgin Mary by the Spanish during the Peninsular War. `The Fighting Ninth.`

Above - Officers` silver shoulder-belt plate - 9th Regiment c1820.

Right - Drum-Major - 2nd Battalion, The Norfolk Regiment, Gibraltar c1908.

The Royal Lincolnshire Regiment

Titles

1685-1751 Known by name of Colonel.
1751-1782 10th Regiment of Foot.
1782-1881 10th (North Lincoln) Regiment of Foot.
1881-1946 The Lincolnshire Regiment of Foot.
1946-1960 The Royal Lincolnshire Regiment.

1st Battalion

Formed in Derby by Colonel John Granville, Earl of Bath, 1685. To the Channel Islands, 1690; Flanders, 1691. Fought at Steenkirk, 1692 and Dottignies, 1693. To England, 1696; Flanders, 1697; Ireland, 1698;

Right - Battalion Headquarters - 2nd Battalion, The Lincolnshire Regiment, near St. Pol, 1940.

Below - Officers` gilt shoulder-belt plate - 10th Regiment, 1847-55.

Holland, 1701. During campaign in Flanders present at Roermond and Liége, 1702; Tongres and Limburg, 1703; Schellenberg and Blenheim, 1704; Helixhem, 1705; Ramillies and Menin, 1706; Oudenarde, 1708; Malplaquet and Tournay, 1709; Bouchain, 1711. To England, 1715; Gibraltar, 1730; Ireland, 1749; North America, 1767. During War of Independence fought at Lexington and Bunker Hill, 1775; Brooklyn and Fort Washington, 1776; Brandywine and Germantown, 1777. To England, 1778; Ireland, 1783; Jamaica, 1786; England then the West Indies, 1795. Took part in operations on Grenada. To England then India, 1798; Egypt, 1801; Malta then Gibraltar, 1803; Sicily, 1807. Took part in expedition to Naples, 1809. To Spain, 1812. Present at Castalla and Tarragona, 1813. To Sicily, 1814; Malta, 1815; the Ionian Islands, 1816; Malta, 1819; England, 1821; Ireland, 1823; Portugal, 1826; Ionian Islands, 1828; Ireland, 1838; England, 1839; India, 1842. Took part in First Sikh War and present at Sabraon, 1846. Fought at Mooltan and Goojerat, 1848-49. During Indian Mutiny present during siege and capture of Lucknow, 1857-58. Lieutenant H.M. Havelock, Private J. Kirk and Private D. Dempsey awarded Victoria Cross. To England, 1859; Ireland, 1862; South Africa, 1864; Japan, 1868; Hong Kong, 1871; Singapore, 1872. Took part in Malayan operations, 1874 and Perak, 1875-76. To England, 1877; Malta, 1895; Egypt, 1897. Took part in Second Sudan War and present at Atbara and Omdurman, 1898. To India, 1898; Aden, 1910; England, 1912. During First World War took part in battles of Mons, Le Cateau, the Aisne, Messines, Armentières and Ypres, 1914; Hooge, 1915; the Somme, 1916; Arras, Ypres and Cambrai, 1917, the Somme, the Lys, Hindenburg Line and the Selle, 1918. To Ireland, 1919; England, 1924; Gibraltar, 1930; Shanghai, 1931; Hong Kong, 1932; India, 1936. During Second World War took part in Arakan operations and fought in Burma, 1945. To Malaya, 1945; England, 1947. Amalgamated with 2nd Battalion in Egypt, 1948. To Germany, 1952; England then Malaya, 1955; England, Aden then Germany, 1958. Amalgamated with 1st Battalion, The Northamptonshire Regiment to form 2nd East Anglian Regiment (Duchess of Gloucester`s Own Royal Lincolnshire and Northamptonshire), 1960.

2nd Battalion

Formed in Essex, 1804. Took part in Walcheren expedition, 1809. To Jersey, Gibraltar then Malta, 1810; Sicily, 1811. Took part in capture of Ponza, 1813. To Malta, 1815. Merged with 1st Battalion, 1816. Re-formed in Ireland, 1858. To South Africa, 1860; India, 1865; Burma, 1871; England, 1873; Malta, 1878; Gibraltar, 1881; India, 1882; Singapore, 1892; England, 1895; South Africa, 1900. Present during operations at Paardeberg and Johannesburg. To England, 1904; Gibraltar, 1911; Nova Scotia, Bermuda then England, 1914. During First World War fought at Neuve Chapelle, 1914 and 1915; Aubers Ridge and Bois Grenier, 1915 (Corporal C. Sharpe awarded Victoria Cross); the Somme, 1916; Ypres and Passchendaele, 1917; the Somme, Lys, Hindenburg Line and the Selle, 1918. To England then India, 1919; the Sudan, 1928; England, 1930; Malta, 1935; Palestine then England, 1936. Fought in France and Belgium, 1939-40. Took part in D-Day landings and fought in North West Europe, 1944-45. To Egypt, 1945. Served in Palestine and amalgamated with 1st Battalion, 1948.

Badges

The Sphinx superscribed `Egypt` - for services in 1801.

Uniform

Blue coats with red facings were worn until 1691. Yellow facings were later adopted, changing to white in 1881.

Nicknames

`The Poachers` - from the regimental march `The Lincolnshire Poacher.`The Springers` - from the quickness that the regiment went into action during the American War of Independence.

Above - Other ranks` Cap badge - The Lincolnshire Regiment prior to 1946.

Left - Cap badges - The Royal Lincolnshire Regiment after 1946. Officers` (left), other ranks` (right).

The Devonshire Regiment

Titles

1685-1751 Known by name of Colonel.
1751-1782 11th Regiment of Foot.
1782-1881 11th (North Devon) Regiment of Foot.
1881-1958 The Devonshire Regiment.

1st Battalion

Raised by Henry, Duke of Beaufort in Bristol, 1685. Present at York and Hull during Monmouth Rebellion, 1688. To Ireland, 1689. Took part in relief of Londonderry, battle of the Boyne, sieges of Athlone and Limerick. To England then took part in operations in the Netherlands, 1703. To Portugal, 1704 and taken prisoner. To England, 1705; Portugal, 1706; Spain, 1707 and present at Yecla and Almanza. To England then Flanders, 1708. Present at siege of Mons, 1709. Took part in operations in France and Flanders, 1710-11. To England then America on Walker Expedition, 1711. Returned to England same year. To France, 1712; England then Scotland, 1714; Ireland then Scotland, 1715. Took part in battles of Sheriffmuir, 1715 and Glenshiel, 1719. To England, 1722; Flanders, 1742; Germany, 1743. Fought

at Dettingen. To Flanders then the Netherlands, 1744. Took part in battle of Fontenoy, 1745. To England, 1745; the Netherlands, 1746 and fought at Rocoux. To England, 1747; Germany, 1760. Present at Warburg and Kloster Kamp, 1760; Vellinghausen, 1761; Wilhelmsthal, 1762. To England, 1763; Minorca, 1764; England, 1771; Ireland, 1775; Gibraltar, 1783; England, 1793. Detachments served with Mediterranean Fleet, 1793-97, present during operations at Toulon and Hyères Bay, 1793; Corsica, 1794 and Genoa, 1795. Took part in expedition to Ostend, 1798. To the West Indies, 1800; England, 1806; Madeira, 1807; Portugal, 1809. During Peninsular War took part in battles of Busaco, 1810; Salamanca, 1812; Pyrenees operations, Nivelle, 1813; Orthez and Toulouse, 1814. To Ireland, 1814; Gibraltar, 1816; England, 1820; Ireland, 1821; Portugal, 1827; the Ionian Islands, 1828; Ireland, 1835; Canada, 1838; England, 1840; Ireland, 1843; England, 1844; New South Wales, 1845; England, 1857; India, 1864; England, 1877; Ireland, 1882; England, 1888; Egypt, 1891; India, 1893. Took part in Tirah and Punjab campaigns, 1897. To South Africa, 1899. Present at Ladysmith and fought at Elandslaagte and Waggon Hill. Lieutenant J.E.I. Masterton awarded Victoria Cross. To India, 1902; Burma, 1905; England, 1908; Jersey, 1911. During First World War fought at Mons, on the Marne, Aisne, at La Bassée and Ypres, 1914; at Ypres, 1915; on the Somme, 1916; at Arras and Ypres, 1917. Moved to Italian Front end of 1917. Returned to France, 1918 and took part in battles of the Lys, Somme, Hindenburg Line and the Selle. Lance Corporal G. Onions awarded Victoria Cross. To England, 1919 then Ireland. To England, 1922; Shanghai then Malta, 1927; India, 1929. During Second World War fought in Burma, 1944-45. Left India for Singapore, 1945. Served in Malaya and then to Hong Kong, 1947. Returned to Singapore and served in Malaya during Emergency, 1948-50. To England, 1950; North Africa, 1951; England, 1952. Served in Kenya during Mau Mau Emergency, 1953-55. To England then Germany, 1955. Amalgamated with 1st Battalion, The Dorset Regiment to form 1st Battalion, The Devonshire and Dorset Regiment, 1958.

Charge of the 2nd Battalion, Devonshire Regiment at Waggon Hill - 6th January, 1900. Illustration by W.T. Maud and taken from a sketch done by him on the spot.

Below - Presentation of Colours to 1st Battalion, The Devonshire Regiment by H.M. King George V at Aldershot - 11th June, 1924.

2nd Battalion

Formed, 1756. Became 64th Regiment, 1758 (see The North Staffordshire Regiment). Another formed in Ireland, 1808 and to England. Took part in Walcheren expedition of 1809. Present during siege of Flushing. To the Channel Islands, 1810; Gibraltar, 1811. Merged with 1st Battalion, 1816. Re-formed, 1857. To the Cape of Good Hope then China. To the Cape of Good Hope, 1866; Ireland, 1870; Scotland, 1872; England, 1873; India, 1877. Took part in Second Afghan War of 1878-80. To Burma, 1890; Egypt then England, 1893; South Africa, 1899. Present at Colenso, Spion Kop, Vaal Krantz and Monte Cristo. To England, 1903; Crete, 1908; Malta, 1910; Egypt, 1912; England, 1914. During First World War fought at Neuve Chapelle, 1914 and 1915; Aubers Ridge and Bois Grenier, 1915; on the Somme, 1916; at Ypres, 1917; on the Somme, at Villers Bretonneux, Bois des Buttes and Arras, 1918. To England, 1919 then India. To Aden, 1926; England, 1927; Malta, 1938. During Second World War remained in Malta till 1943 then served in Sicily and Italy. Returned to England then after Normandy assault landing in June, 1944 fought through North West Europe to Germany. Left Germany for England, 1948 and disbanded.

Badges

The Castle and motto `Semper fidelis` from the Arms of Exeter - taken into use in 1883 and previously a badge of the Devon Militia. A Rose - introduced in 1881.

Uniform

Early facings are described as `Tawny` changing to green by 1742. White was wore after 1881, but the former green was restored in 1905.

Nickname

`The Bloody Eleventh` - after the sever fighting at Salamanca in July, 1812. The regiment`s casualties were more than 300 out of a strength of just over 400.

Below - `D` Company, 1st Battalion, The Devonshire Regiment - Guard of Honour, Malta, 1929.

The Suffolk Regiment

Titles

1685-1751 Known by name of Colonel.
1751-1782 12th Regiment of Foot.
1782-1881 12th (East Suffolk) Regiment of Foot.
1881-1959 The Suffolk Regiment.

1st Battalion

Raised by Henry Howard, 7th Duke of Norfolk at Norwich, 1685. To Ireland, 1689. Present during action at Carrickfergus, battle of the Boyne, capture of Athlone and the fighting at Aughrim. To England, 1691. Served on board ship during operations along French coast and at Ostend, 1692. To Flanders, 1694. Engaged at Fort Kenoque and later surrendered at Dixmude, 1695. To Ireland, 1697; the Leeward Islands, 1701; Jamaica, 1704; England, 1705. Served on board ship during operations along French coast and in Flanders, 1708. Present at Lessinghen. To Portugal, 1710; Spain, 1711; Minorca, 1712; England, 1720; Flanders, 1742. During War of the Austrian Succession fought at Dettingen, 1743 and Fontenoy, 1745. To England, 1745. Served in Holland, 1748. To Minorca, 1749; England, 1751; Germany, 1758. Fought at Minden, 1759; Warburg, 1760 and Fellinghausen, 1761. Also present at Groebenstein and Wilhelmstahl, 1762. To England, 1763; Gibraltar, 1769. Present during Siege of 1779-83.

Above - Light Company officer - 12th Regiment, 1796. Green over red plume, scarlet jacket and waistcoat, yellow facings, gold lace. Illustration by P.W. Reynolds.

Below - Three officers - 12th Regiment, 1825-30. The headdress is the Regency shako worn with tall (12 inch) plumes - white over red (battalion companies), white (grenadier company). Note the officer in blue undress uniform. Plume removed, his shako is covered by a protective canvas bag. Illustration by P.W. Reynolds.

Right - Officers - 1st Battalion, The Suffolk Regiment, Tower of London, 1st August,1895. It is Minden Day and roses are being worn in the caps.

To England, 1783; Jersey and Guernsey, 1788; England, 1790; Ireland, 1791. Flank companies served in West Indies, 1793-95 and engaged during operations on Martinique, St. Lucia and Guadeloupe. Just one officer and two men returning to England. Battalion companies embarked for Flanders, 1794 and engaged in operations around Ypres, and then present at Boxtel and Nimeguen. Later withdrew from Holland into Germany and to England, 1795. Took part in capture of Isle D`Yeu on the French coast October-December, 1795. To India, 1796. In Mysore, 1799 took part in actions at Malleville, Shaw`s Post and storming of Seringapatam. Took part in war in Travancore, 1809. Engaged during fighting for Bourbon and Mauritius, 1810. Left Mauritius for Bourbon, 1813 returning to Mauritius, 1815. To Ireland, 1817; England, 1820; Jersey and Guernsey, 1821; England then Gibraltar, 1823; England, 1834; Ireland, 1835; Mauritius, 1837; England, 1847; Ireland, 1852; Australia, 1854. Took part in New Zealand wars, 1860-66. To England, 1867; Ireland, 1872; India, 1876. Took part in Afghan War, 1878-80 and with Hazara Field Force during Black Mountain expedition, 1888. To England, 1892; Malta, 1897; England then South Africa, 1899. Fought at Colesberg and Belfast. To England, 1902; Malta, 1907; Egypt, 1911; the Sudan then England, 1914. During First World War fought at Ypres and Loos, 1915 then to Egypt. From there transferred to Macedonian front. To Gallipoli, 1918; England then India, 1919. Took part in Malabar operations, 1921-22. To Gibraltar, 1924; England, 1926; Malta, 1937; England, 1939. Fought in France, 1940 and North West Europe, 1944-45. Served in Egypt and Palestine, 1945-48;

Malaya, 1949-53; Cyprus, 1956-59. Amalgamated with 1st Battalion, The Royal Norfolk Regiment to form 1st East Anglian Regiment (Royal Norfolk and Suffolk), 1959.

2nd Battalion.

Raised, 1756 and made independent as 65th Regiment (see The York and Lancaster Regiment), 1758. Another formed, 1811. To Ireland, 1813; England, 1814 and guarded American prisoners at Dartmoor. Stationed in France, 1815. To Ireland, 1816 and disbanded, 1818. A Reserve Battalion, 12th Regiment formed, 1842 and sent to Mauritius via South Africa. To Cape Colony, 1851 and took part in Kaffir War, 1851-53. Detachment on board H.M.S. Birkenhead 24th February, 1852. Designated as 2nd Battalion and to England, 1858. To India, 1864; England, 1877; Jersey, 1880; Ireland, 1882; England, 1888; Egypt, 1889; India, 1891; Burma, 1895; India, 1899; Aden, 1906; England, 1907; Ireland, 1913. Crossed to France, 1914 and engaged during retreat from Mons and later at Ypres. Fought at Hooge, 1915; on the Somme, 1916; Arras and Ypres, 1917; on the Somme, Lys and Hindenburg Line, 1918. To England, 1919; Ireland, 1920; England, 1923; Gibraltar then Hong Kong, 1926. Served with Shanghai Defence Force, 1927-29. To India 1929. Served on North West Frontier and in Burma during Second World War. To England, 1947 and amalgamated with 1st Battalion, 1948.

Badges

The Castle, key and motto of Gibraltar - commemorates the part played by the 12th Foot during the siege of 1779-83.

Uniform

White facings were replaced by yellow before 1742. Regulation white for English regiments was ordered in 1881, but yellow was restored in 1899.

Nicknames

`The Old Dozen` - from the regimental number.

Above - Lance Corporal - The Suffolk Regiment. Note Drummers` arm-badge and special lace edging the shoulder straps and forming an Austrian knot of the cuffs. There are green bugle-cords and three inverted chevrons on the lower left arm denoting more than twelve years good conduct.

Left - 1st Battalion, The Suffolk Regiment - Drums c1904 -1905.

Below - Officer`s Shooting Team - 1st Battalion, The Suffolk Regiment, Malta, 1909. Winners of the Emmanuel Cup - left to right - Lieutenants W.J. Terry (killed in action 1915), D.V.M. Balders, I.R.B. Bond and P.S. Walker.

The Somerset Light Infantry
(Prince Albert's)

Titles

1685-1751 Known by name of Colonel.
1751-1782 13th Regiment of Foot.
1782-1822 13th (1st Somersetshire) Regiment of Foot.
1822-1842 13th (1st Somersetshire) Regiment (Light Infantry).
1842-1881 13th or Prince Albert's Regiment of Light Infantry.
1881-1912 The Prince Albert's (Somersetshire Light Infantry).
1912-1920 Prince Albert's (Somerset Light Infantry).
1921-1959 The Somerset Light Infantry (Prince Albert's).

1st Battalion

Raised by Theophilus, 7th Earl of Huntingdon, 1685. To Scotland, 1689. Fought at Killiekrankie in July and then to Ireland. Took part in battle of the Boyne, 1690 and present at capture of Cork and Kinsale. To England, 1691. Took part in expeditions to Flanders,1692 and Camarett Bay, 1694. To Ireland, 1698; Holland, 1701. Present during siege of Venloo, 1702. Embarked for service in Portugal and Spain, 1704. Present during siege of Gibraltar, 1704-05; fighting at Barcelona, 1705 and San Mateo 1706.

Officers - 2nd Battalion, The Somersetshire Light Infantry prior to leaving for South Africa in 1899. Lieutenant-Colonel E.J. Gallwey (commanding officer) seated third from right

Converted into regiment of dragoons (Pearce's), 1706. Commanding officer and cadre returned to England to re-form. Embarked for service in Portugal and Spain, 1708. Took part in battle of the River Caya, 1709. To Gibraltar, 1711 and present during siege of 1727. To England, 1728; Flanders, 1742. Fought at Dettingen, 1743; Fontenoy, 1745. Sent back to England for rebellion in Scotland. Present during action at Falkirk Muir and battle of Culloden, 1746. Returned to Flanders and fought at Roucoux, 1746 and Lauffeld, 1747. To England, 1747; Gibraltar, 1754; England, 1762; Ireland, 1768; Minorca, 1769; England, 1776; West Indies, 1780; England, 1782; Ireland, 1783; West Indies, 1790. Took part in operations on St. Domingo, 1794 and present at Cape Tiburon, L'Acul and Port Au Prince. To England, 1795; Ireland, 1797; England, 1799. Took part in expedition to Spain. To Egypt, 1800. Took part in action at Roman Camp and battle of Alexandria. To Malta, 1802; Gibraltar, 1803; England, 1805; Ireland, 1807; West Indies, 1808. Took part in capture of Martinique, 1809 and Guadeloupe, 1810. To Canada, 1813; England, Ireland then Channel

Lieutenant - The Somersetshire Light Infantry in full dress. The helmet is the Colonial pattern with green pugaree.

Machine gun detachment - 2nd Battalion, The Somersetshire Light Infantry - Malta, 1911.

Islands, 1815. To England, 1819; Ireland, 1820; England then India, 1822. Took part in First Burma War, 1824-26 gaining battle honour `Ava.` To Afghanistan, 1838. Fought at Ghazni, 1839, present during siege of Jellalabad, 1841-42 and at Kabul, 1842. Returned to India, 1842. Took part in storming of the Heights of Truckee, 1845. To England, 1845; Ireland, 1847; Scotland, 1850; Gibraltar, 1851; Crimea, 1854. Fought at Sevastopol, 1855. To Gibraltar then South Africa, 1856; India, 1857. Took part in action at Azimghur, 1858 - Sergeant W. Napier and Private P. Carlin awarded Victoria Cross. To England, 1864; Ireland, 1866; Gibraltar, 1867; Malta, 1872; South Africa, 1874. During Zulu War of 1879 fought at Kambula and Ulundi. Major W.K. Leet awarded Victoria Cross. To England, 1879; Ireland, 1882; England, 1886; Gibraltar, 1891; India, 1893. Took part in Mohmand campaign of 1897. To England, 1908. During First World War took part in retreat from Mons and battles of Le Cateau, the Marne, the Aisne and Armentières, 1914; Ypres, 1915; the Somme, 1916; Arras and Ypres, 1917; the Somme, Lys, Arras, Hindenburg Line and the Selle, 1918. To England then Ireland, 1919; England, 1923; Egypt, 1926; Hong Kong, 1928; India, 1931. Served in Arakan, 1943-44. To England, 1948; Germany, 1951. Served in Malayan campaign, 1952-55 and Cyprus, 1956-57. Amalgamated with 1st Battalion, The Duke of Cornwall`s Light Infantry to form 1st Battalion, The Somerset and Cornwall Light Infantry, 1959.

2nd Battalion

Formed at Winchester, 1858. To South Africa, 1859; Mauritius, 1863; England, 1867; Ireland, 1871; Scotland, 1875; England, 1876; Malta, 1877; India, 1878; Burma, 1883. Took part in Burma War of 1885-87. To India, 1887; England, 1894; Channel Islands, 1895; England, 1897; South Africa, 1899. Present at Spion Kop, Vaal Krantz and during relief of Ladysmith. To England, 1903; Malta, 1908; North China, 1911; India, 1913. Remained in India throughout First World War. Took part in Third Afghan War of 1919. To the Sudan, 1926; England, 1927; Gibraltar, 1939. Served in Egypt, 1943-44; Italy, 1944; Greece, 1944-45. To Austria, 1947, then England and amalgamated with 1st Battalion, 1948.

Badges

The Sphinx superscribed 'Egypt' - to commemorate services in Egypt, 1801. A Bugle-horn - adopted in 1822 after conversion to light infantry. A Mural Crown superscribed 'Jellalabad'- awarded after the defence of Jellalabad, 1841-42. The Cypher of Prince Albert - adopted after 1842.

Uniform

Yellow facings replaced by blue in 1842

Nicknames

'Jellalabad Heroes' and 'The Illustrious Garrison' - after gallant defence of Jellalabad. 'The Light Bobs' - a traditional name for light infantry. 'The Bleeders' - given to 2nd Battalion just after formation in 1858. The men were given a £3 bounty which they promptly spent of drink.

Above - Glengarry cap badge - 13th Regiment, 1874-1881.

Below - Cap badge - The Somersetshire Light Infantry post 1895.

The West Yorkshire Regiment (The Prince of Wales`s Own)

Titles

1685-1751 Known by name of Colonel.
1751-1782 14th Regiment of Foot.
1782-1809 14th (Bedfordshire) Regiment of Foot.
1809-1876 14th (Buckinghamshire) Regiment of Foot.
1876-1881 14th (Buckinghamshire or The Prince of Wales`s Own) Regiment of Foot.
1881-1920 The Prince of Wales`s Own (West Yorkshire Regiment).
1920-1958 The West Yorkshire Regiment (The Prince of Wales`s Own).

1st Battalion

Formed in Kent, 1685. To Scotland, 1689; Flanders then England, 1692. Took part in expedition to French Coast and then to Flanders, 1693. Fought at Landen, 1693; Huy, 1694; Kenoque and Namur, 1695. To England, 1696; Ireland, 1698; Scotland, 1715; England, 1722; Gibraltar, 1727 and present during siege that year. To England, 1742; Flanders, 1745; Scotland, 1746. Present at battles of Falkirk and Culloden. To England, 1750; Gibraltar, 1752; England, 1759; Nova Scotia, 1766; Massachusetts, 1771; St. Vincent, 1772. Took part in operations against the Caribs, 1772-73. To North America, 1773; England, 1777; Jamaica, 1782; England, 1791; Flanders, 1793. Present at Famars, Valenciennes and Dunkirk, 1793; Landrécies and Tournay, 1794 and Gueldermalsen, 1795. To England, 1795; West Indies, 1796. Took part in capture of St. Lucia and St. Vincent, 1796; Trinidad and attack on Porto Rico, 1797. To England, 1803; Germany, 1805; England then Ireland, 1806; England then India, 1807. Took part in expedition to Traquebar, 1808; capture of Mauritius, 1810 and Java, 1811. Returned to India, 1813. Took part in war in Nepal, 1815-16; capture of Hatrass, 1817 and Third Mahratta War, 1817-18. Fought at Bhurtpore during Jat War, 1825-26. To England, 1831; Ireland, 1832; West Indies, 1836; Canada, 1841; Nova Scotia, 1846; England, 1847; Ireland, 1850; Malta, 1854; the Crimea, 1855. Fought at Sevastopol. To Malta, 1856; the Ionian Islands, 1858; West Indies, 1860; England, 1864; Ireland, 1866; Malta, 1867; India, 1868; Aden, 1878; England, 1879; Ireland, 1883; England, 1891; Gibraltar, 1895; Hong Kong, 1896; Singapore, 1897; India, 1899; England, 1911. During First World War fought on the Aisne and at Armentières, 1914; Hooge, 1915; on the Somme, 1916; battle of Cambrai, 1917; the Somme, Lys, Hindenburg Line and the Selle, 1918. To England, 1919; Ireland, 1920; England then Germany, 1922; Northern Ireland, 1926; West Indies, 1929; Egypt, 1931; India, 1934. Present during earthquake at Quetta, 1935. Served in India and Burma during Second World War. Left Burma for England, 1946 then to Austria. To England, 1952. Served in Egypt, 1952; Malaya, 1952-55; Northern Ireland, 1955-56; Egypt, 1956. Amalgamated with 1st Battalion, The East Yorkshire Regiment (The Duke of York's Own) to form 1st Battalion. The Prince of Wales's Own Regiment of Yorkshire, 1958.

2nd Battalion

Formed at Bedford, 1804. To Ireland, 1806; Spain, 1808. Fought at Corunna and then to England, 1809. Took part in Walcheren expedition, 1809 and present at Flushing. To Malta, 1810; Italy, 1814; France, 1815; Malta then the Ionian Islands, 1816; England, 1817. disbanded, 1817. Reformed in Ireland, 1858. To New Zealand, 1860. Took part in wars of 1860-61 and 1863-66. To Australia, 1866; England, 1870; Ireland, 1876; India, 1878. Took part in Second Afghan War and present at Mazeena, 1880. To Burma, 1893; Aden, 1894. Took part in Ashanti War, 1895 and then to England. To South Africa, 1899. Fought at Willow Grange, Colenso and Tugela Heights operations, relief of Ladysmith, Monte Cristo, Railway Hill (Captain Conwyn Mansell-Jones awarded Victoria Cross), Alleman's Nek and Lake Chrissie (Sergeant W.B. Traynor awarded Victoria Cross). To Ireland, 1904; England, 1906; Malta, 1912. Detachments served in Albania during Balkan War, 1913. To England, 1914. During First World War fought at Neuve Chapelle, 1914 and 1915; Aubers Ridge and Bois Grenier, 1915; on the Some, 1916; at Ypres and Passchendale, 1917; St. Quentin,

Above - 1st Battalion, 14th Regiment - Crimea, 1855-56. Illustration by P.W. Reynolds.

Left - Men of `H` Company, 1st Battalion, The Prince of Wales's Own (West Yorkshire Regiment) wearing foreign service helmets.

Rosières, Villers Bretonneux and Arras, 1918. To England then India, 1919; Iraq, 1923. Took part in operations in Kurdistan. To India, 1924; the Sudan, 1928; England, 1930; Palestine, 1936. Present during Arab rebellion. To England, 1937; Palestine, 1938. During Second world War served in Palestine and the Sudan, 1939-40; Egypt, Palestine, Iraq and Cyprus, 1941; Egypt and Iraq, 1942; India and Burma, 1943-45. Served in Malaya and Indonesia, 1945-48. Returned to England then amalgamated with 1st Battalion in Austria, 1948.

3rd Battalion

Formed, 1813. To Belgium, 1815 and fought at Waterloo. Left France for England, 1815. Disbanded, 1816.

Above - Colonel Frederick W. Kitchener (younger brother of Lord Kitchener), South Africa, 1900.

Right - Artist's impression of the 1st Battalion, The Prince of Wales's Own (West Yorkshire Regiment) attacking during the battle of the Aisne 20th September, 1914. This action resulted in over 600 casualties - killed, wounded or missing.

Badges

The White Horse - an old badge of the 14th Regiment. The Royal Tiger superscribed `India`- for services in India, 1807-31. The Prince of Wales's Coronet, Plume and motto - authorized, 1876.

Uniform

Buff facings changing to white in 1881. Buff restored, 1900.

Nickname

`Calvert's Entire` - General Sir Harry Calvert was Colonel of the 14th Regiment, 1806-26. During this period Calvert's Brewery produced a beer named `Calvert's Entire.`

Above - Cap badge.

Below - Machine gun section, 2nd Battalion, The Prince of Wales's Own (West Yorkshire Regiment) c1897.

The East Yorkshire Regiment (The Duke of York`s Own)

Titles

1685-1751 Known by name of Colonel.
1751-1782 15th Regiment of Foot.
1782-1881 15th (York East Riding) Regiment of Foot.
1881-1935 The East Yorkshire Regiment.
1935-1958 The East Yorkshire Regiment (The Duke of York`s Own).

1st Battalion

Officer - 15th Regiment c1759.
Illustration by Ernest Ibbetson.

Raised in Nottingham by Sir William Clifton, 1685. To Scotland, 1689; England, 1693; Flanders, 1694. Present during capture of Huy, 1694 and siege of Dixmunde, 1695. To England, 1697; Ireland, 1698; Holland, 1701. During campaign in Flanders took part in capture of Venloo, Ruremonde and Liége, 1702. Fought at Huy and Limburg, 1703; Schellenberg and Blenheim, 1704; Ramillies, 1706; Oudenarde, 1708; Malplaquet, 1709. To England, 1714; Scotland, 1714. During Jacobite Rebellion present at Kintail, 1719. To England, 1724; Jamaica, 1740. Took part in expedition to South America and present during attack on Fort St. Lazar, Cartagena in 1741. To England, 1742; Flanders, 1745. After siege of Ostend returned to England same year. Took part in attack on Port L'Orient, 1746. To Ireland, 1749; England, 1755; North America, 1758. Took part in capture of Louisburg, 1758; Quebec, 1759 and present at Sainte Foy, 1760. To the

West Indies, 1761. Fought on Martinique and present at capture of Havannah, 1762. To Canada, 1763; England, 1768; Ireland, 1774; North America, 1776. During American War of Independence fought at Brooklyn, Fort Washington, Danbury, Brandywine and Germantown. To the West Indies and took part in capture of St. Lucia, 1778 and St. Kitts, 1782. To England, 1782; Ireland, 1784; West Indies, 1790. Fought on Martinique and Guadeloupe, 1794. To England, 1796; Ireland, 1800; West Indies, 1805. Took part in operations on Martinique and the Saints Islands, 1809; Guadeloupe, 1810 and 1815. To Nova Scotia, 1817; England, 1821; Ireland, 1822; Canada, 1827; England, 1840; Ireland, 1843; Ceylon, 1845; Ireland, 1855; Gibraltar, 1856; England, 1857; Channel Islands, 1859; Ireland, 1860; New Brunswick, 1862; Bermuda, 1868; Ireland, 1870; Channel Islands, 1873; England, 1874; Ireland, 1878; England, 1883; Gibraltar, 1885; West Indies, 1886; South Africa, 1888; Egypt, 1893; India, 1895; Burma, 1903; England, 1906. Crossed to France and took part in battles of the Aisne and Armentières, 1914; Hooge, 1915; the Somme, 1916; Arras, Ypres and Cambrai, 1917; the Somme, the Lys, Hindenburg Line and the Selle, 1918. To Ireland, 1919; England then Egypt, 1922; North China, 1925; India, 1928. Fought in Burma, 1945. Served in Austria and Germany, 1945-52; Malaya, 1952-56; Germany, 1956-58. Amalgamated with 1st Battalion, The West Yorkshire Regiment (The Prince of Wales`s Own) to form 1st Battalion, The Prince of Wales`s Own Regiment of Yorkshire, 1958.

2nd Battalion

Formed, 1799. To Ireland, 1800. Disbanded, 1802. Re-formed at Scarborough, 1804. To Jersey, 1811. Disbanded, 1814. Re-formed in Guernsey, 1815. Disbanded, 1816. Re-formed, 1858. To Malta, 1859; Gibraltar, 1863; Ireland, 1868; Channel Islands, 1870; England, 1871; India, 1875. Took part in Second Afghan War of 1879-80. To Aden then England, 1888; Ireland, 1894; England then South Africa, 1900. Present during action at Biddulphsberg. Io England, 1902, Burma, 1905; India, 1909; England, 1914. Crossed to France and took part in battles of Ypres and Loos, 1915. Moved to Egypt in October then served on Macedonian Front. To India, 1919; Mesopotamia, 1920. Took part in Iraq operations. To England, 1923; Palestine, 1936; England, 1938. Fought in France and Belgium, 1939-40 and in North West Europe, 1944-45. Took part in D-Day landings 6th June, 1944. Served in Palestine and Egypt, 1945-48. Amalgamated with 1st Battalion, 1948.

Above - Officers` shoulder-belt plate - 15th Regiment.

Right - Cap badge - The East Yorkshire Regiment.

Badges

An eight-pointed Star. The White Rose of York.

Uniform

Yellow facings were replaced by white in 1881.

Nicknames

`The Snappers` - during the battle of Brandywine in 1777 the 15th Regiment became low on ammunition. Not to make this known to the enemy, what ball ammunition was available was passed out among the better shots. The remaining men then moved from position to position firing charges of powder only (`snapping`). `The Poona Guards` - said to be from the 2nd Battalion`s long garrison service at Poona.

The East Yorkshire Regiment c1890.
Illustration by R. Simkin.

The Bedfordshire and Hertfordshire Regiment

Titles

1688-1751 Known by name of Colonel.
1751-1782 16th Regiment of Foot.
1782-1809 16th (Buckinghamshire) Regiment of Foot.
1809-1881 16th (Bedfordshire) Regiment of Foot.
1881-1919 The Bedfordshire Regiment.
1919-1958 The Bedfordshire and Hertfordshire Regiment.

1st Battalion

Raised in southern counties of England, 1688. To Flanders, 1689 and during the War of the League of Augsburg fought at Walcourt, 1689; Steenkirk, 1692; Landen, 1693. Gained earliest battle honour at Namur, 1695. To England, 1697; Ireland, 1698; Flanders, 1701. Present at capture of Liége, 1702; Huy and Limburg, 1703. Moved into Germany and fought at Schellenberg, Blenheim and Landau, 1704; Brabant and the Dyle, 1705; Ramillies, 1706; Oudenarde and Lisle, 1708; Tournai, Malplaquet and Mons, 1709; Pont-a-Vendin, Douai, Aire, St. Venant, 1710; Bouchain, 1711. To Scotland, 1714 and present during suppression of Rebellion, 1715. To England, 1717. Detachment to the West Indies, 1740 and took part in attack on Fort Lazar, Carthagena, 1741. Regiment to Flanders, 1745 and present at Melle. To England, 1746; Ireland, 1749; America, 1767. During the American War of Independence fought at Baton Rouge, 1779. To England, 1782; Ireland, 1783; Nova Scotia then Jamaica, 1791. Took part in Maroon War, 1795. To England, 1796; Ireland, 1800; Barbados, 1804. Engaged during Surinam expedition, April-May. To England, 1812; Ireland, 1813; Canada, 1814; England, Belgium, France then England, 1815; Ireland, 1816; Ceylon, 1820; India, 1829; England, 1841; Ireland, 1843; Gibraltar, 1846; Corfu, 1847; Jamaica, 1851; Canada, 1854; Ireland, 1857; England, 1859; Canada, 1861. Involved in Fenian Raid, 1866. To Ireland, 1870; Jersey, 1872; England, 1873; Ireland, 1877; England, 1882; Ireland, 1887; England, 1888; Malta then India, 1890. Formed part of Chitral Relief Force, 1895 and engaged at Malakand Pass in April. To Aden, 1907; England, 1908; Ireland, 1913. Crossed to France in 1914. Fought at Mons, Le Cateau, battles of the Marne, Aisne and Ypres, 1914-15 (Private E. Warner awarded Victoria Cross). Took part in battle of the Somme, 1916 and operations around Arras and Ypres, 1917. Moved to Italian Front November, 1917. Returned to France, 1918 and engaged during battles of the Lys, Somme and Hindenburg Line. To England, 1919; Ireland, 1920; England, 1922; Malta, 1925; Shanghai, 1927. Formed part of Shanghai

Defence Force, 1927-28, then to North China. Left Hong Kong for India, 1929. To Palestine, 1938 and after operations there to Egypt, 1939. During Second World War served in Palestine, 1939; Egypt, Lemnos, Syria, 1941; Libya, 1941-42; Egypt, 1942; India, 1942-44; Burma, 1944; India, 1944-45. To Tripolitania, 1947; Greece, 1948; England, 1950. Served in Cyprus, 1951; Egypt, 1952-54. To Germany, 1956. Amalgamated with 1st Battalion, The Essex Regiment to form 3rd East Anglian Regiment (16th/44th Foot), 1958.

2nd Battalion

Raised in Ireland, 1858. To Canada, 1861; the West Indies, 1866; England, 1869; India, 1876; Burma, 1881; India, 1885; England, 1891; Ireland, 1898; South Africa, 1899. Took part in operations around Colesberg and Rensburg, 1900. To England, 1903; Gibraltar, 1907; Bermuda, 1910; South Africa, 1912; England, 1914. Crossed to Belgium and after Antwerp operations fought at Ypres. Took part in fighting at Neuve Chapelle, Aubers Ridge and Loos, 1915 (Captain C.C. Foss awarded Victoria Cross); on the Somme, 1916 at Arras and Ypres, 1917; Somme, the Lys and Hindenburg Line, 1918. To England then India, 1919; Iraq, 1925; England, 1926; Egypt, Palestine then England, 1936. Fought in France and Belgium, 1939-40; North Africa, 1943-44; Italy and Greece, 1945. To Egypt then England, 1947. Amalgamated with 1st Battalion, 1948.

1st Battalion, The Bedfordshire Regiment - Church Parade, Aldershot 1913.

Badges

The Star of the Order of the Bath - thought to have been adopted during the Colonelcy (1823-54) of the Viscount Beresford, GCB. A hart crossing a ford - introduced in 1881. The Arms of Bedford.

Uniform

Yellow facings replaced white by 1742, but in 1881 regulation white for English regiments was again in use.

Nicknames

`The Old Bucks` - during the period 1782-1809 when the regiment was associated with Buckinghamshire. There are two main reasons for another nickname in use for many years - `The Peacemakers` - although involved in numerous campaigns, it was not until 1882 that any battle honour appeared under the regiment`s name in the Army List. "Blenheim", Ramillies", "Oudenarde" and "Malplaquet" by then authorized. It was possibly this lack of recognition that led to the nickname and the implication that the 16th had seen no war service. Another theory however, is that the regiment`s strong fighting reputation led the enemy to make peace at the earliest opportunity.

Above - Officer - 16th Regiment, Canada, 1862.

Right - Cap badge - The Bedfordshire and Hertfordshire Regiment.

Top - Officers` silver and gilt glengarry badge
- The Leicestershire Regiment.

Bottom - Lieutenant G. Peevor - 17th
Regiment, who ran the Regimental School in
India, 1816-23.

The Royal Leicestershire Regiment

Titles

1688-1751 Known by name of Colonel.
1751-1782 17th Regiment of Foot.
1782-1881 17th (Leicestershire) Regiment of Foot.
1881-1946 The Leicestershire Regiment.
1946-1964 The Royal Leicestershire Regiment.

1st Battalion

Formed in London by Colonel Solomon Richards, 1688. Sent to Ireland for defence of Londonderry in April, 1689 but returned same month. To Flanders, 1694. Present during action near the Kenoque and siege of Namur, 1695. To Ireland, 1697; Holland, 1701. Fought at Venloo, Ruremonde and Liége, 1701; Huy and Limburg, 1703. To England, 1703; Portugal, 1704. During war in Portugal and Spain fought at Valencia de Alcantara, Albuquerque and Badajoz, 1705; Alcantara and Madrid, 1706 and Almanza, 1707. To England, 1708; Ireland, 1714; Scotland, 1715. Took part in battle of Sheriffmuir. To Ireland, 1721; Minorca, 1725; Ireland, 1749; Nova Scotia, 1757. Took part in siege of Louisburg, 1758 and Ticonderoga, 1759. Stationed in New York then to the West Indies, 1761. Took part in capture of Martinique and Havana, 1762. To North America, 1762; England, 1767; Ireland, 1773; North America, 1775. Fought at Brooklyn and White Plains, 1776; Fort Washington, Princeton, Brandywine and Germantown, 1777; Yorktown, 1781. To Nova Scotia, 1783; England, 1786; Jersey, 1787; England, 1788. Served on board ship as marines, 1790. To Ireland, 1792. Flank companies to West Indies, 1793 and fought at Martinique and Guadeloupe, 1794. Remainder of regiment to St. Domingo, 1795. Fought at Jeremie, 1796. To England, 1798. Took part in Helder expedition of 1799. To Minorca, 1800; Ireland, 1802; England then India, 1804. Took part in operations in Bundelkund, 1806-07 and present during capture of Chunar. Took part in campaign in Nepal, 1814-15. To England, 1823; Ireland, 1826; England, 1829; New South Wales, 1830; India, 1836. Took part in First Afghan War of 1839 and present at capture of Ghuznee and Khelat. To Aden, 1841; India, 1845; England, 1847; Ireland, 1850; Gibraltar then the Crimea, 1854. Took part in fighting at The Redan and Sevastopol. Lance Sergeant Philip Smith awarded Victoria Cross. To Canada, 1856; England, 1865; Ireland, 1867; India, 1870. Took part in Second Afghan War gaining battle honours `Ali Masjid` and `Afghanistan, 1878-79.` To England, 1882; Bermuda, 1888; Nova Scotia, 1891; West Indies, 1893; South Africa, 1895. Took part in attack on Talana Hill and

61

Below - Colour Sergeant - The Leicestershire Regiment c1887.

Right - 1st Battalion, The Leicestershire Regiment - Aldershot, 1911.

action at Lombard`s Kop, 1899; defence of Ladysmith, 1899-1900; capture of Bergendal, 1900. To India, 1902; England, 1906; Ireland, 1912. Crossed to France and fought at battles of the Aisne and Armentières, 1914; Hooge, 1915; the Somme, 1916; Cambrai, 1917; the Somme, Lys, Hindenburg Line and the Selle, 1918. To Ireland, 1920; England, 1923; Egypt, 1925; India, 1927. Fought in Malaya, 1941 and after heavy casualties temporally amalgamated with 2nd Battalion, The East Surrey Regiment as The British Battalion. Captured by the Japanese at Singapore, 1942. Re-formed in England from 8th Battalion, 1942. Fought in North West Europe, 1944-45. Left Germany for England, 1947. To Hong Kong, 1949; Korea, 1951. Gained battle honour `Maryang-San.` To England then Germany, 1952; the Sudan, 1955. Later served in Germany, Cyprus, Brunei, Aden and Malta. Became 4th Battalion, The Royal Anglian Regiment, 1964.

2nd Battalion

Formed and took part in Helder expedition, 1799. To Minorca, 1800. Disbanded, 1802. Formed, 1858. To Ireland then Nova Scotia, 1861. Took part in Fenian operations in Canada, 1866. To Ireland, 1868; Channel Islands, 1869; England, 1870; Ireland, 1874; India, 1876; Burma, 1888; Aden, 1889; England, 1890; Ireland, 1896; Egypt, 1900; Channel Islands, 1902; England, 1904; India, 1906; France, 1914. Fought at battles of La Bassée, 1914; Neuve Chapelle (Private William Buckingham awarded Victoria Cross), Festubert and Loos, 1915. To Egypt then Mesopotamia, 1915. Fought at Kut Al Amara, 1917 then to Egypt and Palestine. To India, 1919; the Sudan, 1923; England, 1925; Germany, 1927; ; England, 1929; Northern Ireland, 1932; England, 1936; Palestine, 1938. Fought in the Western Desert, 1940-41; Crete, Damascus and Tobruk, 1941. To Ceylon, 1942; India, 1943. Fought in Burma, 1944. Left India for England, 1947. Amalgamated with 1st Battalion, 1948.

Badges

The Royal Tiger superscribed `Hindoostan` - for services in India, 1804-23. An Irish Harp - introduced in 1881 and an old badge of the Leicestershire Militia.

Uniform

Facings were first described as `pearl-grey` and later as white. Pearl-grey was restored in 1931.

Nicknames

`The Bengal Tigers` - from the badge. `The Lillywhites` - from the facings.

Colours - 2nd Battalion, The Leicestershire Regiment c1936.

The Green Howards (Alexandra, Princess of Wales`s Own Yorkshire Regiment)

Titles

1688-1751 Known by name of Colonel.
1751-1782 19th Regiment of Foot.
1782-1875 19th (1st York. North Riding) Regiment of Foot.
1875-1881 19th (1st York. North Riding) Princess of Wales`s Own Regiment of Foot.
1881-1902 The Princess of Wales`s Own (Yorkshire Regiment).
1902-1920 Alexandra, Princess of Wales`s Own (Yorkshire Regiment).
1920 The Green Howards (Alexandra, Princess of Wales`s Own Yorkshire Regiment).

1st Battalion

Formed in Exeter by Colonel Francis Luttrell, 1688. To Flanders, 1692. Fought at Steenkirk, 1692; Landen, 1693 and Namur, 1695. To England, 1696; Flanders then England, 1697; Ireland, 1699. As marines took part in Cadiz expedition of 1702 and in the West Indies present during attack on Guadeloupe, 1703. Returned to Ireland, 1704. To England, 1705; Flanders, 1707. Fought at Malplaquet, 1709; Douai and Béthune, 1710; Bouchain, 1711. To England, 1714; Ireland, 1715. Took part in Vigo expedition of 1719. To England, 1727; Ireland, 1731; Scotland, 1739; England, 1741; Flanders, 1744. Fought at Fontenoy, 1745. To England, 1754; Flanders,

64

Left - 2nd Battalion, The Green Howards - Larnaca, Cyprus, 1955. The Guard of Honour, of which almost every man was a National Serviceman, is being inspected by the departing Governor of Cyprus, Sir Robert Armitage. (Green Howards Museum).

Below - Lieutenant - 19th Regiment, 1823.

1746. Fought at Roucoux, 1746 and Lauffeld, 1747. To England, 1748; Gibraltar, 1749; England, 1752. Took part in expedition to Belle Isle, 1761. To Gibraltar, 1763; England, 1771; Ireland, 1775; North America, 1781. Fought at Eutaw Springs in September. To Jamaica, 1782; England, 1791; Flanders then England, 1793; Flanders, 1794. Fought at Geldermalsen. To England, 1795; India then Ceylon, 1796. Took part in operations against the Kandians, 1803; the Travancore War, 1809 and Kandian War, 1815-1818. To England, 1820; Ireland, 1821; West Indies, 1826; Ireland, 1836; Malta, 1840; the Ionian Islands, 1843; West Indies, 1845; Canada, 1848; England, 1851; the Crimea, 1854. Gained battle honours `Alma`, `Inkerman` and `Sevastopol.` Privates Samuel Evans and John Lyons awarded Victoria Cross. To England, 1856; India, 1857. Served during the Indian Mutiny, part of Hazara Field Force, 1868 and took part in Black Mountain expedition. To England, 1871; Burma, 1877; Nova Scotia, 1880; Malta then Egypt, 1884. Part of Nile expedition and present at Ginnis, 1885. To Cyprus, 1888; Egypt then England, 1889; Jersey, 1892; Ireland, 1895; Gibraltar, 1898; England then South Africa, 1899. Took part in operations near Colesberg, relief of Kimberley, battles of Paardeberg (Sergeant A. Atkinson awarded Victoria Cross), Driefontein, Johannesburg, Diamond Hill and Belfast. To England, 1902; Egypt, 1908; the Sudan, 1911; India, 1912. Remained in India throughout First World War. Took part in Third Afghan War, 1919. To Palestine, 1919; India, 1920; Egypt, 1926; England then Shanghai, 1927; England, 1928; Malta, 1936; Palestine, 1938; England, 1939. During Second World War in France, 1939-40 and fought in Norway, 1940. To India, 1942. Served in Iraq and Persia, 1942-43; Egypt, Syria and Sicily, 1943; Italy, 1943-44; Egypt, Palestine and Syria, 1944-45; North West Europe, 1945. Left Germany for England, 1947. To the Sudan, 1948. Served in Malaya, 1949-52; Austria and Germany, 1953-56; Hong Kong, 1956-59; Germany, 1959-63; Libya, 1963-66; British Honduras, 1968. Since 1969 the regiment has carried out numerous tours of Germany and Northern Ireland, was in Cyprus, 1981 and the Falkland Islands, 1989-90.

1st Battalion, The Green Howards - Transport, Shanghai, 1927. (Green Howards Museum).

2nd Battalion

Formed in Dorset by Colonel Thomas Erle, 1689 and to Ireland. Fought in battle of the Boyne, 1690 and present at Athlone and Aughrim, 1691. To England, 1692. Took part in raids along French coast, 1694. Disbanded, 1697. Re-formed at Morpeth, 1756. Became 66th Regiment (see The Royal Berkshire Regiment), 1758. Re-formed at Exeter, 1858. To Ireland, 1861; Burma, 1863; India, 1868; England, 1876; Ireland, 1881; England, 1886; India, 1890; Burma, 1892. Detachments served in Katchin Hills operations, 1893. To India, 1897. Took part in Tirah expedition and present during attack on Karuppa, 1897. To South Africa, 1906; England, 1909; Guernsey, 1913. During First World War took part in battles of Ypres, 1914; Neuve Chapelle (Corporal William Anderson awarded Victoria Cross), Aubers Ridge, Festubert and Loos, 1915; the Somme, 1916; Arras and Ypres, 1917; the Somme, Lys, Arras and Hindenburg Line, 1918. To Ireland, 1919; England then the West Indies 1925; Egypt, 1927; Palestine then Shanghai, 1929; India, 1930. Took part in Waziristan operations, 1937-38. During Second World War remained in India until 1944 then to Burma. Served in Egypt and the Sudan, 1947. Disbanded, 1949. Re-formed, 1952 at Barnard Castle. To Egypt, 1953; Cyprus, 1954; England, 1955. Placed into suspended animation, 1956.

Badges

The Princess of Wales's Cypher and Coronet and Dannebrog Cross - authorized in 1882.

Uniform

At first, blue coats with yellow facings (the livery of Colonel Francis Luttrell) were worn. Scarlet was quickly introduced and the facings green by 1742. White was worn from 1881, green being restore in 1899.

Nicknames

`The Green Howards` - from the colour of the facings and name of colonel - Hon. Charles Howard (1738-48). Around the same period the colonel of the 3rd Regiment (`the Buff Howards`) was also named Howard. The nickname was incorporated into the official title of the regiment in 1920.

1st Battalion, The Green Howards on Exercise `Gryphons Flight` at Catterick, North Yorkshire, 1990. The vehicle is an All Terrain Mobile Platform.
Note Regimental badge. (Green Howards Museum).

The Lancashire Fusiliers

Titles

1688-1751 Known by name of Colonel.
1751-1782 20th Regiment of Foot.
1782-1881 20th (East Devonshire) Regiment of Foot.
1881-1968 The Lancashire Fusiliers.

1st Battalion

Raised by Sir Robert Peyton, 1688. To Ireland, 1689 and took part in battle of the Boyne, 1690. Also engaged at Athlone and Aghrim, 1691. Left Ireland for sea service around Spain, 1702. Took part in Cadiz expedition and present during action in Vigo Bay. Later same year moved to the West Indies and took part in operations at Guadeloupe, 1703. To Ireland, 1704; Portugal, 1707. Fought in Spain and present at La Gudina, 1709. To Gibraltar, 1713 and present during siege of 1727. To Ireland, 1728; England then Flanders, 1742. Took part in War of the Austrian Succession and gained first battle honour at Dettingen, 1743. Also present at Fontenoy and Melle, 1745. Recalled due to Jacobite rebellion in Scotland, 1745. Moved north and took part in battle of Culloden, 1746. Left

Left - Colonel F.C. Evelegh, CB, 20th Regiment. Fought in the Crimea and wounded during attack on the Redan.

Below - Cap badge - The Lancashire Fusiliers.

Scotland for England, 1753. Took part in expeditions to Rochefort, 1757 and St. Malo, 1758. To Germany, 1758. Fought at Minden, 1759 and also present at Warburg and Kloster Kampen, 1760 and Vellinghausen, 1761. To England then Gibraltar, 1763; England, 1769; Ireland, 1774; Canada, 1776. Served in Quebec operations and later Burgoyne campaign. In action at Bemis Heights September, 1777 and interned at Saratoga. To England, 1781; Ireland, 1783; Nova Scotia, 1789; Jamaica, 1792; St. Domingo, 1793. Took part in attacks on Tiburon and L`Acul, 1794. To England, 1796. Took part in Helder campaign of 1799. Engaged at Zype Canal and Egmont-op-Zee. To Ireland, 1800 then took part in expedition to Belle Isle. To Minorca and then Egypt, 1801. Fought at Alexandria. To Malta, 1801; Italy, 1805. Took part in battle of Maida, 1806. To England, 1807; Portugal, 1808. Fought at Vimiera and Corunna returning to England, 1809. Took part in Walcheren expedition of 1809. To Ireland, 1810; Portugal, 1812.

Fought at Vittoria, during the Pyrenees operations and Nivelle, 1813; Orthes and Toulouse, 1814. To Ireland, 1814; St. Helena, 1819. Began guard duty over Napoleon. Twelve men of the Grenadier Company carried Napoleon's coffin to his grave in May, 1821. To India, 1822; England, 1837; Ireland, 1840; Bermuda, 1841; Nova Scotia then Canada, 1847; England, 1853; the Crimea, 1854. Gained battle honours "Alma", "Inkerman" and "Sevastopol". Took part in capture of Kinburn, 1855. To England, 1856; India, 1857. Served in Oudh operations, 1858 and engaged at Sultanpore, Lucknow and Dhondiakhera. To England, 1867; Ireland, 1869; Bermuda, 1873; Nova Scotia, 1876; Cyprus, 1878; Malta, 1880; Ireland, 1881; England, 1885; Ireland, 1891; England, 1897; Malta then Crete, 1899; Gibraltar, 1902; Malta, 1905; Egypt then Malta, 1906; India, 1907; England via Aden, 1914. During First World War fought at Gallipoli. Moved to France and took part in battles of the Somme, 1916; Arras, Ypres and Cambrai, 1917 and Lys, 1918. To England then Ireland, 1919; England, 1923; Egypt, 1927; Gibraltar, 1929; England, 1930; China, 1936; India, 1938. Served in India and Burma (Chindits operations) during Second World War. Since Second World War served in Egypt, 1950-52; Kenya during emergency, 1952-54; Cyprus, 1957-60. Became 4th Battalion, The Royal Regiment of Fusiliers, 1968.

2nd Battalion

Formed, 1756. Became 67th Regiment of Foot, 1758 (see The Royal Hampshire Regiment). Another formed, 1799 and served with 1st Battalion during Helder campaign. To Ireland, 1800 and took part in expedition to Belle Isle. Went on to Minorca and landed in Egypt, 1801. Fought at Alexandria. To Malta, 1801 and disbanded, 1802. A Reserve (or 2nd Battalion) formed, 1842 and to Bermuda. To Nova Scotia then Canada, 1847. Merged with 1st Battalion, 1850. New 2nd Battalion formed in Ireland, 1858. To England, 1861; India then Hong Kong, 1863; Japan, 1864; Hong Kong, 1866; South Africa, 1867; Mauritius, 1870; Ireland, 1872; England, 1874; Ireland, 1879; India, 1881; Egypt, 1898. Took part in Second Sudan War and present at Omdurman 4th September. Returned to Egypt and then via Crete to Malta. To South Africa, 1899. Engaged at Tugela Heights, present at Spion Kop, and during relief of Ladysmith. To

Above - Captain R.R. Willis leading a party through wire entanglements west of Cape Helles, Gallipoli, 25th April, 1915. Captain Willis was awarded the Victoria Cross for his gallantry, that day, along with five other members of 1st Battalion, The Lancashire Fusiliers.

Right - The Lancashire Fusiliers, 1913. Lieutenant and colour sergeant, full dress; sergeant and private service dress, marching order. The officer wears the Queen's South Africa Medal and the colour sergeant the Sudan, Queen's and King's South Africa Medals.

England, 1902. During First World War took part in the retreat from Mons and battle of the Aisne, 1914; battles of Ypres, 1915; the Somme, 1916; Arras and Ypres, 1917; the Somme, Lys, Arras and Hindenburg Line, 1918. To India, 1919; Palestine, 1935; England, 1936. Fought in France and Belgium, 1939-40. Later served in North Africa, Sicily, Italy and Austria. Amalgamated with 1st Battalion, 1948. Re-formed, 1952 and served as garrison troops in Trieste. Disbanded, 1955.

3rd Battalion

Formed, 1898 and to Malta. To Barbados, 1901; South Africa, 1903; England and disbanded, 1906.

4th Battalion

Formed, 1900. To Ireland, 1902. Disbanded, 1906.

Badges

The Sphinx superscribed "Egypt" - for service in Egypt during 1801.

Uniform

Yellow facings were being worn by 1740. The regulation white for English regiments adopted in 1881. .

Nicknames

`Kingsley`s Stand` - after the battle of Minden an order was issued to the effect that the 20th Regiment, in view of its severe losses, should stand down and be relieved from duty. Major-General William Kingsley who commanded the regiment would not accept this and insisted that his men should take their place in the line. `The Minden Boys.` `The Two Tens.`

Above - 1st Battalion, The Lancashire Fusiliers - Regimental Policeman, India, 1911. Note Truncheon carried in leather case on left side.

Below - Drums, 1st Battalion, The Lancashire Fusiliers - Tientsin, China, Minden Day, 1937. Lieutenant-Colonel R.F.H. Massy-Westrop, MC (Commanding Officer) seated centre. Note custom of decorating the drums and headdress with roses.

The Cheshire Regiment

Titles

1689-1751 Known by name of Colonel.
1751-1782 22nd Regiment of Foot.
1782-1881 22nd (Cheshire) Regiment of Foot.
1881   The Cheshire Regiment.

1st Battalion

Raised by Henry, Duke of Norfolk, 1689. Moved to Ireland and present at siege of Carrickfergus, 1689; battle of the Boyne, 1690; Ballymore, Athlone, Aghrim, Galway and Limerick, 1691. To Flanders, 1695; England, 1696; Ireland, 1698; Jamaica, 1702; England, 1714; Ireland, 1718; Minorca, 1726. Detachments to Gibraltar and present during siege of 1727. To Ireland, 1749; Nova Scotia, 1756. Took part in siege of Louisburg and capture of Cape Breton, 1758; battle of Quebec, 1759. Left New York for the West Indies, 1761. Took part in capture of Dominica, 1761; Martinique and Fort Moro, Havanna, 1762. To West Florida, 1763; England, 1765; Ireland, 1773; North America, 1775. During American War

of Independence fought at Bunker Hill, Brooklyn, Fort Washington and operations on Rhode Island. To England, 1783; Channel Islands then England, 1787; Ireland, 1790; West Indies, 1793. Took part in capture of Martinique, Guadeloupe and St. Domingo, 1794. To England, 1795; Guernsey, 1798; England, 1799; Cape of Good Hope, 1800; India, 1802. During Second Mahratta War flank companies joined Cuttack Field Force, 1803 and present at capture of Fort Barrubatta; Deeg and siege of Bhurtpore, 1804. Took part in capture of Mauritius, 1810. To Bourbon, 1811; Mauritius then Bourbon, 1812; Mauritius, 1813; England, 1819; Ireland, 1821; Jamaica, 1826; Ireland, 1837; England, 1840; India, 1841. Took part in Scinde campaign of 1843 and present at Meeanee and Hyderabad. During Kolhapur operations, 1844-45 fought at Forts Punalla and Pownghur, operations in the Sawunt-Warree district, Forts Monuhurr and Monsentosh and capture of Seevapore. Took part in operations against the Afridis, 1853. To England, 1855; Ireland, 1859; Malta, 1860; New Brunswick, 1866; Ireland, 1869; Channel Islands, 1871; England, 1872; Ireland, 1877; Channel Islands, 1881; England, 1883; Gibraltar, 1885; Egypt, 1886; India then Burma, 1887. Took part in Chin-Lushai campaign, 1890. To India, 1891; England, 1904; Ireland, 1909. During First World War fought at battles of Mons, Le Cateau, the Marne, Aisne, Armentières and Ypres, 1914; Ypres, 1915; the Somme, 1916; Arras and Ypres, 1917. Moved to Italian Front December, 1917. Returned to France April, 1918 and fought at the Lys, Somme, Hindenburg Line and the Selle. To England, 1919; Ireland, 1920; England then India, 1922; the Sudan, 1938. During the Second World War served in Egypt, 1940; Malta, 1941-43; North West Europe, 1944-45. Placed into suspended animation, 1947. 2nd Battalion stationed in England renumbered as 1st, 1948. To Cyprus, 1950; Egypt, 1951, England, 1954; Germany, 1955; England, 1956; Malaya, 1957; Singapore, 1958; England then Northern Ireland, 1960; Germany, 1962; Cyprus, 1964; Germany then England, 1965; Bahrain, 1968; England, 1969; Northern Ireland then Germany, 1970; England, 1972. Stationed in Northern Ireland and Germany, 1973-1979 then to England. Served in Belize, 1980; Northern Ireland, 1982-84; Hong Kong, 1984-86; Belize, 1986-87; Falkland Islands, 1988-89; Northern Ireland, 1990; Bosnia, 1992-93.

Top - Cap badge - The Cheshire Regiment, 1881-1922.

Bottom - Lieutenant C. May Hayes Newington - 1st Battalion, 22nd Regiment, New Brunswick, 1866.

Officers, R.S.M, Bandmaster and Drum Major - 2nd Battalion, The Cheshire Regiment, Tidworth, 1927. Lieutenant-Colonel E.G. Hamilton, C.M.G., D.S.O., M.C. (Commanding Officer) seated centre.

2nd Battalion

Formed and disbanded, 1814. Re-formed, 1858. To Malta, 1859; Gibraltar then Mauritius, 1865; England, 1867; India, 1873; Burma, 1887; England, 1889; Ireland, 1895, South Africa, 1900. Present during action at Karee Sidings, Zand River and Johannesburg operations. To England, 1902; India, 1904; England, 1914. During First World War took part in battles of Ypres and Loos, 1915. Moved to Egypt end of year and from there served rest of the war on Macedonian Front. To England then Constantinople, 1919; England, 1920; Ireland, 1921; England, 1923; Malta, 1930; England, 1935; Egypt and Palestine then England, 1936. During Second World War fought in France and Belgium, 1939-40; Egypt, Cyprus and Iraq, 1941; Syria, Egypt and Libya, 1942; Libya, North Africa, Egypt and Sicily, 1943; North West Europe, 1944. To Egypt then Palestine, 1946; England, 1947. Renumbered as 1st Battalion, 1948.

Badges

An Acorn with oak-leaves - origins uncertain. The Prince of Wales's Plume, Coronet and Motto - and A Rose - in use after 1881.

Uniform

Buff facings were replaced with regulation white for English regiments in 1881. Buff being restored in 1904.

Nicknames

`The Red Knights` - an all-red uniform - jackets, waistcoats and breeches was worn in 1795. `The Lightning Conductors` - from an incident in Ireland, 1899 when part of the 2nd Battalion were struck by lightning. `The Two-Twos` - from the number.

The Royal Welch Fusiliers

Titles

1689-1702 Known by name of Colonel.
1702-1713 The Welsh Regiment of Fusiliers.
1713-1714 The Royal Regiment of Welsh Fusiliers.
1714-1727 The Prince of Wales`s Own Royal Regiment of Welsh Fusiliers.
1727-1751 The Royal Welsh Fusiliers.
1751-1881 23rd (Royal Welsh Fusiliers) Regiment of Foot.
1881-1920 The Royal Welsh Fusiliers.
1920-   The Royal Welch Fusiliers.

1st Battalion

Raised by Henry, Lord Herbert of Chirbury for service in Ireland, 1689. Present at battle of the Boyne, 1690 and Aughrim, 1691. To England, 1691; Flanders then England, 1692; Flanders, 1694 and present at surrender of Namur, 1695. To England, 1697; Ireland, 1698; Flanders, 1701. Took part in capture of Liége, 1702 and Huy, 1703. During War of The Spanish Succession fought at Schellenberg and Blenheim, 1704; Ramillies and siege of Menin, 1706; Oudenarde, Lille and Wynendaele, 1708; Tournay and Malplaquet, 1709; Douai, 1710; Bouchain, 1711. To Ireland, 1713; England, 1715; Ireland, 1718; England, 1719. Served in Scotland, 1735-37 and present during Edinburgh riots. To Flanders, 1742. Fought at Dettingen, 1743; Fontenoy and Ghent, 1745 then to England. To Flanders, 1747 taking part in battle of Lauffeld. To Scotland, 1748; England, 1742; Minorca, 1754. Engaged during siege of Fort St. Philip, 1756. To England, 1756. Took part in expedition to St. Malo, 1758. To Germany, 1758. Fought at Minden, 1759; Warburg and Kloster Kampen, 1760; Kirsh Denkern, 1761; Wilhelmsthal, 1762. To England, 1763; America, 1773. During American War of Independence fought at Lexington and Bunker Hill, 1775. Took part in New York operations, 1776 and in action at Ridgefield and Brandywine, 1777; Rhode Island, 1778. Served as marines, 1778, took part in capture of Fort Lafayette, 1779; siege of Charleston and fighting at Camden, 1780; action at Guildford Court House and surrender of Yorktown, 1781. To England, 1783; Ireland, 1790; West Indies, 1793. Flank companies engaged during operations in Martinique; St. Lucia and Guadeloupe, 1794. To England, 1796. Took part in Helder Campaign of 1799 and present at Egmont-op-Zee. Took part in attack on Ferrol, 1800. Fought in Egyptian campaign, 1801 and saw action at Aboukir Bay, Roman Camp and Alexandria. To Gibraltar, 1801; England, 1803. Took part in expeditions to North Germany, 1805 and Copenhagen, 1807. To Nova

Above - Officer - 23rd Regiment, 1855. The large grenade badge being worn on the Albert shako is that seen below. Illustration by P.W. Reynolds.

Right - 23rd Regiment escorting prisoners - Fort William, India, 1857. Engraving from The Illustrated London News.

Below - Gilt grenade with silver Prince of Wales's Plumes etc. worn on the Albert shako 1844-55 - 23rd Regiment.

Scotia, 1808 and at end of year moved to Barbados. Fought in Martinique campaign, 1809. To Nova Scotia in March then Portugal, 1810. Fought at Albuhera and Aldea da Ponte, 1811; Badajoz and Salamanca, 1812; Vittoria, Pyrenees operations and battle of Nivelle, 1813; Orthes and Toulouse, 1814. To England, 1814; Belgium, 1815. Fought at Waterloo and during capture of Cambrai. To England from France, then to Ireland, 1818; Gibraltar, 1823; Portugal, 1827; Gibraltar, 1828; England, 1834; Ireland, 1836; Nova Scotia, 1838; Canada, 1841; West Indies, 1843; Nova Scotia, 1847; England, 1848. A Reserve Battalion, 23rd Foot formed, 1842 at Chichester and sent to 1st Battalion in Canada. Returned to England and absorbed into 1st Battalion, 1853. To the Crimea, 1854. Took part in battles of the Alma and Inkerman. Engaged during attack on the Redan, 1855. To England, 1856; China, 1857. Diverted to India due to Indian Mutiny. Took part in relief of Lucknow and fighting at Cawnpore. To England, 1869; Ireland, 1875; India, 1880. Took part in Burma Campaign, 1885-87. Returned to India and in Hazara expedition, 1891. To Aden, 1896; England, 1897; South Africa, 1899. Fought at Colenso, capture of Hussar Hill and during relief of Ladysmith. To England, 1903; Ireland, 1907; England, 1912; Malta in January, 1914, returning to England in September. Crossed to Belgium and after operations at Antwerp took part in battles of Ypres. Engaged at Neuve Chapelle; Aubers Ridge and Loos, 1915; on the Somme, 1916; at Ypres, 1917. Moved to Italian Front November, 1917. To England then India, 1919 and took part in Waziristan Campaigns, 1919-24. To the Sudan, 1930; England, 1932. Fought in France and Belgium, 1940; India and Burma, 1942-45. Since the Second World War served in the West Indies, 1951-54; Cyprus, 1958-59; Singapore, 1962-63; Cyprus, 1966; Hong Kong, 1969-72; Belize, 1974, the Falklands, 1985 in addition to numerous tours in Germany and Northern Ireland..

2nd Battalion

Formed at Leicester, 1756 and took part in expedition to St. Malo, 1758. Became 68th Regiment of Foot (see The Durham Light Infantry) same year. New 2nd Battalion formed, 1804 and recruited in North Wales. To Ireland,

Above - Captain Annesley Cary - 2nd Battalion, 23rd Regiment, Canada, 1866-67. Captain Cary served in the India Mutiny, 1857-58. Note cold weather cap and jacket.

Left - Captain E.W.D. Bell - 23rd Foot, winning the Victoria Cross at the battle of Alma 29th September, 1854. Engraving after L.W. Desanges.

Below - Officer - 23rd Regiment in blue patrol uniform. The headdress and badge would date this photograph sometime between 1874 and 1881. Glengarry caps were also worn for a time by non-Scottish regiments. The photograph was taken by a Woolwich photographer, the 1st Battalion, 23rd arriving there from Ireland in May, 1879.

1807; Spain, 1808, returning to England after fighting at Corunna, 1809. Later took part in expedition to Walcheren. Disbanded, 1814. Re-formed at Newport, Mon., 1858. To Malta, 1859; Gibraltar, 1863; Canada, 1866; England 1867; Ireland, 1872. Took part in Ashanti expedition, 1873-74. To Gibraltar, 1874; England, 1880; Ireland, 1883; North Wales then England, 1892; Malta, 1896; Crete, 1897; Egypt then Hong Kong, 1898. Took part in Tientsin operations and relief of Pekin, 1900. Left China for India, 1902 then to Burma, 1907. Returned to India, 1911 and to England, 1914. Crossed to France and took part in the battle and retreat from Mons, battles of the Marne and Aisne. Fought at Ypres and Loos, 1915; on the Somme, 1916; at Arras and Ypres, 1917; Somme and Hindenburg Line, 1918. To Wales then Ireland, 1919; Wales, 1922; Germany, 1926; England, 1929; Gibraltar, 1931; Hong Kong, 1934; Shanghai, 1937; Hong Kong, 1938; the Sudan then India, 1938. During Second World War served in India, until 1940; Madagascar, 1942; India and Burma, 1943-45. Left India for Japan, 1946. To Malaya, 1947; England and disbanded, 1948. Re-formed at Tidworth, 1952. Stationed in Germany, 1953-54; Malaya, 1954-57. Returned to England and disbanded.

Above - Group of officers - 23rd Regiment, Newport Barracks c1870. The party also includes officers from the 21st Regiment who`s Depot was attached to the 23rd at the time. (Royal Welch Fusiliers Museum).

Below - The Royal Welsh Fusiliers. Coloured post card showing sergeant, corporal and drummer c1913. Note the white hackle and Flash. Illustration by Harry Payne.

Right - Drum Major and drummer - The Royal Welsh Fusiliers with Regimental Goat c1898.

Badges

The Coronet, Plume and motto of the Prince of Wales, the Red Dragon and the Rising Sun - granted in 1714. The White Horse of Hanover, with motto Nec aspera terrent (Nor do difficulties appal) - awarded after the battle of Dettingen in 1743. The Sphinx superscribed "Egypt" - for the campaign of 1801.

Uniform

Blue facings.

The South Wales Borderers

Titles

1689-1751 Known by name of Colonel.
1751-1782 24th Regiment of Foot.
1782-1881 24th (2nd Warwickshire) Regiment of Foot.
1881-1969 The South Wales Borderers.

1st Battalion

Raised by Sir Edward Dering, 1689. Sent to Ireland and engaged during rebellion, 1689-91. Served on board ship and took part in operations along French coast, 1692-97. To Holland, 1701 and during War of The Spanish Succession fought at Schellenberg and Blenheim, 1704; Ramillies, 1706; Oudenarde and Lille, 1708; Malplaquet, 1709; Douai, 1710 and Bouchain, 1711. To Ireland. 1714; Scotland, 1715 and served during rebellion, then returned to Ireland. Took part in Vigo expedition of 1719 then returned to Ireland. To England, 1734; Ireland, 1735; England, 1739; Jamaica, 1740. Took part in expedition to Fort St. Lazar in Cartagena, 1741. To England, 1742. Served in Scotland during rebellion, 1746. Left Scotland for England, 1749. To Minorca, 1752. Took part in defence of Minorca, 1756 then returned to England. Took part in operations along French coast, 1758 - St. Malo, Cherbourg. To Germany, 1760. Fought at Corbach and Warburg, 1760; Vellinghausen, 1761 and Wilhelmsthal, 1762. To Gibraltar, 1763; Ireland, 1769; Canada, 1776. Took part in relief of Quebec and present during operations on Lake Champlain. Fought at Bemis Heights, 1777 and later forced to surrender at Saratoga. To England, 1782; Ireland, 1785; Canada, 1789; Nova Scotia, 1799; England, 1800. Served in Egyptian campaign of 1801 then to Malta. To England, 1802; Cape of Good Hope, 1805 and took part in capture of Cape Town, 1806. To India, 1810. Attacked by French warships on voyage from Cape Town and most of battalion held prisoner on Mauritius until released, 1811. Took part in Nepal campaign, 1814-18. To England, 1823; Ireland, 1825; England then Canada, 1829; England, 1841; Ireland, 1844; India, 1846. Took part in Second Sikh War and fought at Ramnagar and Sadullapur, 1848, Chillanwallah and Goojerat, 1849. To England, 1861; Ireland, 1865; Malta, 1866; Gibraltar, 1872; South Africa, 1875. Engaged during Kaffir War, 1877-78. In Zulu War fought at Isandhlwana January, 1879. Lieutenants T. Melvill and N.J.A. Coghill awarded Victoria Cross. To England, 1880; Ireland, 1883; England, 1889; Gibraltar, 1895; India, 1897; England, 1910. Crossed to France, 1914. Engaged during retreat from Mons and battles of the Marne, Aisne and Ypres. Fought at Aubers Ridge and Loos, 1915; on the Somme, 1916;

Right - Officers - 2nd Battalion, 24th Regiment - South Africa, 1878. Among the group (seated second from left, second row) is Lieutenant G.S.Bromhead who would receive the Victoria Cross for his gallantry at Rorke`s Drift in 1879. Note the various orders of dress, badges of rank being worn on the collars and cap numerals.

Below - Officer - 24th Regiment, 1850. The headdress was that in use between 1844-55 and is that shown on page 81. The oblong gilt shoulder-belt plate has in silver the Sphinx above the numerals 24 all within a crowned wreath. From Historical Records of the 24th Regiment, 1892.

at Ypres, 1917. Took part in battles of the Lys, Arras and Hindenburg Line, 1918. To England, 1919; Ireland, 1920; England, 1922; Egypt, 1928. Took part in operations in Palestine, 1929. To Hong Kong, 1930; India, 1934. Took part in Waziristan operations, 1937. Moved to Iraq, 1941 and fought in Libya, 1942. Received heavy casualties and later disbanded in Cyprus. Reconstituted at Wimborne, Dorset December, 1942. Stationed in Palestine, 1945-46; Cyprus, 1946-49 and then to the Sudan. Moved to Eritrea and took part in operations against the Shifta, 1950-52. Stationed in Germany, 1953-55. Took part in Malayan campaign, 1955-58. Stationed in Germany, Hong Kong and Aden, 1959-67. Amalgamated with 1st Battalion, The Welch Regiment to form 1st Battalion, The Royal Regiment of Wales (24th/41st Foot), 1969.

2nd Battalion

A 2nd Battalion, 24th Regiment formed, 1757. Took part in Rocheford expedition of 1757. Became 69th Regiment, 1758 (see The Welch Regiment). Another raised at Warwick, 1804. To Guernsey, 1808; Portugal, 1809. During Peninsular War gained battle honours "Talavera", "Busaco", "Fuentes d`Onor", "Salamanca", "Vittoria", "Pyrenees", "Nivelle" and "Orthes". Left France for England, 1814 and disbanded. Re-raised at Sheffield, 1858. To Mauritius, 1860; Burma, 1865. Five Victoria Crosses awarded for gallantry in the Andaman Islands May, 1867. To India, 1869; England, 1872; South Africa, 1878. Engaged during Kaffir War. In Zulu War, 1879 "G" Company present with 1st Battalion at Isandhlwana and "B" Company in defence of Rorke`s Drift. Seven Victoria Crosses awarded. To Gibraltar then India, 1880. Took part in Burma campaign, 1886-88 and then to India. To Aden, 1892; England, 1893; Ireland then South Africa, 1899. Took part in relief of Kimberley and present during operations at Jacobsdal and Johannesburg. To England, 1904; South Africa, 1910; Tientsin, North China, 1912. Took part in fighting at Tsingtao,

September-November, 1914. Left Hong Kong for England, December, 1914. Embarked for Egypt, 1915 and from there landed at Gallipoli. Moved to France March, 1916 and later took part in Somme operations. Fought at battles of Arras, Ypres and Cambrai, 1917; the Lys, 1918. To England them India, 1919 Aden, 1927; England, 1929; Malta, 1935; Palestine then England, 1936. Fought in Norway, 1940 and after landing on D-Day - North-West Europe, 1944-45. Disbanded, 1948.

Badges

The Sphinx superscribed `Egypt` - awarded to 1st Battalion, 24th Regiment for its services during 1801. A Silver Wreath of Immortelles - when the 1st Battalion returned home after the Zulu War, Queen Victoria requested to see the Colour defended by Lieutenants Melvill and Coghill. To commemorate their gallantry, and that of the defence of Rorke's Drift, she place a wreath of immortelles upon the staff. It was then directed that a silver wreath be borne round the staff of the Queen's Colour of each battalion. The Welsh Dragon.

Uniform

White facings were ordered to be worn in 1881. The grass green in use prior to then being restored in 1905.

Nicknames

`Howards Greens` - from the colour of the facings and Thomas Howard, Colonel of the 24th, 1717-37. `The Bengal Tigers` - from service during the Sikh War, 1848-49.

Above - Engraving from front page of The Illustrated London News for 29th March, 1879. The Queen's Colour of the 1st Battalion, 24th Regiment having been lost after Isandhlwana was later found just below where Lieutenants Melvill and Coghill had crossed the Buffalo River. The illustration shows the Colour being handed over to what remained of the battalion at Helpmakaar.

Left - Albert Shako, 1844-55, 24th Regiment. Gilt plate, white over red ball-tuft.

Below - Private A. Edwards - 1st Battalion, The South Wales Borderers, Hong Kong, 1964.

Cap badge and Back Badge - The Gloucestershire Regiment.

Cap badge and Back Badge - The Gloucestershire Regiment.

Grenadiers of the 28th Regiment attacking at Louisburg 1758. Illustration by A.C. Lovett

The Gloucestershire Regiment

Titles

1694-1751 Known by name of Colonel.
1751-1782 28th Regiment of Foot.
1782-1881 28th (North Gloucestershire) Regiment of Foot.

1756-1758 2nd Battalion, 3rd Regiment of Foot.
1758-1782 61st Regiment of Foot.
1782-1881 61st (South Gloucestershire) of Foot.

1881-1994 The Gloucestershire Regiment

28th Regiment

Raised at Portsmouth by Colonel John Gibson, 1694. Took part in expedition to Newfoundland, 1697. To Ireland, 1702; Flanders, 1704. Gained first battle honour at Ramillies 23rd May, 1706. To England in July and then to Portugal. Fought at Almanza,1707; Tarragona, 1708 then to England. Took Part in Vigo expedition, 1719 then to Ireland. To Flanders, 1743. Sent back to England after fighting at Fontenoy May, 1745. Took part in expedition to Lorient, 1746 and present during operations at Hulst, 1747. To Ireland, 1749; America, 1757. Fought at Louisburg, 1758; Quebec, 1759; Sainte Foy, 1760. To the West Indies, 1761. Fought in Martinique and Cuba, 1762. To America, 1763; Ireland, 1767; America, 1775. Fought at Brooklyn, White Plains and Fort Washington, 1776; Brandywine, Germantown, 1777. To the West Indies, 1778 and took part in capture of St. Lucia. Took part in St. Kitts operations, 1782. To England, 1783; Ireland, 1786; Jersey, 1793; England then Flanders, 1794. Fought at Nejmegen and Geldermansel. To England, 1795; the West Indies, 1795. Regiment divided during storm at sea - part reached Barbados, part returned home and then to Gibraltar. Took part in capture of Minorca, 1798. To Malta, 1800; Egypt, 1801. Took part in landing at Aboukir and fighting at Roman Camp; Mandora and Alexandria. To England, 1802. Took part in expedition to Copenhagen, 1807. To Portugal, 1808. Took part in retreat to Corunna, returning to England January, 1809 (detachments remained in the Peninsular and present at the Douro, Talavera and Busaco). Took part in expedition to Walcheren, 1809. To Gibraltar, 1810; the Peninsular and fought at Barrosa and Arroyo dos Molinos, 1811; Burgos, 1812; Vittoria, Pyrenees operations, Nivelle, the Nive, 1813; Orthez and Toulouse, 1814. To Ireland, 1814. *A 2nd Battalion, 28th Regiment formed at Plymouth, 1803. Left Ireland for the Peninsular and present at Busaco, 1810 and Albuhera, 1811. Disbanded, 1814.* To Belgium, 1815 and fought at Quatre Bras and Waterloo. Left France for England, 1816. To Malta,

Above - Officers` shoulder-belt plate - 28th Regiment. Gilt plate with silver Royal Crest and numerals.

Left - 28th Regiment fighting back to back at Alexandria 21st March, 1801.

Below - Officers` shako plate 1816-29.

1817; the Ionian Islands, 1818; Ireland, 1829; Australia, 1835; India, 1842. Took part in Scinde campaign, 1843. To England, 1848; the Crimea, 1854. Took part in battles of the Alma, Inkerman and siege of Sevastopol. To Malta, 1855; India, 1858; England, 1865; Gibraltar, 1868; Malta, 1872; Hong Kong, 1876; Malay, 1878; Ireland, 1879. Became 1st Battalion, The Gloucestershire Regiment, 1881.

61st Regiment

Raised in 1756 at Chatham as 2nd Battalion, 3rd Regiment (see The Buffs, Royal East Kent Regiment). Became independent and designated 61st Regiment, 1758 and then to the West Indies. Won first battle honour at Guadeloupe, 1759. To England, 1760; the Channel Islands, 1762; Ireland, 1763; Minorca, 1771; England, 1782; Ireland, 1783; Gibraltar, 1792; West Indies, 1794. Fought in St. Lucia, 1795 and 1796. To England, 1796; Channel Islands, 1797; Cape Colony, 1798. Part of regiment sent to India, 1801 and took part in capture of Broach, 1803. Remainder to Egypt, 1801. To Malta, 1803; Italy, 1805; Sicily, 1806. Flank companies took part in battle of Maida in July. To Gibraltar, 1807; Portugal, 1809. Fought at Talavera in July. Present at Busaco, 1810; Fuentes d` Onoro, 1811; Salamanca and Burgos, 1812; Vittoria, Pyrenees, Nivelle and Nive operations, 1813; Orthes and Toulouse, 1814. *A 2nd Battalion, 61st Regiment formed, 1803 in Durham and Northumberland and disbanded, 1814.* To Ireland, 1814; Jamaica, 1816; England, 1822; Ceylon, 1828; England, 1840; India, 1845. Took part in Punjab Campaign, 1848-49 and present at battles of Ramnagar, Chilianwala and Goojerat. Served during Indian Mutiny gaining battle honour "Delhi 1857." Surgeon H.T. Reade awarded the Victoria Cross. To Mauritius, 1859; England, 1860; Channel Islands, 1863; Ireland, 1864; Bermuda, 1866; Canada, 1870; Ireland, 1872; Channel Islands, 1875; England, 1876; Malta, 1878; India, 1880. Became 2nd Battalion, The Gloucestershire Regiment, 1881.

1st Battalion

Formed from the 28th Regiment of Foot stationed in Ireland, 1881. To Malta, 1893; Egypt, 1895; India, 1897; South Africa, 1899. Fought at Rietfontein, Cainguba Hill and Ladysmith. To Ceylon guarding Boer prisoners, 1900; India, 1903, England, 1910. During First World War took part in battles of Mons, the Marne, Aisne and Ypres, 1914; Aubers Ridge and Loos, 1915; the Somme, 1916; operations on the Flanders coast and battle of Passchendaele, 1917; battles of the Lys, Arras and Hindenburg Line, 1918. Served in Ireland, 1920-22; Upper Silesia and Cologne, 1922-23; Egypt, 1928-31; Singapore, 1931-32; India, 1931-38, then to Burma. Fought in Burma to 1943, then to India. To England, 1947. Amalgamated with 2nd Battalion in Jamaica, 1948. To England, 1949. Served in Korea, 1950-51, fighting at Hill 327 and at the Imjin River. Colonel J.P. Carne awarded Victoria Cross and Distinguished Service Order. Served in Kenya, 1955-56; Aden and Bahrain, 1956; Cyprus, 1957-58; Germany, 1958-60; Cyprus, 1962-65; Swaziland, 1965-66; Germany, 1967-69. Amalgamation with 1st Battalion, The Royal Hampshire Regiment ordered in 1968 but cancelled, 1970. The regiment has had several tours of duty in Northern Ireland and served in Belize, 1975. Amalgamated with 1st Battalion, The Duke of Edinburgh`s Royal Regiment (Berkshire and Wiltshire) to form 1st Battalion, The Royal Gloucestershire, Berkshire and Wiltshire Regiment, 1994.

2nd Battalion

Formed from the 61st Regiment of Foot stationed in India, 1881. To Aden, 1893; England, 1894; Channel Islands, 1897; England, 1899. Embarked for South Africa and fought at Paardeberg February, 1900. Remained in Bloemfontein area, returning to England, 1904. To Malta, 1910; North China, 1913; England, 1914. Crossed to France and fought in Ypres battles of 1915. Moved to Macedonian Front end of year. Served in Bulgaria, 1918; Armenia and Russia, 1919, then to India. Part of Shanghai Defence force, 1927. To England, 1928; Egypt, 1936; England, 1937. During Second World War fought in France and Belgium, 1939-40; North-West Europe, 1944-45 taking part D-Day landings. Left Germany for England, 1946, then to the West Indies. Amalgamated with 1st Battalion, 1948.

Above - Drum-Major and Drummer, 28th Regiment, 1844. Note Sphinx Back Badge. Illustration by A.C. Lovett.

Right - The Gloucestershire Regiment c1895. Note Back Badge.

Badges

The Royal Crest - an old badge of the 28th. The Sphinx superscribed `Egypt` - awarded to both the 28th and 61st for service in Egypt during 1801. The Arms of the City of Gloucester - introduced in 1881.

Uniform

28th Regiment - bright yellow facings. 61st Regiment - buff. The Gloucestershire Regiment - white until 1929, then primrose yellow.

Nicknames

`The Old Braggs` - Philip Bragg, Colonel of the 28th, 1734-1759. `The Slashers` - after and incident in 1764 when a Montreal magistrate`s ear was cut off, and from the fighting at White Plain in 1776. `The Silver-tailed Dandies` - the 61st are said to have worn in the Peninsular longer coat-tails than other regiments, decorated with silver ornaments. `The Flowers of Toulouse` - the 61st Regiment from the many red-coated dead left on the field after the battle of Toulouse 10th April, 1814. `The Glorious Glosters.'

Above - Major S. Humphrey - 1st Battalion, The Gloucestershire Regiment. Taken prisoner in South Africa October, 1899. Note cap badge - Sphinx above arms of the City of Gloucester. Gilt and red enamel.

Left - Second Lieutenant S. R. Crisp, 2nd Battalion, The Gloucestershire Regiment 1945. Note formation badges - 49th West Riding Division (top), 56th Infantry Brigade (bottom). Overseas service chevrons are worn on the lower right arm and a wound strip on the left.

The Worcestershire Regiment

Titles

1694-1751	Known by name of Colonel.	1701-1751	Known by name of Colonel.
1751-1782	29th Regiment of Foot.	1751-1782	36th Regiment of Foot.
1782-1881	29th (Worcestershire) Regiment of Foot.	1782-1881	36th (Herefordshire) Regiment of Foot.

1881-1970   The Worcestershire Regiment.

29th Regiment

Raised by Colonel Thomas Farrington in London, 1694. To Ireland, 1702; Flanders, 1704. Fought at Elixheim, 1705 and Ramillies, 1706. To Portugal, 1706; England, 1707; Flanders, 1708; England, 1709; Gibraltar, 1711;

86

Ireland, 1713; Gibraltar, 1727; Cape Breton, 1745; Ireland, 1750; Nova Scotia, 1765; Boston, 1768. Present during `Boston Massacre` in 1770. To England, 1773; Canada, 1776. Flank companies took part in Burgoyne expedition and captured at Saratoga, 1777. To England, 1787. Detachments served as marines, taking part in operations in the West Indies and with Lord Howe`s Channel Fleet present on the `Glorious 1st of June.` To the West Indies, 1795. Took part in operations on Grenada, 1795-96. *A 2nd Battalion, 29th Regiment formed in Jersey, 1795. To England and disbanded, 1796.* To England, 1796; Ireland, 1798; England, 1799. Took part in Helder Campaign of 1799 and present at Alkmaar, Egmont-op-Zee and Bergen. To Nova Scotia, 1802; England, 1807. Took part in operations along Spanish coast, 1808 then to Portugal. Fought at Rolica and Vimiera, 1808; the Douro and Talavera, 1809; Albuhera, 1811. To England, 1811; Cadiz, 1813; Gibraltar then Nova Scotia, 1814; England then France, 1815; Ireland, 1819; England, 1820; Ireland, 1821; Mauritius, 1826; England, 1827; Ireland, 1841; India, 1842. Took part in Setlej campaign, 1845-46 and present at Firuzshahar and Sabraon. In Punjab campaign, 1848-49 fought at Chilianwala and Goojerat. To England, 1859; Ireland, 1863;

Lieutenant J.W. Leckie - 2nd Battalion, The Worcestershire Regiment, c1885.

2nd Battalion, The Worcestershire Regiment passing through 1st South Wales Borderers at Château Gheluvelt - 31st October, 1914.

Malta, 1865; Canada, 1867; West Indies, 1869; Ireland, 1873; Jersey, 1875; England, 1876; India, 1879. Became 1st Battalion, The Worcestershire Regiment, 1881.

36th Regiment

Raised by Lord Charlemont in Ireland, 1701. Took part in expeditions to Cadiz, 1702 - in action at Vigo Bay and the West Indies - present during attack on Guadeloupe, 1703. To Ireland, 1704; Spain, 1705. Fought at Barcelona, 1705 and Almanza, 1707. To England, 1707. Took part in 1711 expedition to Canada and present during operations at Quebec. To France, 1712; Ireland, 1714; Scotland, 1715. Present at Dunblane. To Ireland, 1718; England, 1719; Ireland, 1720; England, 1739. Detachments served in the West Indies, 1740-41 and fought at St. Lazar, Cartagena, 1741. To Flanders, 1744; Scotland, 1745. Present at Culloden, 1746. To Flanders, 1747 and present at Lauffeld. To England, 1748; Gibraltar, 1749; Scotland, 1754; England, 1755. Took part in raids along French coast, 1758 - attack on Cherburg-St. Vast, and in 1761 fought at Belle Isle. *A 2nd Battalion, 36th Regiment formed, 1756. Became 74th Regiment, 1758.* To the West Indies, 1764; England, 1773; Ireland, 1775; England, 1782; India, 1783. During Third Mysore War fought at Cheyoor, 1790; Bangalore, Arikera and Nundy Droog, 1791; Seringaptam, 1792. To England, 1798. Took part in expedition to Quiberon and then to Minorca, 1800. To Ireland, 1803; Germany then England, 1806; South America then Ireland, 1807; Portugal, 1808. Fought at Rolica and Vimiero, 1808. After Corunna, 1809 moved to England then took part in expedition to Walcheren. Returned to the Peninsular, 1811. Fought at Salamanca, 1812; during Pyrenees operations, battles of Nivelle and the Nive, 1813; Orthes and Toulouse, 1814. *A 2nd*

Battalion, 36th Regiment formed, 1804 in Durham. Disbanded, 1814. To Ireland, 1814; France then England, 1815; Malta, 1817; Ionian Islands, 1821; England, 1825; Ireland, 1827; West Indies, 1830; Nova Scotia, 1838; New Brunswick, 1840; Ireland, 1842; England, 1845; Ionian Islands, 1847; West Indies, 1851; England, 1857; Ireland, 1860; India, 1863; England, 1875; Ireland, 1880. Became 2nd Battalion, The Worcestershire Regiment, 1881.

1st Battalion

Formed from the 29th Regiment stationed in India, 1881. To Burma, 1894; Aden, 1895; England, 1896; South Africa, 1900. Served in Cape Colony operations. To Ireland, 1903; England, 1908; Egypt, 1913; England, 1914. During First World War fought at Neuve Chapelle, 1914 and 1915; Aubers Ridge and Bois Grenier, 1915; on the Somme, 1916; at Ypres, 1917; St. Quentin, Rosières, Villers Bretonneux, on the Aisne and Scarpe, 1918 (Lieutenant-Colonel G.W. St. G. Grogan and Captain F.C. Roberts awarded Victoria Cross). To England then India, 1919; Shanghai, 1929; England, 1931; Palestine, 1938. Present during Arab rebellion. To the Sudan, 1939. During Second World War served in the Sudan, Eritrea and North Africa. Captured at Tobruk, 1942. Re-formed in England from 11th Battalion, 1943. Fought in North West Europe, 1944-45. Left Germany for England, 1950. Served in Malaya, 1950-53; Germany, 1954-56; West Indies, 1957-60; Germany, 1962-64; Gibraltar, 1965-67. Amalgamated with 1st Battalion, The Sherwood Foresters to form 1st Battalion, The Worcestershire and Sherwood Foresters Regiment (29th/45th Foot), 1970.

2nd Battalion

Formed from the 36th Regiment stationed in Ireland, 1881. To England, 1893; Malta, 1895; Bermuda, 1897; South Africa, 1899. Present during Colesberg operations. To Ceylon, 1904; India, 1906; England, 1913. During First World War took part in battles of Mons, the Marne, Aisne and Ypres, 1914; Festubert, Loos and the Hohenzollern Redoubt, 1915; the Somme, 1916 (Lieutenant E.P. Bennett awarded Victoria Cross); Arras and Ypres, 1917; the Lys (Lieutenant J.J. Crowe awarded Victoria Cross), Hindenburg Line and the Selle, 1918. To England then Ireland, 1919; England, 1923; Germany, 1926; England, 1928; Malta, 1930; Shanghai, 1933; Tientsin, 1934; India, 1936. During Second World War served in India then Burma, 1944-45. Left Burma for England, 1947. Amalgamated with 1st Battalion, 1948.

3rd Battalion

Formed, 1900. To Ireland, 1902; England, 1904; South Africa, 1907; England, 1908. During First World War took part in battles of Mons, Le Cateau, the Marne, Aisne, Messines, Armentières and Ypres, 1914; Hooge, 1915; the Somme, 1916; Messines and Ypres, 1917; the Somme, Lys; Selle and Sambre, 1918. To England then Ireland, 1919; England then India, 1920; England, 1922. Disbanded, 1923.

Presentation bugle bearing Worcestershire Regiment badge.

4th Battalion

Formed, 1900. To Bermuda, 1902; Barbados, 1903; Malta, 1905; India, 1909; Burma, 1914; England, 1915. During First World War fought at Gallipoli, 1915-16 (Second- Lieutenant H. James awarded Victoria Cross); on the Somme, 1916; battles of Arras, Ypres (Private G.F. Dancox awarded Victoria Cross) and Cambrai, 1917; Messines, Bailleul, Ypres and Courtrai, 1918. To England, 1919; Germany, 1920; Scotland then Ireland, 1921; England, 1922 and disbanded.

Badges

The Lion - Ancient badge of the 29th Regiment. The Garter Star - another Ancient badge of the 29th Regiment. A Naval Crown superscribed `1st June, 1794` - from the 29th Regiment. The motto `Firm` - of the 36th Regiment. The Royal Crest - old badge of the 36th Regiment. A Round Tower of Worcester Castle - introduced in 1881. A Rose - introduced in 1881.

Uniform

29th Regiment - yellow facings. 36th Regiment - green facings. Worcestershire Regiment - white, changing to green in 1920.

Nicknames

`Guards of the Line` - the 29th Regiment was raised by a Guardsman and was long associated with the Coldstream Guards in training, equipment, dress etc. `The Ever-Sworded 29th` - During service in North America in 1746, the regiment was attacked while at Mess. The custom of wearing swords at Mess was then introduced. `The Vein-openers` - given to the 29th Regiment after the `Boston Massacre` in 1770. `The Two and Hook` - from the number 29. `The Saucy Greens` - from the 36th Regiment's facings.

The East Lancashire Regiment

Titles

1689-1751	Known by name of Colonel.	1755-1757	61st Regiment of Foot.
1751-1782	30th Regiment of Foot.	1757-1782	59th Regiment of Foot.
1782-1881	30th (Cambridgeshire) Regiment of Foot.	1782-1881	59th (2nd Nottinghamshire)

1881-1958   The East Lancashire Regiment.

30th Regiment

Raised in Lincolnshire, 1689. To Flanders, 1691 and fought at Namur, 1695. To England, 1697. Disbanded, 1698. Re-formed in Lincolnshire as a regiment of marines, 1702. Took part in capture of Gibraltar and battle of Malaga, 1704; capture of Barcelona, 1705; capture of Alicante, 1706; Sardinia and Minorca, 1708. Also present during the defeat of French Fleet in the Firth of Forth. Disbanded, 1714. Re-formed and to Ireland, 1715. To Minorca, 1718; Gibraltar, 1725. Present during siege of 1727. To Ireland, 1728; England, 1744. As marines, took part in expedition to Lorient, 1746 and action at Cape Finisterre, 1747. To Ireland, 1749; England, 1755. Took part in attacks along French coast - Cherburg, St. Cast, St. Malo, 1757-58; capture of Belle Isle, 1761. To Gibraltar, 1763; England, 1771; Ireland, 1775; North America, 1781. Took part in campaign in Carolina. Flank companies present at Eutaw Springs. To the West Indies, 1782. Stationed in Dominica, 1784-1791 and engaged during slave uprisings of 1788 and 1791. To England, 1791. Served as marines in the Mediterranean, 1793-96. Took part in occupation of Toulon, attack on Fort Mulgrave and Aresnes, 1793; capture of Bastia, Calvi and Corsica, 1794. To England then Ireland, 1796; Minorca, Italy then Malta, 1799. Took part in capture of Valetta. Took part in Egyptian campaign of 1801 and fought at Mandora, Alexandria and Rahmanieh. Returned to Malta then to England, 1802; Ireland, 1804; Germany, 1805; England then India, 1806. Detachments served in expedition to Java, 1807 and occupation of Macao, 1808. Took part in Pindari War, 1817-19 and present at Asseerghur. *A 2nd Battalion, 30th Regiment formed, 1803. To Ireland, 1804; Portugal then Gibraltar, 1809, Spain then Portugal, 1810. Present at Torres Vedras, 1810; Fuentes d` Onor, 1811; Badajoz and Salamanca, 1812. To England then Jersey, 1813; Holland then Belgium, 1814. Fought at Quatre Bras and Waterloo, 1815. Left France for England, 1815. To Ireland, 1816. Disbanded, 1817.* To England, 1829; Ireland, 1831; Bermuda, 1834; Nova Scotia, 1841; Ireland, 1843; England,

2nd Battalion, 30th Regiment in square at Waterloo from a painting by G.P. Jazet.

1846; Ionian Islands, 1851; Gibraltar, 1853; the Crimea, 1854. Present at the Alma, Inkerman (Lieutenant Mark Walker awarded Victoria Cross) and Sevastopol. To Gibraltar, 1856; Ireland, 1857; Channel Islands, 1860; England then Canada, 1861; Nova Scotia, 1868; Ireland, 1869; Jersey, 1871; England, 1872; India, 1880. Became 1st Battalion, The East Lancashire Regiment, 1881.

59th Regiment

Formed in Leicestershire and Nottinghamshire, 1755 and then to Ireland. To Nova Scotia, 1763, Boston, Massachusets, 1772. Fought at Lexington and Bunker Hill, 1775. To England, 1775; Gibraltar, 1782; England, 1792; Channel Islands, 1793; Flanders, 1794 and fought at Nijmegen. To England then the West Indies, 1795. Fought at St. Vincent, 1796. To England, 1802; Cape of Good Hope, 1805. Took part in operations against the Dutch. To India, 1806. Took part in capture of Mauritius, 1810 and Java, 1811. Left Java for India, 1815. *A 2nd Battalion, 59th Regiment formed, 1804 in Derbyshire. Served in Ireland and the Channel Islands then to Spain, 1808. Fought at Corunna. Returned to England then took part in Walcheren expedition, 1809. To Ireland, 1810; England, 1811; Spain, 1812. Present at Vittoria, San Sebastian, Bidassoa, the Nivelle and Nive, 1813. To Ireland then Belgium and France, 1815. Returned to England and disbanded, 1816. To Ceylon, 1817; India, 1818. Took part in Third Mahratta War, 1818-19 and present at Bhurtpore during Jat War, 1826. To England, 1829;*

Above - Cap badge - The East Lancashire Regiment

Left - Officers` waist-belt clasp - 59th Regiment.

Below - Drummer Spencer John Bent - 1st Battalion, The East Lancashire Regiment who won the Victoria Cross near Le Gheer, Belgium 2nd November, 1914.

Ireland, 1831; England, 1834; Malta, 1836; West Indies, 1841; England, 1843; Ireland, 1846; China, 1849. Took part in Second China War. Fought at Canton, 1857 and Nantow, 1858. To South Africa, 1858; England, 1861; Ireland, 1865; Ceylon, 1867; India, 1869. Took part in Afghan War, 1878-80. Captain E.H. Sartorius awarded Victoria Cross at Shahjui, 1879; present at Ahmed Khel, 1880. To England, 1880. Became 2nd Battalion, The East Lancashire Regiment, 1881.

1st Battalion

Formed from the 30th Regiment stationed in India, 1881. Took part in Chitral relief expedition, 1895. To Burma, 1896; England, 1897; South Africa, 1900. fought at Karee Siding, Zand River and Johannesberg. To Ireland, 1902; England, 1908. During First World War took part in retreat from Mons and battles of the Marne, Aisne and Armentières, 1914 (Drummer S.J. Bent awarded Victoria Cross); Ypres, 1915; the Some, 1916; Arras and Ypres, 1917; St. Quentin, the Lys; Selle and Valenciennes, 1918. To England, 1919; Jamaica and Bermuda, 1921; Malta, 1923; Egypt, 1924; the Sudan, 1925; India, 1926; Shanghai, 1932; England, 1933; Egypt, 1936; Northern Ireland, 1937. During Second World War fought in France and Belgium, 1939-40 and North West Europe, 1944-45. Left Germany for England, 1947. To the Sudan, 1950; Egypt, 1951; England, 1953; Germany, 1954; England then Hong Kong, 1957. Amalgamated with 1st Battalion, The South Lancashire Regiment to form 1st Battalion, The Lancashire Regiment (Prince of Wales`s Volunteers), 1958.

2nd Battalion

Formed from the 59th Regiment stationed in England 1881. To Ireland, 1885; Gibraltar, 1893; England, 1895; India, 1897; South Africa, 1911; England, 1914. During First World War took part in battles of Neuve Chapelle, 1914 and 1915; Aubers Ridge and Bois Grenier, 1915; the Somme, 1916; Ypres, 1917; St. Quentin, Rosiäres, Villers Bretonneux and the Scarpe, 1918. To England, 1919; Ireland, 1920; England, 1923; Hong Kong, 1933; India, 1937; England, 1940. During Second World War served in South Africa, Madagascar and East Africa, 1942; India, 1943-44; Burma, 1944-45. Left India for England, 1947. Amalgamated with 1st Battalion, 1948.

DRUMMER SPENCER JOHN BENT

Below - Ammunition mule - 2nd Battalion, The East Lancashire Regiment c1897.

Badges

The Sphinx superscribed `Egypt` - for the services of the 30th Regiment in Egypt, 1801. The Red Rose of Lancaster - adopted in 1881.

Uniform

30th Regiment - yellow facings. 59th Regiment - light crimson (purple) changing to white in 1776. East Lancashire Regiment - white.

Nicknames

`The Triple X`s` and `The Three Tens` - from the number of the 30th Regiment. `The Lilywhites` from the facings of the 59th Regiment.

Cap badge - The East Surrey Regiment.

2nd Battalion, 31st Regiment at Albuhera
16th May, 1811. Illustration by Harry Payne.

The East Surrey Regiment

Titles

1702-1751	Known by name of Colonel.	1756-1758	2nd Battalion, 31st Foot.
1751-1782	31st Regiment of Foot.		Regiment of Foot.
1782-1881	31st (Huntingdonshire)	1758-1782	70th Regiment of Foot.
	Regiment of Foot.	1782-1812	70th (Surrey) Regiment of Foot.
		1812-1825	70th (Glasgow Lowland)
		1825-1881	70th (Surrey) Regiment of Foot.

1881-1959 The East Surrey Regiment.

31st Regiment of Foot

Raised as marines, 1702. Served during early stages of the War of the Spanish Succession taking part in Cadiz expedition and capture of Spanish warships in Vigo Bay. Gained first battle honour for capture and subsequent defence of Gibraltar, 1704-05. Engaged at Barcelona, 1705; Toulon, 1707; Cagliari and Minorca, 1708. To England, 1711 and as a line regiment in Scotland during rebellion, 1715. To Ireland, 1716; England, 1739; Flanders, 1742. Fought at Dettingen, 1743; Fontenoy and Melle, 1745. To England, 1745; Minorca, 1749; England, 1752; West Florida,

Second-Lieutenant B.H. Geary, 4th Battalion, The East Surrey Regiment who won the Victoria Cross at Hill 60 during the night of 20th/21st April, 1915 while attached to the 1st Battalion.

1765; the West Indies, 1772 and fought in St. Vincent against the Caribs. To England then Ireland, 1774; Canada, 1776. Garrisoned Quebec during American War of Independence. Flank companies fought under General Burgoyne and present at Saratoga, 1777. To England, 1787; Ireland, 1792. Flank companies to West Indies, 1793 and engaged during capture of Martinique and fighting at St. Lucia and Guadeloupe 1794. Battalion served in Holland, 1794-95 and then to the West Indies. Fought in St. Lucia, 1796 and present at La Vigie in May. To England, 1797. Took part in Helder campaign of 1799 and present at Egmont-op-Zee, Bergen and Kastrikum. To Ireland, then the Isle de Huat, 1800; Minorca, 1801; England, 1802; Jersey, 1803; England, 1804; Sicily, 1806. Took part in 1807 expedition to Egypt and present at Rosetta. Returned to Sicily and to Malta, 1808. *A Second Battalion, 31st Regiment raised, 1804. To the Channel Islands then Ireland, 1807; Portugal, 1808. During Peninsular War gained battle honours "Talavera", "Albuhera", "Vittoria"; "Pyrenees", "Nivelle", "Nive" and "Orthes." To Ireland and disbanded, 1814.* To Sicily, 1810; Malta then Sicily, 1811; Genoa, Corsica then Sicily, 1814; Naples then Genoa, 1815; Malta, 1816; England, 1818; Ireland, 1821; England, 1824; India, 1825. Fought in First Afghan War and gained battle honour "Cabool 1842". Later in Sutlej campaign receiving further honours at Moodkee and Ferozeshah, 1845; Aliwal and Sobraon, 1846. To England, 1846; Ireland, 1848; the Ionian Islands, 1853; the Crimea, 1855. Present during operations at Sevastopol. To Gozo, 1856; Malta then Gibraltar, 1857; South Africa then India, 1858; China, 1860. Served in North China campaign, 1860 and took part in action at Sinho and capture of Taku Forts. Later served in operations against the Taepings, 1862 and present at Nanhsiang, Kadin, Tsinpoo, Tsolin and Najow. To England, 1863; Ireland, 1866; Malta, 1867; Gibraltar, 1872; England, 1876; Ireland, 1880. Became 1st Battalion, The East Surrey Regiment, 1881.

70th Regiment of Foot

Formed in Glasgow as 2nd Battalion, 31st Regiment of Foot, 1756. Made independent and designated 70th Regiment, 1758. To England, 1759; Ireland, 1763; West Indies, 1764; England, 1774; North America, 1778. Flank companies served in New York operations and present at capture of Fort Lafayette and Charleston. To England, 1784; Ireland, 1787; West Indies, 1793. Took part in capture of Martini and Guadeloupe, 1794. To England then Gibraltar, 1795; West Indies, 1800; Jersey then England, 1801; West Indies, 1803. Took part in capture of Guadeloupe, 1810. To Scotland, 1812; Ireland then Canada, 1813; Ireland, 1827; Gibraltar, 1834; Malta, 1836; the West Indies, 1838; Canada, 1841; England, 1843; Ireland, 1845; India, 1849. Stationed on Peshawar Frontier during Indian Mutiny. To New Zealand, 1861 and took part in Maori wars, 1863-65. To England, 1866; Ireland, 1868; India, 1871. Took part in Afghan campaign, 1878-79, serving first with the Candahar Column and then with the Thull Chotiali Field Force. Became 2nd Battalion, The East Surrey Regiment, 1881.

1st Battalion

Formed from the 31st Regiment stationed in Ireland, 1881. To Gibraltar, 1882; England, 1883; Gibraltar then India, 1884; England, 1903; Jersey, 1906; England, 1908; Ireland, 1910. Crossed to France, 1914 and engaged during retreat from Mons and battle of the Aisne. Fought at Ypres, 1914-15; on the Somme, 1916 and at Arras and Ypres, 1917. Moved to

Italian Front November, 1917, returning to France April, 1918. Took part in battles of the Lys; Somme and Hindenburg Line. Later served in North Russia and gained battle honour "Murman 1919". To England then Ireland, 1919; England, 1920; Palestine, 1921; Egypt, 1922; Hong Kong, 1923; India, 1926; the Sudan, 1937; England, 1938. Fought in France and Belgium, 1939-40. Later in North Africa, Sicily and Italy. Served in Greece, 1946-49. To Somaliland, 1949; England, 1950. Served in Libya and Egypt, 1951-53; Germany, 1955-58; Cyprus and Libya, 1958. Amalgamated with 1st Battalion, The Queen's Royal Regiment (West Surrey) to form 1st Battalion, The Queen's Royal Surrey Regiment, 1959.

Major-General Arthur Fitzroy Hart, C.B. and his sons - Captain A.H.S. Hart (left) and Lieutenant R.V. Hart (right) prior to leaving for South Africa in 1899. All three officers served with The East Surrey Regiment. The General joined the 31st Regiment as an ensign in 1864 and saw "special service" in the Ashanti war of 1873-74; Zulu war, 1879; in South Africa, 1881 and Egypt, 1882. Both Captain Hart and Lieutenant Hart won the Distinguished Service Order in South Africa. Captain Hart also served in the 1st World War, losing both legs in 1918 and receiving a Bar to his D.S.O.

Officers` silver and gilt shoulder-belt plate - 31st Regiment c1830-1847.

2nd Battalion

Formed from the 70th Regiment stationed in India, 1881. To Egypt, 1884. Took part in Suakin operations, 1885 and present at Hasheen and Tamai. To England, 1885; Guernsey, 1888; Ireland, 1891; Malta, 1893; England, 1895; South Africa, 1899. Fought at Colenso December, 1899 and later in action at Spion Kop, Monte Cristo Hill, Wynne`s Hill and Pieter`s Hill. To India, 1903; Burma, 1911; India then England, 1914. During First World War took part in operations around Ypres and at Loos, 1915. Moved to Egypt October, 1915 and from there to Salonika. Fought on Macedonian Front for remainder of war. To Constantinople, 1918; England, 1919; Egypt, Turkey then Ireland, 1920; England, 1922; Jersey, 1924; Gibraltar, 1927; England, 1929; Shanghai, 1938; Malaya, 1940. After heavy casualties, temporally amalgamated with 2nd Battalion, The Leicestershire Regiment under title of "The British Battalion." Captured by the Japanese at Singapore, 1942. Reconstructed from 11th Battalion and served in Palestine and Egypt, 1946-48. To England then amalgamated with 1st Battalion in Greece.

Badges

The Arms of Guildford - the county town of Surrey, and The eight-pointed Star of the Order of the Garter - previously worn by the 3rd Royal Surrey Militia.

Uniform

31st Regiment - buff facings. 70th Regiment - grey to black by 1763. The East Surrey Regiment - white.

Nicknames

`The Young Buffs` - originated at Dettingen. During the battle, George II in seeing their buff facings and thinking they were the 3rd Regiment, called out to the 31st, "Bravo Old Butts". His mistake having been pointed out he quickly amended his congratulatory remark to "Then bravo Young Buffs." Early recruitment in Glasgow and the colour of its facings brought the 70th Regiment the nickname `The Glasgow Greys.`

The Duke of Cornwall`s Light Infantry

Titles

1702-1751	Known by name of Colonel.	1741-1751	Known by name of Colonel
1751-1782	32nd Regiment of Foot.	1751-1782	46th Regiment of Foot.
1782-1858	32nd (Cornwall) Regiment of Foot.	1782-1881	46th (South Devonshire)
1858-1881	32nd (Cornwall) Light Infantry.		Regiment of Foot.

1881-1959 The Duke of Cornwall`s Light Infantry

32nd Regiment of Foot

Raised in 1702 as one of several regiments of marines for service in the War of the Spanish Succession. Moved to Spain taking part first in Cadiz expedition and later in attack on Vigo. First battle honour gained for the capture and subsequent siege of Gibraltar, 1704-05. Also present at battle off Malaga. Later saw action at Barcelona, 1705 and Almanza, 1707. Returned to England and disbanded, 1713. Re-formed and to Ireland as a regiment of the line, 1715. To England, 1734; Ireland, 1736 and by 1741 in Scotland. During War of the Austrian Succession fought at Dettingen,1743 and Fontenoy,1745. To England,1745 and employed first in Lancashire during Jacobite Rebellion before moving north to the Highlands. Returned to Flanders,1746 and took part in battle of Lauffeld, 1747. To England, 1748; Gibraltar, 1749; England, 1753. *A 2nd Battalion, 32nd Regiment raised in Scotland, 1756 and made independent as 71st Regiment of Foot, 1758.* To St. Vincent, 1763; England, 1773; Ireland, 1775. Troopship the Rockingham Castle wrecked just outside Cork harbour with loss of ninety men and much of the regiment`s property. To Gibraltar, 1783; West Indies, 1792; England then Jersey, 1793; England, 1794; Ireland, 1795. Took part in 1796 expedition to St. Domingo. Engaged during operations to suppress revolt being staged by slaves from local plantations. Returned to England then to Ireland. To England, 1807 then took part in expedition to Copenhagen. Served in Spain and Portugal, 1808-09 - present at battles of Rolica and Vimiera and during retreat to Corunna. Returned to England and soon sent on 1809 expedition to Walcheren. To Guernsey, 1810. Returned to the Peninsular, 1811 and took part in fighting at Salamanca and Burgos, 1812; battles of the Pyrenees, Nivelle and the Nive, 1813. Last Peninsular battle honour gained at Orthes February, 1814 then to Ireland. *A 2nd Battalion, 32nd Regiment formed, 1804. To Guernsey, 1807; Ireland, 1809 and disbanded, 1814.* To Belgium,

Officers` shako - 46th Regiment, 1829-44.

Three regimental badges - The Duke of Cornwall`s Light Infantry - cap badge (left), collar badge (right), undress cap badge (top).

1815 and fought at Quatre Bras and Waterloo. Left France for England, 1816. To the Ionian Islands, 1817; England, 1825; Ireland, 1827; Canada, 1830; England, 1841; Ireland, 1845; India,1846. Took part in Second Sikh War, 1848-49 and involved in operations at Mooltan and Gujerat. Served on early expeditions into Yusufzai territory, 1852-53. During Indian Mutiny sustained over three hundred and seventy killed and two hundred wounded during siege of Lucknow. Four Victoria Crosses awarded and Light Infantry title conferred as mark of recognition for gallantry shown at Lucknow. Also present at Cawnpore operations November-December, 1857. To England, 1859; Ireland, 1863; Gibraltar, 1865; Mauritius, 1866. Stationed in Mauritius and South Africa until, 1877 then to England. To Jersey, 1879; England, 1880. Became 1st Battalion, The Duke of Cornwall`s Light Infantry, 1881.

46th Regiment of Foot

Raised as Colonel John Price`s Regiment, 1741. To Scotland, 1742 and present during Young Pretender`s Rebellion. Formed part of General Cope`s force at Prestonpans, 1745. To England, 1746; Jersey, 1747; Ireland; 1749; Nova Scotia, 1757. Took part in attack on Fort Ticonderoga, 1758 and capture of Fort Niagara, 1759. To the West Indies, 1761 and took part in capture of Martinique and Havannah, 1762. To Canada, 1763; Ireland, 1767; North America, 1776. Engaged in operations at Long Island, Brooklyn and White Plains. Took part in expedition to Philadelphia, 1777 and battles at Brandywine and Paoli. To the West Indies, 1778 and engaged during December attack on St. Lucia. Flank companies fought at La Vigie. To England, 1782; Ireland, 1784; Gibraltar, 1792; the West Indies, 1794. Helped in suppression of native uprising (the Caribs) at St. Vincent, 1795-96. To England, 1796; Ireland, 1799; West Indies, 1804. Took part in

Lieutenant Henry Thomas Cantan - 2nd Battalion, Duke of Cornwall`s Light Infantry. This officer was first gazetted in May, 1892 and was appointed Superintendent of Gymnasia, Dublin in March, 1896. In addition to insignia of the shoulder cords, rank was also indicated by lace on the collar and cuffs.

Top Right - Band - 2nd Battalion, The Duke of Cornwall's Light Infantry, 1910.

Bottom Right - 1st Battalion, The Duke of Cornwall's Light Infantry, front line, Messines Ridge January, 1915.

Below - Private - 32nd Regiment c1854. The shako is that in use between 1844-55 and has a green ball-tuft and brass plate (see page 104). The red jacket has distinctive "light infantry" shoulder wings.

defence of Dominica,1805, capture of Martinique, 1809 and fighting at Guadeloupe, 1810. To England, 1811; Jersey, 1812; England, 1813; Australia, 1814; India, 1817; England, 1833; Ireland, 1834; Gibraltar, 1837; West Indies, 1842; Nova Scotia then Canada, 1845; Nova Scotia, 1847; England, 1848; the Crimean, 1854. Present at Alma, Inkerman and Sevastopol. To Corfu, 1856; India, 1858; England, 1869; Ireland; 1873; Bermuda, 1876; Gibraltar, 1880. Became 2nd Battalion, The Duke of Cornwall's Light Infantry, 1881.

1st Battalion

Formed from the 32nd Regiment stationed in England, 1881. To Ireland, 1883; Malta. 1885; India, 1888; Burma, 1891 and took part in Wunthoo expedition. To India, 1893. Served in reserve brigade during Tirah Campaign, 1897. Guarded Boer prisoners in Ceylon during war in South Africa. To South Africa, 1902; England, 1906; Ireland, 1913. Crossed to France August, 1914 and fought throughout the retreat from Mons and battle of the Aisne. Took part in Ypres operations, 1914-15; battle of the

Band 2nd Battn Duke of Cornwall's L.I.

Somme, 1916; Arras and Ypres operations, 1917. Moved to Italy November, 1917. Returned to France April, 1918 and engaged during battles of the Lys, Somme and Hindenburg Line. To England, 1919 then Ireland. To India, 1922. Moved via Iraq to Egypt, 1941. After heavy casualties at Tobruk cadre of eleven men returned to England where battalion was brought up to strength by 6th D.C.L.I. Since Second World War served in Middle East, Cyprus, Somaliland, 1945-48; Germany and the West Indies, 1951-59. Amalgamated with 1st Battalion, The Somerset Light Infantry to form 1st Battalion, The Somerset and Cornwall Light Infantry, 1959.

2nd Battalion

Formed from the 46th Regiment stationed in Gibraltar, 1881. To Egypt, 1882 and present at Ramleh, Tel-el-Mahuta, El Magfar, Kassassin and Tel-el-Kebir. Took part in Nile expedition,1884-85. To England, 1886; Ireland, 1891; England, 1898; South Africa, 1899. Fought at Paardeberg and also present at Doornkop. To England, 1902; Gibraltar, 1905; Bermuda, 1907; South Africa, 1910; Hong Kong, 1913; England, 1914. During First World War took part in Ypres battles, 1915. Transferred to Macedonia front, November, 1915. To India, 1919; Ireland, 1921; Germany, 1922; Guernsey, 1924; England, 1927; Gibraltar, 1932; England, 1935. Fought in France and Belgium, 1939-40. Later in Tunisia, Italy and Greece. Amalgamated with 1st Battalion,1950.

Top - Band - 2nd Battalion, The Duke of Cornwall`s Light Infantry, Cologne, 1924.

Bottom - Guard - 1st Battalion, The Duke of Cornwall`s Light Infantry, India, 1922.

Badges

A Bugle-horn - adopted by the 32nd after grant of Light Infantry distinction in 1858. Two red feathers - after a surprise attack by the light company of the 46th Regiment in September, 1777 (see also nicknames), the Americans promised revenge on all those that had taken part. As a mark of contempt and to show that they were not afraid, the men died their white feathers red. The idea being that the enemy could easily distinguish them from other troops. The Shield and Motto (One and All) of the County of Cornwall. A Turreted Archway - represents the gateway of Launceston Castle, part of the Great Seal of the Duke of Cornwall. The Coronet of the Duke of Cornwall. .

Uniform

32nd Regiment - green facings at first, later changing to white. 46th Regiment - yellow. The Duke of Cornwall`s Light Infantry - white.

Nicknames

`Murray`s Bucks` - the 46th, while under the command of Lieutenant-General the Hon Thomas Murray (1743-1764). `The Lacedemonians` - a later commanding officer in a speech to his regiment just before going into action during the American War of Independence, made reference to the discipline of the Lacedemonians of ancient Greece and in doing so originated the nickname.`The Red Feathers` (see badges) and `The Surprisers` - the 46th Regiment after the commando style raid of 20th September, 1777. `The Docs.`

Above - Brass shako badge - 32nd Regiment, 1844-55 as seen on page 102. (D. Endean Ivall).

Right - Colours - 1st Battalion, The Duke of Cornwall`s Light Infantry, Tidworth, 1912.

The Duke of Wellington's Regiment (West Riding)

Titles

1702-1751	Known by name of Colonel.	1787-1807	76th Regiment of Foot.
1751-1782	33rd Regiment of Foot.	1807-1812	76th (Hindoostan) Regiment of Foot.
1782-1853	33rd (1st Yorkshire West Riding) Regiment of Foot.	1812-1881	76th Regiment of Foot.
1853-1881	33rd (The Duke of Wellington's) Regiment of Foot.		

1881-1920   The Duke of Wellington's (West Riding Regiment).
1920   The Duke of Wellington's Regiment (West Riding)

33rd Regiment

Formed by the Earl of Huntingdon in the Gloucestershire area, 1702 and then to Flanders. Present at Venloo in September. To Portugal, 1704 and in Spain fought at Valencia d' Alcantara, 1705; Alcantara, 1706. Surrendered after heavy casualties at Almanza, 1707. Fought at Saragossa and Brihuega, 1710. To Ireland, 1713. Disbanded, 1714 but re-raised and to England, 1715. Took part in expedition to Vigo, 1719. To Ireland, 1730; Flanders, 1742. Fought at Dettingen, 1743 and Fontenoy, 1745. Recalled to England, 1745 and in Scotland during Young Pretender's Rebellion. Returned to Flanders, 1746 and present at Roucoux in October and Lauffeld, 1747. To Minorca, 1749; England, 1753. Took part in raids along French coast, 1758 - St. Malo, Cherbourg and St. Cast. To Germany, 1760 and present at Warburg in July, Kloster Kamp, October and Wilhelmsthal, 1762. To England, 1763. *A 2nd Battalion, 33rd Regiment formed, 1756. Became 72nd Regiment, 1758.* To Minorca, 1764; England, 1769; Ireland, 1774; America, 1776. Fought at Brooklyn and Fort Washington, 1776; Brandywine and Germantown, 1777; Charleston and Camden, 1780; Guildford and Yorktown, 1781. To Canada, 1783; England, 1786; Ireland, 1792. (Flank companies to the West Indies, 1793 and engaged during operations in Martinique and Guadeloupe, 1794.) Served in Netherlands campaign of 1794-95 and present at Boxtel and Geldermalsen. To South Africa, 1796; India, 1797. Fought in Mysore War of 1799 and present at Seringapatam. (Flank companies took part in Mauritius expedition December, 1810.) To England, 1812; Holland, 1813. Fought at Bergen-op-Zoom, 1814. Moved into Belgium and at Quatre Bras and Waterloo June, 1815. From France to England in December. To Ireland, 1821; Jamaica, 1822; England, 1832; Ireland, 1835; Gibraltar, 1836; West Indies, 1841; Canada, 1843; Scotland, 1848. Left Manchester for Ireland, 1853. To the

Above - Drum Major and Drummer - 33rd Regiment 1852. Note black coverings on drum and staff for the funeral procession of the Duke of Wellington.
Illustration by P.W. Reynolds.

Below - 1st Battalion, The Duke of Wellington's Regiment - Dover, 1898. Note the Pioneer bottom right.

Crimea, 1854. Gained battle honours `Alma`, `Inkerman` and `Sevastopol.` To England then Ireland, 1856; Mauritius then India, 1857. Served in Central India during Indian Mutiny. Took part in expedition to Abyssinia, 1867 and fall of Magdala, 1868. Victoria Crosses awarded to Drummer Michael Magner and Private James Bergin. To England, 1868; Ireland, 1873; India, 1875. Became 1st Battalion, The Duke of Wellington's (West Riding Regiment), 1881.

76th Regiment

Raised for service in India by Colonel Thomas Musgrave, 1787. To India, 1788. Took part in Third Mysor War and present at Bangalore and Arikera, 1791 and Seringapatam, 1792. During Mahratta Wars took part in capture of Ally Ghur, battle of Delhi, surrender of Agra and fighting at Leswarree, 1803; battle of Deig, 1804 and siege of Bhurtpore, 1805. To England, 1806; Jersey, 1807; England then Spain, 1808. Engaged during retreat to Corunna. Returned to England and took part in expedition to Walcheren, 1809. To Ireland, 1810; Spain then France, 1813. Fought at the Nive in December. To Canada, 1814 and fought at Plattsburg. To Ireland, 1827; the West Indies, 1834; Canada, 1841; Ireland, 1842; England, 1844; Corfu, 1848; Malta, 1850. *(A Reserve Battalion, 76th Regiment formed, 1847 and to Corfu, 1848. Disbanded, 1850.)* To Canada, 1853; Ireland, 1856; Scotland, 1861, England, 1862; India, 1863; Burma, 1868; India, 1870; England, 1876; Ireland, 1879. Became 2nd Battalion, The Duke of Wellington's (West Riding Regiment), 1881.

1st Battalion

Formed from the 33rd Regiment stationed in India, 1881. To Aden, 1888; England, 1889; Malta, 1895; England, 1898; South Africa, 1899. Took part in relief of Kimberley and fighting at Paardeberg and Bloemfontein. Victoria Cross awarded to Sergeant James Firth. To England, 1902; India, 1905. Remained in India during First World War. Took part in Third Afghan War,

Left - 33rd Regiment, 1855.
Illustration by H. Martens.

Below - Post card showing the Honorary
Colours of the 76th Regiment.

1919. Served in Egypt and Palestine, 1920 and to England then Ireland, 1921. To England, 1922. Served in Gibraltar, and Constantinople, 1923 then to England. To Malta, 1935; England, 1937. Fought in France and Belgium, 1939-40; North Africa and Pantellaria, 1943; Italy, 1944-45 (Private Richard Burton awarded Victoria Cross); Palestine and Syria, 1945. Stationed in Egypt, 1946 then to Palestine. To England, 1947; Germany, 1951; England then Korea, 1952. Present during the fighting at `The Hook` in 1953. Since the Korean War the regiment has served in Gibraltar, Cyprus, Kenya, British Honduras, Germany, Hong Kong, Belize and the Falklands in addition to several operational tours of Northern Ireland. Sent to Bosnia, 1994.

2nd Battalion

Formed from the 76th Regiment stationed in Ireland, 1881. To England, 1885; Bermuda, 1886; Canada, 1888; Barbados, 1891; South Africa, 1893. Formed part of Mashonaland Field Force, 1896. To India, 1898; Burma, 1899; India, 1902; England, 1905; Ireland, 1911. Crossed to France, 1914 and fought at battles of Mons, the Marne, Aisne, Messines, Armentières and Ypres. Took part in battle of the Somme, 1916; Arras and Ypres, 1917; the Somme, Lys, Arras, Hindenburg Line and the Selle, 1918. Left Germany for England, 1919. To Ireland, 1920; England then Egypt, 1922; Singapore,

1926; India, 1928. Took part in Mohmand campaign, 1935. Served in India and Burma during the Second World War returning to England, 1947. Amalgamated with 1st Battalion, 1948.

Badges

The Crest and Motto of the Duke of Wellington - The Hon Arthur Wesley (later Duke of Wellington) joined the 33rd Regiment in 1793 and commanded it until 1802. He served as its Colonel, 1806-12. The regiment took the Duke`s name just after his death in 1852. The Elephant with Howdah - Conferred on the 76th Regiment in 1807 to commemorate its service in India from 1788 to 1806.

Uniform

33rd and 76th Regiments - Red (or scarlet) facings. The Duke of Wellington`s Regiment - white, 1881-1905 then scarlet.

Nicknames

`Havercake Lads` - To entice recruits, sergeants of the 33rd Regiment placed `havers` (or oatcakes) on the points of their swords. `The Immortals` - From the rate in which the wounded of the 76th Regiment reappeared on the field during the Mahratta War of 1803-05. `The Seven and Sixpennies` - From the number. `The Duke`s`.

Above - Cap badge - The Duke of Wellington`s Regiment.

Right - Officers - 2nd Battalion, The Duke of Wellingtons`s Regiment, South Africa, 1896. Commanding officer, Lieutenant-Colonel C.W. Gore seated centre. The photograph includes both sets of Colours.

Left - Various uniforms as worn by the 85th Regiment and King's (Shropshire Light Infantry), 1865-1912. Print published in 1913 from a painting by P.W. Reynolds.

Below - The 23rd (Royal Welsh Fusiliers) Regiment. Lithograph showing various uniforms of the 1840's. Note Pioneer with apron and axe, and 'Flash' attached to back of collar.

Left - Officer's shoulder-belt plate - 2nd (Queen's Royal) Regiment, 1843-54.

Below Left - The 23rd (Royal Welsh Fusiliers) Regiment - Colours c1850.

Below - The 66th (Berkshire) Regiment of Foot c1874. Section from a calendar published by Raphael Tuck & Sons showing Field Officer and Sergeant Major.
From a painting by Harry Payne.

Left - The King's Royal Rifle Corps Skirmishing. From a water colour by Richard Simkin. The regiment wore the helmet for the period 1878-1890.

Below - The 3rd (East Kent) Regiment of Foot (The Buffs) - during Peninsular War, 1813. Note Dragon badge on valise and drummer's coat which is buff with scarlet facings and the reverse of that normally worn by the regiment. From a painting by R. Simkin.

Left - Grenadier - 23rd (Royal Welsh Fusiliers) Regiment, 1742. Lithograph published in 1850.

Below Left - Drum Major and Drummer - 41st (The Welch) Regiment of Foot c1856. From a painting by P.W. Reynolds.

Below - The Death of Lieutenant H. Tryon of The Rifle Brigade at 'The Ovens' (Crimean War), 20th November, 1854. Painting by Harry Payne.

Left - The 48th (Northamptonshire) Regiment - Talavera, 28th July, 1809. The illustration, which is by Ernest Ibbetson, recalls an incident in the battle where Colonel Donellan, having been wounded, handed over command of the regiment to Major Middlemore.

Below - "The Infantry Will Advance" - a painting by Peter Archer depicting the 19th Regiment storming the Great Redoubt during the battle of the Alma, 20th September, 1854. (Courtesy the Officer's Mess, 1st Battalion, The Green Howards).

Left - Private - 19th (1st York, North Riding) Regiment, 1832. Print published in 1911 from a painting by P.W. Reynolds.

Below Left - Grenadier - 66th Regiment, 1768.

Below - The 7th (Royal Fusiliers) Regiment, 1769-1780 - from left to right, Officer, Fusilier and Corporal of Grenadier Company. Watercolour by H. Oakes Jones.

Left - Band - 12th (East Suffolk) Regiment c1861-71. Illustration by P.W. Reynolds published in 1914.

Below - The York and Lancaster Regiment - post card published c1913. Illustration by Ernest Ibbetson.

THE YORK & LANCASTER REGIMENT
Dipping the Colours in a Royal Salute.

Left - Post card produced in aid of the Banner Fund - Salisbury Branch, National Union of Railwaymen.

Below Left - Drum Major and Drums, The West Yorkshire Regiment. One of a set of six postcards published just prior to the First World War from a painting by Ernest Ibbetson.

Below - 1st Battalion, The Duke of Wellington's Regiment - Bosnia, 1994. (Courtesy 1st Battalion, Duke of Wellington's Regiment).

Left and Below - 1st Battalion, The Duke of Wellington's Regiment - Bosnia, 1994. (Courtesy 1st Battalion, Duke of Wellington's Regiment).

THE LATE LIEUT. DEASE.

Left - Lieutenant M.J. Dease and Private S.F. Godley, 4th Battalion, The Royal Fusiliers who were among the first to be awarded the Victoria Cross during the First World War - 23rd August, 1914 at Mons.

Below - The Storming of the Taku Forts by the 67th Regiment, China War, 1860.

PRIVATE S.F. GODLEY.

Left - 50th (Queen's Own) Regiment c1850.

Below - Soldiers of the 34th (Cumberland) Regiment playing skittles with French Zouaves - Crimea, 1855. Painting by A. Protain. (Courtesy Border Regiment Museum.)

Left - Musicians - 37th (North Hampshire) Regiment c1815. Water-colour by E.A. Campbell 1937.

Below Left - Lance-Corporal F.W. Holmes, 2nd Battalion, The King's Own (Yorkshire Light Infantry) who won the Victoria Cross at Le Cateau, 26th August, 1914. From set of cigarette cards 'Victoria Cross Heroes' published by W.D. & H.O. Wills

Below - Sergeant - The Royal Sussex Regiment. Print published during the 1890s and from a painting by Frank Feller.

LANCE CORPORAL HOLMES.

Left - Officer's shako plate 1869-1878 - 8th (The King's) Regiment of Foot.

Below - Contingent from the 19th (1st York, North Riding) Regiment forming up for the funeral of The Duke of Wellington, 18th November, 1852. Illustration by R. Ebsworth.

Left - The 36th Regiment of Foot c1742. Grenadier (left), Private (right).

Left Below - Captain - 33rd Regiment c1825. (Courtesy 1st Bn. The Duke of Wellington's Regiment)

Below - The King's Royal Rifle Corps - Officers and Private 1904. From a painting by P.W. Reynolds.

Left - The Manchester Regiment. Plate from 'Types of the British Army' series by Richard Simkin published in 1895.

Below Left - Officers, 4th (The King's Own) and 5th (Northumberland) Regiments, 1829. Published in 1829 and from a series of plates after W. Henry Heath.

Below - Officers, 7th (Royal Fusiliers) and 8th (The King's) Regiment, 1829. Published in 1830 and from a series of plates after W. and Henry Heath.

Following Page - The Duke of Edinburgh's Wiltshire Regiment From 'Types of the British Army' series by Richard Simkin published in 1895.

The Border Regiment

Titles

1702-1751	Known by name of Colonel.
1751-1782	34th Regiment of Foot.
1782-1881	34th (Cumberland) Regiment of Foot.

1755-1757	57th Regiment of Foot.
1757-1782	55th Regiment of Foot.
1782-1881	55th (Westmoreland) Regiment of Foot.

1881-1959   The Border Regiment

34th Regiment of Foot

Raised by Lord Lucas, 1702 and recruited throughout East Anglia. To Portugal, 1705 and later in Spain fought at Barcelona, 1705 and Montjuich, 1706. To England, 1707. Served as marines then in Flanders and Germany. Present at Douai, 1710 and Siege of Bouchain, 1711. To England, 1713; Ireland, 1717. Took part in Vigo expedition, 1719 then returned to Ireland. To Gibraltar, 1727 and took part in siege. Returned home and then served in England and Ireland. To Flanders and covered retreat at Fontenoy, 1745. To England, 1745 and in Scotland fought at Falkirk and Culloden, 1746. To Minorca, 1752 and present during siege of St. Philip, 1756 then via Gibraltar to England. Took part in operations along French coast, 1758 - St Malo and Cherbourg. To the West Indies, 1762 and took part in assault on Fort Moro, Havannah. *A 2nd Battalion, 34th Regiment raised, 1757 which became 73rd Regiment, 1758.* To West Florida, 1763; Ireland, 1767; Canada, 1776 and joined garrison at Quebec, then under siege. Took part in Burgoyne`s expedition and at Saratoga, 1777. To England, 1786. To the West Indies and engaged during operations in St. Lucia and St. Vincent, 1796. To Cape of Good Hope, 1800 and took part in Kaffir War. To India, 1802. *A 2nd Battalion, 34th Regiment raised at Ashford in Kent, 1805 and served in Hanover. Took part in Peninsular campaign, 1810-14 gaining battle honours - "Albuhera", "Arroyo Dos Molinos", "Vittoria", "Pyrenees", "Nivelle", "Nive", "Orthes" and "Peninsular". Returned home and disbanded in Ireland, 1817.* Took part in Pindari War, 1817-19. To England, 1823; Ireland, 1824; North America, 1829. Present during Canadian Rebellion of 1838. To England, 1842; then Ireland. To the Ionian Islands, 1845; the West Indies, 1848;. Ionian Islands, 1854; the Crimean, 1855. Fought at The Redan and gained battle honour - "Sevastapol". To England, 1856; India, 1857. Took part in Indian Mutiny and engaged at Cawnpore and Lucknow. Present during operations at Azimghur and Oude. To England, 1867; Ireland, 1872; India, 1875. Became 1st Battalion, The Border Regiment, 1881.

55th Regiment of Foot

Raised as 57th Regiment of Foot by Colonel George Perry at Stirling, 1755 and re-numbered, 1757. To Nova Scotia, 1757 and in 1758 took part in the action at Ticonderoga. Fought at Niagara and again at Ticonderoga, 1759. Took part in expedition to Montreal, 1760. Later spent fifteen months under siege by Indians at Fort Detroit then to Ireland. To America, 1775. During American War of Independence present at Brooklyn, 1776; Princeton, Brandywine and Germantown, 1777. To the West Indies, 1778. Engaged during capture of St. Lucia. To England, 1785; Ireland, 1791; Holland, 1793. During campaign in the Austrian Netherlands main part of regiment served in West Flanders and engaged at Nijmegen in November, 1794. Flank companies in the meantime returned to the West Indies and fought at Martinique, St. Lucia and Guadeloupe, 1794 before being almost

Above - Cap badge, The Border Regiment.

Right - Assault of the 55th Regiment on The Redan, 1855. Illustration by Wal Paget.

totally wiped out by yellow fever and forced to surrender. Regiment to West Indies, 1795 and fought at St. Lucia and St Vincent, 1796. To England, 1797. Served in Ostend, 1798 and in the Helder campaign in Holland saw action at Groete Ketan, Egmont-op-Zee and Bergen, 1799. To England, 1800; West Indies, 1802; England, 1812; Holland, 1813. Took part in assault on Bergen-op-Zoom, 1814. To England, 1814; Ireland, 1820; England then South Africa, 1821. Took part in operations against the Kaffirs. To India, 1830 and took part in fighting at Coorg, 1834. To China, 1840 and took part in war of 1840-42. Present during capture of Chusan, operations round Chinghae and Ningpo and attack on Nankin. To England, 1844; Ireland, 1846; Gibraltar, 1851; the Crimea, 1854. Gained battle honours - "Alma", "Inkerman" and "Sevastapol". Also heavily engaged during the fighting at The Redan, 1855. To Gibraltar, 1856; England then Ireland, 1857; England, 1860; India, 1863. Took part in Bhootan operations, 1864. To Aden, 1876; England, 1877. Became 2nd Battalion, The Border Regiment, 1881.

1st Battalion

Formed from the 34th Regiment stationed in India, 1881. To Burma, 1889; England, 1890; Malta, 1897. Sent two companies to restore order in Crete. To South Africa and engaged at Tugela River and Colenso December, 1899; Spion Kop, during relief of Ladysmith and Megaliesburg, 1900. To England, 1902; Gibraltar, 1906; India, 1908; Burma, 1910; England, 1914. During First World War moved to Egypt then Gallipoli. To France, 1916 and took part in battle of the Somme. Engaged during Arras, Ypres and Cambrai operations, 1917 and battle of the Lys, 1918. To England then India, 1919. Took part in Waziristan campaign, 1922-23. To Aden, 1924;

The 34th Regiment leaving the Crimea for England. Engraving published in the Illustrated London News for 23rd August, 1856.

Illustration by Richard Simkin showing Drum-major and Drummer, 1st Battalion, Border Regiment, with Colours and French drums captured at Arroyo dos Molinos.

England, 1925; Shanghai, 1927. Served in Shanghai Defence Force. To England, 1928; Northern Ireland, 1933; Palestine, 1936; England, 1939. Fought in France and Belgium, 1939-40. As part of 1st Air Landing Brigade, 1st Airborne Division, took part in invasion of Sicily, 1943. Later fought in Italy and was at Arnhem, 1944 and in Norway, 1945. After Second World War served in Trieste, 1946-47; Palestine, 1947-48; Somaliland, 1948-50. Later in Cyprus, the Canal Zone and Germany. Amalgamated with 1st Battalion, The King`s Own Royal Regiment (Lancaster) to form 1st Battalion, The King`s Own Border Regiment, 1959.

2nd Battalion

Formed from the 55th Regiment stationed in England, 1881. To Ireland, 1882; Guernsey, 1887; Malta, 1888; India, 1890. Took part in Waziristan operations, 1894. To Burma. 1902; South Africa, 1905; England, 1907. Crossed to France, 1914 and took part in Ypres battles, 1914 (two Victoria Crosses awarded), battles of the Somme, 1916 and Ypres, 1917. Moved to

Italy November, 1917. To England, 1919 then Ireland; England, 1922; Malta, 1924; the Sudan then Malta, 1926; North China, 1927; India, 1929. Took part in operations on the North-West Frontier, 1930-31. Served in India and Burma during Second World War. Returned to England and amalgamated with 1st Battalion, 1950.

Badges

A Laurel Wreath - which is traditionally associated with the 34th's involvement at the battle of Fontenoy in April, 1745. A Maltese Cross - another old badge of the 34th. The Dragon superscribed "China" - commemorates the services of the 55th Regiment in the China War of 1840-42. The Star of the Order of the Garter - one of the badges of the old Royal Westmorland Militia which became 3rd Battalion, The Border Regiment in 1881. A Glider - awarded in respect of 1st Border's services with the 1st Air Landing Brigade during the invasion of Sicily July, 1943. The first occasion in which British gliderbourne troops took part in a major tactical operation.

Uniform

34th Regiment - at first wore coats lined with grey. Facings later changed, first to white, and then light yellow. 55th Regiment - dark green facings, but these were later changed to Lincoln green. The Border Regiment - white facings changing to yellow in 1913.

Nicknames

`The Cattle Reavers` - an early nickname for both the 34th and 55th, the association being with that of the old cattle thieves that operated across the border between England and Scotland. `The Harry Lauders` - rhyming slang for `The Borders`. `The Cumberland Gentlemen`.

Above - Cloth arm badge awarded to 1st Battalion, The Border Regiment for its part in the first gliderborne operation, 9th/10th July, 1943. The letters and glider are in yellow on a maroon ground.

Left - Boy drummers with Arroyo dos Molinos Drums.

The Royal Sussex Regiment

Titles

1701-1751	Known by name of Colonel.	1853-1858	3rd Bengal European Infantry Regiment.
1751-1782	35th Regiment of Foot.		
1782-1804	35th (Dorsetshire) Regiment. of Foot.	1858-1861	3rd Bengal Light Infantry Regiment.
1804-1832	35th (Sussex) Regiment of Foot.	1861-1881	107th (Bengal Infantry)
1832-1881	35th (Royal Sussex) Regiment of Foot.		Regiment of Foot.

1881-1966   The Royal Sussex Regiment

35th Regiment

THE ROYAL SUSSEX REGIMENT

Regtl. Medal, 1800

Officers' Collar Badge

Raised in Belfast by the Earl of Donegall, 1701. Served as marines and took part in operations along Spanish coast, including Cadiz expedition, 1702. To the West Indies, 1703 and fought at Guadeloupe. First battle honour gained for service in Gibraltar, 1704-05. Fought at Barcelona, 1705; San Mateo, 1706 and Almanza, 1707. To Ireland, 1708; Minorca, 1719; Ireland, 1725. *A 2nd Battalion, 35th Regiment formed, 1748 and disbanded, 1749.* To England then North America, 1756. Forced to surrender at Fort William Henry, 1757. Present at Louisburg, 1758 and took part in capture of Quebec, 1759. Present at Sainte Foy, 1760. To the West Indies and took part in fighting on Martinique, 1761 and Havannah, 1762. To West Florida, 1763; England, 1765; Ireland, 1773; America, 1775. Present at Bunker Hill in June, Brooklyn and White Plains, 1776. To the West Indies, 1777 and took part in capture of St. Lucia, 1778. To England, 1785; Ireland, 1791; West Indies, 1794. Engaged during capture of Martinique, St, Lucia and Guadeloupe. To Gibraltar, 1795; England, 1796. A 2nd Battalion, 35th Regiment raised from members of the Sussex Militia, 1799. Both battalions embarked for Holland and the Helder campaign. Present at Alkmaar, Egmont-op-Zee and Bergen. Took part in capture of Malta, 1800. Second Battalion returned home, 1801 and disbanded, 1803. Left Malta for Sicily, 1805. Took part in expedition to Calabria, 1806 and present at Maida, 4th July. Took part in 1807 expedition to Egypt and engaged in operations at Alexandria, Rosetta and El Hamed then to Italy. Took part in capture of the Ionian Islands, 1809. Two companies served in Northern Italy, 1813-14. To Malta, 1816; England then Ireland, 1817. *Second Battalion re-formed at Winchester, 1805 and joined 1st Battalion in Sicily, 1806. Took part in 1807 expedition to Egypt and engaged in operations at Alexandria, Rosetta and El Hamed. To Italy then England, 1808. Took part in Walcheren expedition,*

1809 and present at capture of Flushing. To Flanders, 1813; Holland, 1814. Present at siege of Antwerp and attack on Bergen-op-Zoom. Formed part of Reserve Army at Turbige, near Hal during Battle of Waterloo. Later took part in capture of Cambrai. To England, 1815; Ireland and disbanded, 1817. To the West Indies, 1820; England, 1832; Ireland, 1834; Mauritius, 1837; England then Ireland, 1848; England, 1852; India, 1854; Burma, 1856; India, 1857; England, 1867; Ireland, 1873; Barbados, 1875; Malta, 1879; Cyprus, 1880. Became 1st Battalion, The Royal Sussex Regiment, 1881.

107th Regiment

Formed by the Honourable East India Company at Chinsurah, 1853 and titled 3rd Bengal European Light Infantry. Took part in Indian Mutiny. Joined British Army as 107th Regiment, 1861 and to England, 1875. To Guernsey, 1879; Ireland, 1880. Became 2nd Battalion, The Royal Sussex Regiment, 1881.

1st Battalion

Formed from the 35th Regiment of Foot stationed in Cyprus, 1881. To Egypt, 1882 and engaged during operations around Alexandria. Took part in Suakin Expedition, 1884 and fought at El Teb and Tamai. Formed part of column sent to Khartoum, 1885 and present at Abu Klea, El Gubat and Metemneh. To England, 1885; Ireland, 1891; England, 1896; Malta, 1899; South Africa, 1900. Moved forward to Pretoria. Engaged at Zand River and Doornkop. Later fought at Diamond Hill and Retief`s Nek. To India, 1902. Remained in India throughout First World War taking part in operations along North West Frontier. Mobilized for Third Afghan War, 1919 and engaged at Orange Patch Ridge (later re-named Sussex Ridge). To England then Germany, 1920; England then Ireland, 1921; England, 1926; Palestine, 1936. Fought in Western Desert, 1940; Eritrea and Abyssinia, 1941; North Africa, 1941-42 and Italy. Served in Greece, Austria, Palestine and Egypt. To England, 1953. Became 3rd Battalion, The Queen`s Regiment, 1966.

2nd Battalion

Formed from the107th Regiment stationed in Ireland, 1881. To Malta, 1882; Egypt then India, 1885. Took part in Black Mountain Expedition, 1888 and with Tirah Field Force, 1897-98. To England, 1902; Malta, 1904; Crete, 1905; Ireland, 1907; England, 1912. During the First World War took part in retreat from Mons and battles of the Aisne and Ypres, 1914. Fought at Aubers Ridge, 1915 and on the Somme, 1916. Took part in operations on the Flanders Coast and Second Battle of Passchendaele, 1917. Fought at the Lys, Arras and the Hindenburg Line, 1918. Left Germany for England, 1919 then to the West Indies. To Malta, 1921. Sent to guard neutral zone south of the Dardanelles, 1922, operating around Chanak and Eastern Thrace. Returned to Malta, 1923 and then to Singapore. To India, 1926; Egypt, 1935; the Sudan, England then Northern Ireland, 1936. Fought in Belgium and France, 1940. Moved to North Africa, 1942. Stationed in Trieste and Malta Amalgamated with 1st Battalion, 1948.

Colours, 1st Battalion, The Royal Sussex Regiment in Malta, 1899. Note condition. This set was presented in 1860 and carried until 1928.

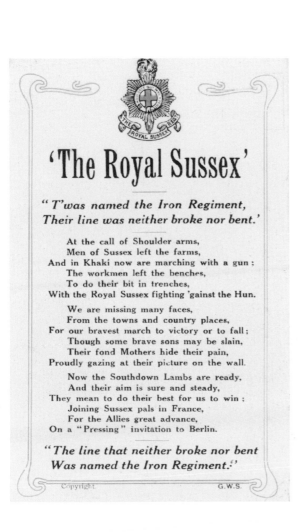

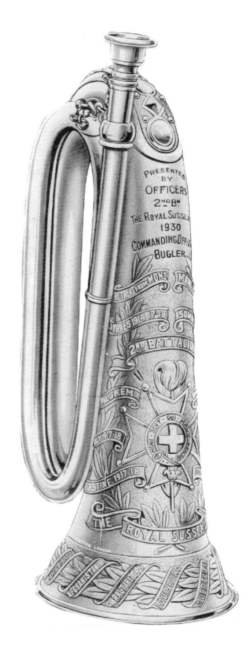

Left - Post card showing soldiers` pay c1910.

Bottom Left - War-time post card making use of the 2nd Battalion`s recently acquired nickname - `The Iron Regiment`.

Below - Presentation bugle - 2nd Battalion, The Royal Sussex Regiment, 1930.

The Royal Sussex Regiment. Post card published in 1914 from the artwork of Ernest Ibbetson.

Badges

A White Plume - commemorates defeat of the French Royal Roussillon Regiment at Quebec in 1759. The 35th Regiment are said to have taken the plumes from the enemy after the battle and placed them in their own caps. The Star of the Order of the Garter - origins are not clear, but official authorization for its use was given in 1879. A Maltese Cross - a badge of the 3rd Bengal European Light Infantry, and later, the107th Regiment.

Uniform

35th Regiment - orange facings changing to blue in 1832. 107th Regiment - white. The Royal Sussex Regiment - blue.

Nicknames

`The Belfast Regiment` - an early nickname of the 35th Regiment after its formation there in 1701. `The Orange Lilies` - from the facings of the 35th Regiment. `The Iron Regiment` - German prisoners taken at Ypres by the 2nd Battalion during the First World War called their captors The Iron Regiment.

The Royal Hampshire Regiment

Titles

1702-1751	Known by name of Colonel.	1756-1758	2nd Battalion, 20th Regiment of Foot.
1751-1782	37th Regiment of Foot.		
1782-1881	37th (North Hampshire) Regiment of Foot.	1758-1782	67th Regiment of Foot.
		1782-1881	67th (South Hampshire) Regiment of Foot.

1881-1946   The Hampshire Regiment
1946-1992   The Royal Hampshire Regiment.

37th Regiment

Raised in Ireland, 1702. To Holland and during War of the Spanish Succession fought at Blenheim, 1704; Ramillies, 1706; Oudenarde, 1708; siege of Tournai and Malplaquet, 1709. To America, 1711. Over 260 lost in shipwreck in St. Lawrence River. Returned to England, 1711 and to Ireland, 1718. Took part in Vigo expedition of 1719. To England, 1726; Ireland, 1727; Flanders, 1742. Fought at Dettingen, 1743. Returned to England, 1745 and then to Scotland. Fought at Culloden April, 1746. Returned to Flanders and present at Lauffeld June, 1747. To England, 1748; Minorca, 1749; England, 1745. *A 2nd Battalion, 37th Regiment formed, 1756,*

Officers - 2nd Battalion, Hampshire Regiment at Mandalay, Burma, 1886.

served as marines, 1757 and became 75th Regiment, 1758. To Germany, 1758. Fought at Minden, 1759; Warburg, 1760; Vellinghausen, 1761 and Wilhelmsthal, 1762. To England then Minorca, 1763; England, 1769; Ireland, 1774; America, 1776. Took part in operations around New York and present at Brooklyn. Fought at Brandywine and Germantown, 1777. To Canada, 1783; England, 1789; Flanders, 1793 and present at Famars and fighting around Dunkirk. Engaged at Tourcoing, Tournai and Druten, 1794. To England, 1795; Gibraltar, 1796; West Indies, 1800; England, 1809; Gibraltar, 1812; France then Canada, 1814. *A 2nd Battalion, 37th Regiment formed in England, 1813 and sent to Holland. Fought at Bergen-op-Zoom, 1814 then moved into Belgium. To Ireland, 1816 and disbanded, 1817.* To England, 1825; Ireland, 1826; Bermuda, 1830; Jamaica, 1832; Canada, 1839; Ireland, 1842; England, 1843; Ceylon, 1846; India, 1857. During Indian Mutiny took part in operations around Azimghur and Arrah. To England, 1861; Ireland, 1865; India, 1866; England, 1875; Ireland, 1880. Became 1st Battalion, The Hampshire Regiment 1881.

67th Regiment

Formed as 2nd Battalion, 20th Regiment (see The Lancashire Fusiliers) in 1756. Became 67th Regiment, 1758 and sent on operations along the French coast - St. Malo and St. Cast. Fought at Belle Isle, 1761. To Portugal, 1762; Minorca, 1763; England, 1771; Ireland, 1776; West Indies, 1785; England, 1794; West Indies, 1795. Took part in fighting on St. Domingo and then to Jamaica, 1798. To England, 1801; Ireland then Guernsey, 1803; England, 1804; India, 1805. Took part in Mahratta War and present at Asseerghur, 1819. To England, 1826. *A 2nd Battalion, 67th Regiment formed in Ireland, 1803. To Guernsey, 1804; Alderney, 1807; Spain, 1810. Fought at Cadiz and Barrosa, 1811 and later at Carthagena, Tarragona and Barcelona. To Gibraltar, 1814; England and disbandment, 1817.* To Ireland, 1830; Gibraltar, 1832; West Indies, 1833; Canada, 1840; England, 1842; Ireland, 1844. A Reserve Battalion formed, 1846 and both battalions to Gibraltar. Battalions merged, 1848. To the West Indies, 1851; England, 1857; India, 1858. Took part in China War of 1860. Present at storming of Taku Forts (four Victoria Crosses awarded) and Pekin. Remained in China, service during troubles in Shanghai, 1862 and in Japan. Left China for South Africa, 1865. To Ireland, 1866; England, 1868; Burma, 1872; India, 1876. Took part in Second Afghan War, 1878-80 - present at Charasia and Kabul. Became 2nd Battalion, The Hampshire Regiment, 1881.

1st Battalion

Formed from the 37th Regiment stationed in Ireland, 1881. To England, 1883; Malta, 1884; India, 1886. Took part in operations in Burma, 1888 then to India, 1891. Took part in operations on North West Frontier. To Aden, 1903 and engaged during operations in the Aden Hinterland and Somaliland. To England, 1904; France, 1914. During First World War took part in retreat from Mons, battles of Le Cateau, the Marne, Aisne, Armentières and Messines, 1914. Fought in Ypres battles of 1915; on the Somme, 1916; at Arras and Ypres, 1917; Arras, the Lys, the Scarpe, Hindenburg Line and the Selle, 1918. To England, 1919; Turkey, 1920; Egypt, 1921; India, 1925. Served in Mohmand campaign, 1935 and Waziristan operations, 1936-37. To Palestine, 1938; Egypt, 1939; Malta, 1941. Fought in Sicily and Italy before returning to England, 1943. Took part in D-Day assault landings on 6th June, 1944, returning to England from Holland in November. To the Middle East, 1945 and served in Palestine, 1946-47. To Germany, 1951. Took part in operations in Malaya, 1953-56. To Germany, 1957; West Indies, 1960; Germany, 1962; England, 1965. Served in Hong Kong, Borneo and Malaya, 1966-67. Later served in Gibraltar, Hong Kong, Germany, the Falkland Islands and numerous tours of operational duty in Northern Ireland. Amalgamated with The Queen's Regiment to form The Princess of Wales' Royal Regiment (Queen's and Royal Hampshires), 1992.

2nd Battalion

Formed from the 67th Regiment stationed in India, 1881. To Burma, 1885 and present during surrender of Mandalay. To India, 1887; England, 1888; Ireland, 1893; South Africa, 1900. Took part in Paardeberg operations and present during actions at Waterval Drift, Karree Siding and Thabanchu. To

Above - Pioneer Corporal - 37th Regiment (left), Band Sergeant, 67th Regiment (right), 1865. Illustration by E.A. Campbell.

Left - Machine Gun drill - 2nd Battalion, The Hampshire Regiment, Catterick, 1931 (Royal Hampshire Regiment Museum).

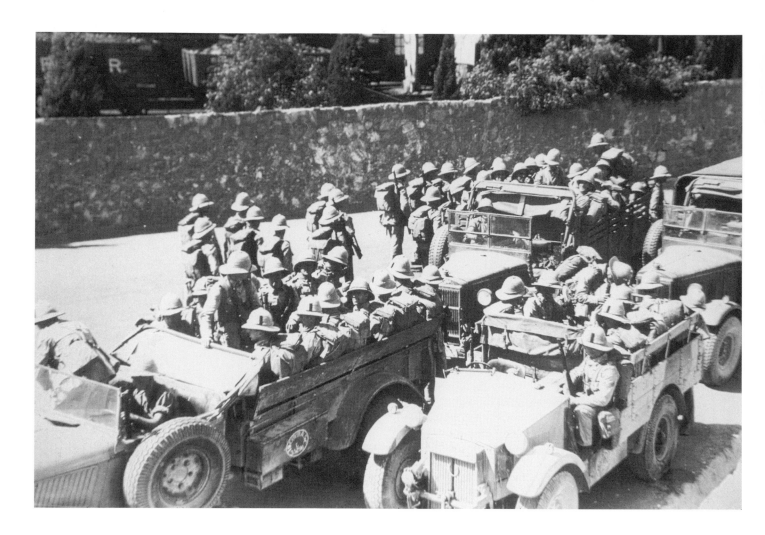

England, 1902; Malta, 1903; Bermuda, 1905; South Africa, 1907; Mauritius, 1911; India, 1913; England, 1914. Fought at Gallipoli, 1915-16; on the Somme, 1916; at Arras, Ypres and Cambrai, 1917; during the battles of the Lys and Ypres, 1918. To England, 1919, detachment serving in North Russia. Stationed in Ireland, 1919-22. To Germany, 1928; England, 1929; Palestine, 1936. Present during Arab rebellion. To England, 1938. Fought in France and Belgium, 1939-40; North Africa, 1942; Italy, 1943-44. Served in Greece and Austria returning to England, 1948. Amalgamated with 1st Battalion, 1949.

Badges

The Royal Tiger superscribed `India` - awarded to the 67th Regiment for its service in India, 1805-26. The Hampshire Rose - an old badge of The Hampshire Militia taken into use after 1881.

Uniform

37th Regiment - yellow facings, 67th Regiment - yellow, The Hampshire Regiment - white from 1881, yellow restored, 1904.

Nickname

The Tigers - from the badge.

Facing page: Top - 1st Battalion, The Hampshire Regiment - Palestine, 1938. (Royal Hampshire Regiment Museum).

Facing page: Bottom - Men of 1st Battalion, The Hampshire Regiment - Arromanches, D-Day 6th June, 1944. (Royal Hampshire Regiment Museum).

Below - 1st Battalion, The Royal Hampshire Regiment - relieving US Army Guard, Spandau Prison, West Berlin, 1984. (Royal Hampshire Regiment Museum).

The South Staffordshire Regiment

Titles

1705-1751	Known by name of Colonel.	1793-1881	80th (Staffordshire Volunteers) Regiment of Foot.
1751-1782	38th Regiment of Foot.		
1782-1881	38th (1st Staffordshire) Regiment of Foot.		

1881-1959 The South Staffordshire Regiment

38th Regiment

Formed at Lichfield, 1705 as Colonel Luke Lillingston's Regiment and to Ireland. To Antigua, 1707 and began a total of fifty-seven years continued service in the West Indies. Saw action at Montserrat and gained first battle honours - "Guadeloupe 1759" and "Martinique 1762." To Ireland, 1764; America, 1774. Fought in the American War of Independence and engaged at Lexington, Bunker Hill and throughout operations in New York. Saw action at Fort Washington. To England, 1783; Ireland, 1790. Light and Grenadier Companies to West Indies,1794 and took part in capture of Martinique, St. Lucia and Guadeloupe. Regiment served in Flanders campaign, 1794-95. To Barbados, 1796; the Saintes Islands, 1797;

England, 1800; Ireland, 1801; Cape of Good Hope and then South America, 1806. Took part in capture of Maldonado and present at Monte Video and Buenos Aires, 1807. To Ireland, 1807; Portugal, 1808. Gained battle honours - "Rolica", "Vimiera", "Corunna" during first phase of Peninsular campaign, 1808-09. Also saw action at Oporto and Talavera and took part in Walcheren Expedition, 1809. To Ireland, 1809. Returned to Portugal,1812 and fought at Salamanca. Further battle honours added for operations at Vittoria, St. Sebastian and the River Nive. To Ireland, 1814. *A 2nd Battalion, 38th Regiment formed at Lichfield,1804. To Ireland then England, 1807; Guernsey, 1809. Took part in Peninsular War, 1810-13 gaining battle honours - "Busaco", "Badajoz" and "Salamanca." To England and disbanded, 1814.* Served as part of the Army of Occupation in Paris, 1815 then to England. To South Africa, 1818 and engaged during Kaffir operations. To India, 1822 and took part in First Burmese War, 1824-26. Present at Donobyu and Napadi, 1825 and received battle honour "Ava." Left India for England, 1836. To Ireland, 1837; the Ionian Islands, 1840; Gibraltar, 1841; Jamaica, 1845. Detachments served in Nicaragua campaign, 1848. To Nova Scotia, 1848; England, 1851; the Crimea, 1854. Present at the Alma, Inkerman, and Sevastopol. To Ireland, 1856; India, 1857. Took part in Indian Mutiny. Present at Cawnpore and Lucknow.

Above - Officers' shako plate - 38th Regiment, 1844-55.

Left - Officers - 38th Regiment, 1853. The shako plate is that shown above. Illustration by H. Martens.

Above - Other ranks' shako plate - 80th Regiment, 1844-55.

Below - Presentation of Burmese medals to members of the 80th Regiment at Southsea Common, 1855. Engraving from Illustrated London News for 30th June, 1855.

Served with the Hazara Field Force in the Black Mountain expedition, 1868. To England, 1871; Ireland, 1877; Malta, 1880. Became 1st Battalion, The South Staffordshire Regiment, 1881.

80th Regiment of Foot

Formed from members of the Staffordshire Militia at Chatham by Lord Henry William Paget, 1793. To Guernsey, 1794. Took part in Flanders campaign, 1794-95 and Isle Dieu expedition, 1795. To South Africa, 1796; Ceylon, 1797; Egypt, 1801; India, 1802. Took part in operations in Southern Mahratta, 1803-04; campaign against Nairs of Wynaud, 1805. To England, 1817; Gibraltar, 1821; Malta, 1822; Ionian Islands, 1828; England, 1831; Ireland, 1832; England, 1834. Detailed to escorted convicts to Australia,1836. Remained on guard duty in New South Wales with detachments serving on Norfolk Island and in New Zealand. To India, 1845 - part of regiment being shipwrecked in the Andaman Islands for fifty days on voyage. Took part in First Sikh War, 1845-46 receiving battle honours "Moodkee", "Ferozeshah" and "Sobraon." To Burma taking part in capture of Pegu, 1852 and returning to India, 1853. To Scotland, 1854; England, 1855; South Africa, 1856; India, 1857. Served during Indian Mutiny receiving battle honour "Central India." Formed part of Bhutan Field Force, 1865. To England, 1866; Ireland, 1869; Singapore then Hong Kong, 1872. Three companies engaged in Perak campaign, 1875-76. To Singapore, 1876; South Africa, 1877. Took part in Zulu War, 1878-79, and present at Ulundi 4th July, 1879. To Ireland, 1880. Became 2nd Battalion, The South Staffordshire Regiment, 1881.

1st Battalion

Formed from the 38th Regiment stationed in Malta, 1881. Took part in Egyptian campaign of 1882 returning to Malta, 1883. To Egypt, 1884 and took part in Nile expedition, 1884-85. Present at Kirbekan. To Gibraltar, 1886; Egypt, 1891; England, 1893; Ireland, 1898; Gibraltar, 1899. Served in South African War, remaining in Orange River Colony and the Transvaal. To Ireland, 1904; England, 1906; Gibraltar, 1911; South Africa, 1913; England, 1914. During First World War took part in Ypres battles, 1914-15, battles of the Somme, 1916, Ypres, 1917. Moved to Italy November, 1917. To England then Singapore, 1919; Burma, 1922; India, 1925; England, 1929; Palestine, 1938. Served in Palestine, North Africa, Egypt, Syria, India and Burma (Chindit operations) during Second World War. Left India for England, 1948. To Hong Kong, 1949; Northern Ireland, 1951; Germany, 1952; Egypt, 1954; Cyprus, 1955; Germany, 1957. Amalgamated with 1st Battalion, The North Staffordshire Regiment (The Prince of Wales`s) to form 1st Battalion, The Staffordshire Regiment (The Prince of Wales`s), 1959.

2nd Battalion

Formed from the 80th Regiment stationed in Ireland, 1881. To England, 1883; Ireland, 1889; England, 1891; Egypt, 1893; India, 1895; Burma, 1897; India, 1900; South Africa, 1907; England, 1911. Crossed to France, 1914 and engaged during retreat from Mons and battles of the Aisne and Ypres, battles of the Somme, 1916; Arras and Cambrai operations, 1917; operations on the Somme and battle of the Hindenburg Line, 1918. Left Germany for England, 1919. To Ireland, 1920; England, 1923; Malta, 1928; Palestine, 1929; Egypt, 1930; India, 1932. Served on North West Frontier, 1939-40 then to England. With 1st Air Landing Brigade took part in landings in Sicily, 1943, operations in Italy, and Arnhem, 1944. To Norway, 1945; Germany, 1946; England, 1948 and amalgamated with 1st Battalion, 1948.

Above - General Hardinge presenting new Colours to 1st Battalion, The South Staffordshire Regiment, Gibraltar January, 1887.

Below - Officer - The South Staffordshire Regiment in patrol uniform c1885.

Badges

The Sphinx superscribed "Egypt" - commemorates services of the 80th Regiment in Egypt, 1801. The Staffordshire Knot - worn by both regiments. The Round Tower of Windsor - was a distinction of the old King's Own Staffordshire Militia which became 3rd Battalion, The South Staffordshire Regiment in 1881. A Glider - recalls 2nd Battalion's service with 1st Air Landing Brigade, 1st Airborne Division during the Sicily Landing in 1943.

Uniform

38th and 80th Regiments - yellow facing. The South Staffordshire Regiment - regulation white facings, yellow being restored in 1936.

Nickname

`The Staffordshire Knots.`

Above - Sergeant - The South Staffordshire Regiment in mess dress c1885.

Below - Band - 1st Battalion, The South Staffordshire Regiment, 1897.

The Dorset Regiment

Titles

1702-1751	Know by name of Colonel.	1755-1757	56th Regiment.
1751-1782	39th Regiment.	1757-1782	54th Regiment.
1782-1807	39th (East Middlesex) Regiment.	1782-1881	54th (West Norfolk)
1807-1881	39th (Dorsetshire) Regiment.		Regiment.

1881-1951   The Dorsetshire Regiment.
1951-1958   The Dorset Regiment.

39th Regiment

Formed in Ireland by Colonel Richard Coote, 1702. To Portugal, 1707. Took part in War of the Spanish Succession - engaged at La Caya, 1709. To Gibraltar and Minorca, 1713. Served as Marines with Sir George Byng`s Fleet and saw action against the Spanish off Cape Passaro, 1718. To Ireland, 1719; Gibraltar, 1727. Present during siege. To Jamaica, 1730; Ireland, 1732; England, 1744. Served once more as Marines, 1744-48, landing at L`Orient, 1746. To Ireland, 1748; India, 1754. Fought at Hooghly, Mahratta Ditch and Plassey, 1757. To Ireland, 1758; Gibraltar, 1769.

Right - Grenadiers - 39th Regiment during siege of Gibraltar, 1779-83. This illustration was copied from the patio wall of the Governor`s Residence at Gibraltar in 1870 by Lieutenant John Marsham, 28th Regiment.

Below - Presentation of new Colours to the 39th Regiment at Salford Barracks 8th September, 1866. Engraving from Illustrated London News.

Present during Great Siege of 1779-83. To England, 1783; Ireland, 1789; the West Indies, 1793. Took part in capture of Martinique and fighting on Guadeloupe, 1794. Heavy casualties at Berville Camp forced surrender, 6th October. To Ireland, 1795. Re-formed and back to the West Indies, 1796. Served in St. Domingo, Demerara, Surinam and Antigua. To England, 1803; Malta, 1805; Sicily, 1810; Portugal, 1811. During Peninsular War gained battle honours - "Vittoria", "Pyrenees", "Nivelle", "Nive" and "Orthez." Formed part of expedition to Canada, 1814-15. Stationed in France, 1815-18. *A 2nd Battalion, 39th Regiment formed, 1803 and to Guernsey, 1804; Ireland, 1806; Guernsey, 1808; Portugal, 1809. During the Peninsular War fought at Albuhera and Arroyo Dos Molinos, 1811. To England, 1812 and disbanded, 1815.* To England then Ireland, 1818; England the Australia, 1825. Began duty guarding prisoners. To India, 1832. Took part in Coorg (1834) and Maharajpore (1843) campaigns. To England, 1847; Ireland, 1850; Gibraltar then the Crimea, 1854. Received battle honour "Sevastopol". To Canada, 1856; Bermuda, 1859; England, 1864; Ireland, 1866; India, 1869. Became 1st Battalion, The Dorsetshire Regiment, 1881.

54th Regiment

Formed at Salisbury by Lieutenant-Colonel John Campbell, 1755. To Gibraltar, 1756. Saw service as marines with Admiral Byng's Mediterranean Fleet. To Ireland, 1768; North America, 1776. Took part in operations around New York and Rhode Island and in action at New London, 1781. To Canada, 1783; England, 1790; Guernsey, 1793; England, 1794. Took part in campaign in Flanders, 1794-95. To the West Indies and fought at St. Vincent, 1795. To England, 1796; Ireland, 1797; England, 1800. Divided into two battalions at Winchester. Later involved in attacks of Spanish naval bases at Ferrol and Cadiz. Took part in Egyptian campaign of 1801-02. Engaged during landings at Aboukir and then in fighting for Alexandria. Gained unique battle honour "Marabout" for operations of 21st August. To Gibraltar and 2nd Battalion disbanded, 1802. To England, 1805; West Indies, 1807. Detachments fought at Buenos Ayres and Montevideo, 1807;

PLAYER'S CIGARETTES.

1808.
Time of Peninsular War.

Above - Private - 54th Regiment c1808. Cigarette card by John Player & Sons.

Left - Officers - 2nd Battalion, The Dorsetshire Regiment, 1897.

San Domingo, 1809. Regiment reduced to one company in the West Indies while reforming in England. Sent from England to garrison Stralsund in Sweden, 1810. To North Germany, 1813 then The Netherlands and Belgium. Present during attack and capture of Merxem, 1814. In reserve at Hal during Waterloo campaign and later at Cambrai. Left France for England, , 1816. To South Africa, 1819 and took part in operations against the Kaffirs. To India, 1822. Took part in Burma War of 1824-25, fighting at Arakan and receiving battle honour "Ava." Left India for England, 1840. To Ireland, 1842; Gibraltar, 1845; Malta, 1847; West Indies, 1848; Canada, 1851; England then Gibraltar, 1854; England, 1856; India, 1857. Took part in Indian Mutiny. To England, 1866; Ireland, 1868; India, 1871. Became 2nd Battalion, The Dorsetshire Regiment, 1881.

Below - Officers - 2nd Battalion, The Dorsetshire Regiment just prior to embarkation to South Africa, 1899. The Commanding Officer - Lieutenant-Colonel C.H. Law is seated centre.

Above - 2nd Battalion, The Dorsetshire Regiment attacking Turkish redoubts at Kut al Amara, 1915. Illustration by Christopher Clark.

1st Battalion

Formed from the 39th Regiment stationed in India, 1881. To England, Malta then England, 1882; Malta then Egypt, 1885; England, 1886; Malta, 1888; Egypt, 1889; India, 1893. Took part in Tirah expedition of 1897 being engaged at Dargai and Saran Sar. To England, 1906; Ireland, 1913. Crossed to France, 1914 and fought during retreat from Mons and battle of the Aisne. Engaged during Ypres operations, 1914-15; battle of the Somme,1916; operations on the Flanders coast and defence of Nieuport, 1917; battles of the Somme and Hindenburg Line, 1918. One company sent to North Russia, 1919. Stationed in Ireland, 1919-21. To Malta, 1922; Egypt then the Sudan, 1924; Malta then India, 1926; Malta, 1939. Moved to Egypt, 1943 and from there took part in invasion of Sicily and Italy. Returned to England November, 1943 and fought in North-West Europe, 1944. Served in Germany, Austria and Hong Kong then to Korea, 1953 and Germany, 1954. Amalgamated with 1st Battalion, The Devonshire Regiment to form 1st Battalion, The Devonshire and Dorset Regiment, 1958.

2nd Battalion

Formed from the 54th Regiment stationed in India, 1881. To Aden, 1885; England, 1886; Malta, 1897. Sent detachment to Crete, 1898 for

operations against the Bashi-Bazouks. To England, 1899. Fought in South Africa, 1899-1902. Saw action during relief of Ladysmith at Spion Kop, Vaal Krantz and Alleman's Nek. To India, 1906. Sent to Mesopotamia October, 1914 and later besieged at Kut al Amara. Taken prisoner April, 1916. Reformed from drafts July, 1916 and later served in Egypt and Palestine. To India, 1919. Took part in Moplah Rebellion of 1921. To the Sudan, 1922; Egypt; 1923; England, 1924; Germany, 1927; England, 1929. Served in Egypt and Palestine, 1936. Fought in France and Belgium, 1939-40. To India, 1942 and took part in battle of Kohima Ridge, 1944. Later fought in Burma. Stationed in Japan, 1946-47; Malaya, 1947. Amalgamated with 1st Battalion, 1948.

Badges

The Castle, Key and Motto of Gibraltar - commemorates the part played by the 39th Regiment during the great siege of Gibraltar, 1779-1783. The Sphinx superscribed 'Marabout' - for the services of the 54th Regiment on 21st August, 1801. 'Primus in Indis' - When the 39th went to India in 1754 they were the first British regiment to serve there and to commemorate this the motto Primus in Indis (First in India) was conferred.

Above - Officers' forage cap badge - The Dorsetshire Regiment. Worn 1881 to the mid 1890s. Silver, gilt and green enamel.

Below - Cap badge - The Dorsetshire Regiment. The title-scroll was amended to read "Dorset" after 1951.

Left: Top - 1st Battalion, The Dorsetshire Regiment on guard duty at Stockingford Station near Nuneaton, Warwickshire during the docks and railways strike August, 1911. Note full dress helmets being worn for protection.

Left: Below - Indian servants - Sergeants' Mess, The Dorsetshire Regiment. Note cap badges and chevrons being worn in the turbans.

Selection of Dorset Regiment badges on display at the Dorset Military Museum, Dorchester.

Uniform

39th Regiment - green facings, the shade being at various times described as "pale", "willow", "popinjay" and "light". 54th Regiment - at first popinjay green, later changing to grass green. The Dorset Regiment - white facings at first, grass green being restored in 1904.

Nicknames

`Sankey`s Horse` - Nicholas Sankey was Colonel of the 39th during its service in Spain and the War of the Spanish Succession. The regiment received the nickname after, it is said, it was mounted on mules to enable it to reach the battle of Almanza. As the regiment were still in Ireland at the time, this legend must be discounted. It is more likely, it is thought by the regimental historian - C.T. Atkinson, that the name came about as a result of the 39th`s close association at the time with Barrymore`s Regiment (13th Foot) which had been converted to dragoons. `The Flamers` - given to the 54th regiment after burning New London in 1781 during the American War of Independence. `The Green Linnets` - the 39th Regiment from its facings. While the 2nd Battalion was besiege at Kut al Amara in 1916, a composite battalion consisting of drafts for the Dorsetshire and the 2nd Norfolk was formed at El Orah and named `The Norsets.`

The South Lancashire Regiment (The Prince of Wales`s Volunteers)

Titles

1717-1751	Known by name of Colonel.
1751-1782	40th Regiment of Foot.
1782-1881	40th (2nd Somersetshire) Regiment of Foot.
1793-1881	82nd (Prince of Wales`s Volunteers) Regiment of Foot.

1881-1938   The Prince of Wales`s Volunteers (South Lancashire Regiment).
1938-1958   The South Lancashire Regiment (The Prince of Wales`s Volunteers).

40th Regiment

Formed from eight independent companies serving in Nova Scotia, 1717. Took part in conquest of Canada and present at Beau Sejour, 1755; Louisburg, 1758 and Quebec, 1759. To the West Indies, 1761. Took part in capture of Martinique and Havannah, 1762. To Nova Scotia, 1763; Ireland, 1764; Boston, Massachusetts, 1775; Nova Scotia, 1776. During American War of Independence fought at Brooklyn and New York operations, 1776; Princeton, Brandywine and Germantown, 1777. To the West Indies, 1778 and took part in capture of St. Lucia. To America, 1781 and present during assault of Fort Griswold. To England, 1783; Ireland, 1789. Flank companies to the West Indies, 1793 and present during attacks on Martinique and Guadeloupe, 1794. Battalion companies took part in expedition to Holland, 1784 then to the West Indies, 1795. Fought at St. Vincent, 1795-96 and

St. Domingo, 1797-98. To England, 1798. Took part in Helder campaign of 1799. Present at Zype Canal and Alkmaar. To Minorca then Malta, 1800. Flank companies took part in Egyptian campaign of 1801 and present at Aboukir and Alexandria. To Minorca, 1801; England, 1802. *A 2nd Battalion, 40th Regiment formed, 1799 and with 1st Battalion took part in Helder expedition. To Minorca then Malta, 1800. Flank companies served in Egypt, 1801. To Minorca, 1801; England, 1802 and disbanded.* To South America, 1806. Took part in capture of Monte Video and San Pedro, 1807. To Ireland, 1807; Portugal, 1808. During the Peninsular War fought at Rolica and Vimiero, 1808; Talavera, 1809; Busaco, 1810; Olivenca, 1811; Ciudad Rodrigo, Badajoz and Salamanca, 1812; Vittoria, San Sebastian, battles in the Pyrenees and Nivelle, 1813; Orthez and Toulouse, 1814. To Ireland then America, 1814; England then Belgium, 1815. Fought at Waterloo. *A 2nd Battalion, 40th Regiment formed, 1804. To Ireland, 1806; England and disbanded, 1815.* Left France for Scotland, 1817. To England then Ireland, 1820; England, 1823. Began moving in detachments on prison ships to New South Wales. To India, 1828. Took part in First Afghan War and present at defence of Kandahar and capture of Ghuznee and Kabul, 1842. Fought at Maharajpore during Gwalior campaign of 1843. To England, 1845; Ireland, 1847; New South Wales, 1852; New Zealand,

Above - Grenadier, 40th Regiment 1751. Illustration by P.W. Reynolds.

Right - Colours - 1st Battalion, The Prince of Wales's Volunteers (South Lancashire), Dover, 1937.

1860. Fought in Maori Wars of 1860-61 (Colour-sergeant John Lucas awarded Victoria Cross) and 1863-66. To England, 1866; Ireland, 1869; India, 1872. Became 1st Battalion, The Prince of Wales's Volunteers (South Lancashire Regiment), 1881.

82nd Regiment

Formed, 1793. To Gibraltar then San Domingo, 1795. *A 2nd Battalion, 82nd Regiment formed shortly after 1st. Amalgamated with 1st at Gibraltar, 1795.* To England, 1797; Ireland, 1800; Minorca, 1801; Ireland, 1802; England, 1807. Took part in 1807 expedition to Copenhagen. To Portugal, 1808 and present at Roleia, Vimiera and retreat to Corunna. To England, 1809. Took part in 1809 expedition to Walcheren. To Gibraltar then Portugal, 1812. Fought at Vittoria, San Sebastian, Pyrenees battles, San Marcial and Nivelle, 1813 and Orthes, 1814. To Canada, 1814 and present during capture of Niagara. To Belgium, France then England, 1815. *A 2nd Battalion, 82nd Regiment formed, 1804 and disbanded, 1815.* To Ireland, 1816; Mauritius, 1819; England, 1831; Ireland, 1834; Gibraltar, 1837; West Indies, 1839; North America, 1843; Nova Scotia, 1847; England, 1848; Ionian Islands then the Crimea, 1855. Fought at

Above - Bandmaster - The South Lancashire Regiment.

Left - 1st Battalion, The Prince of Wales's Volunteers (South Lancashire) on public duties, London September, 1928.

Sevastopol. To England, 1856; India, 1857. During Indian Mutiny present at Lucknow, Cawnpore and Rohilcund. To Aden, 1869; England, 1870; Ireland, 1875; England, 1880. Became 2nd Battalion, The Prince of Wales`s Volunteers (South Lancashire Regiment), 1881.

1st Battalion

Formed from the 40th Regiment stationed in India. To Aden, 1884; England, 1886; Jersey, 1890; Ireland, 1892; England, 1898; South Africa, 1899. Fought at Tugela Heights, relief of Ladysmith, Botha`s Pass and Laing`s Nek. To India, 1903. During First World War remained in India serving on the North West Frontier. fought at Baluchistan, 1918 and during Third Afghan War, 1919. To England then Ireland, 1920; England, 1923; Germany, 1928; England, 1929. During Second World War served in France, 1939-40 and North West Europe, 1944-45. Took part in D-Day landings, 6th June, 1944. Served in Egypt and Palestine, 1946-47 then To Trieste. Served in the Sudan, 1951-53; Germany, 1956-57 then to Hong Kong. Amalgamated with 1st Battalion, The East Lancashire Regiment to form 1st Battalion, The Lancashire Regiment (Prince of Wales`s Volunteers), 1958.

2nd Battalion

Formed from the 82nd Regiment stationed in England, 1881. To South Africa, 1884; Straits Settlements, 1887; Gibraltar, 1889; Malta, 1892; Egypt, 1893; India, 1895; England, 1903; Ireland, 1908; England, 1913. During First World War took part in battles of Mons, Marne, Aisne, Messines (Private W. Ratcliffe awarded Victoria Cross) and Ypres, 1914; Bellewaarde and Hooge, 1915; Somme, 1916; Messines and Ypres, 1917; Somme, Lys, Neuve Eglise, Ypres and Courtrai, 1918. To England, 1919; Ireland then Palestine, 1920; India, 1922. Served on North West Frontier, 1930. To England, 1940. Served in South Africa, Madagascar and East Africa, 1943-43; India and Burma, 1943-45. To England then Malta, 1946; Trieste, 1947. Amalgamated with 1st Battalion, 1948.

Badges

The Prince of Wales`s Coronet, Plumes and motto - from the 82nd Regiment. The Sphinx superscribed `Egypt` - commemorates the services of the 40th Regiment in Egypt, 1801.

Uniform

40th Regiment - buff facings. 82nd Regiment - yellow. South Lancashire Regiment - white until 1934 when buff was restored.

Nicknames

`The Excellers` - from the number XL. `The Fighting Fortieth.`

Cap badge.

The Welch Regiment

Titles

1719-1751	The Regiment of Invalids.	1756-1758	2nd Battalion, 24th Regiment of Foot.
1751-1787	41st Regiment of Foot. (or Invalids)	1758-1782	69th Regiment of Foot.
1787-1831	41st Regiment of Foot.	1782-1881	69th (South Lincolnshire) Regiment of Foot.
1831-1838	41st or the Welch Regiment of Foot.		
1838-1881	41st (The Welch) Regiment of Foot.		

1881-1920   The Welsh Regiment.
1920-1969   The Welch Regiment.

41st Regiment

Formed by Colonel Edmund Fielding from out pensioners of The Royal Hospital, Chelsea. Comprised companies stationed in Portsmouth area and in the Channel Islands. Regiment ceased to comprise invalids, 1787. To Ireland, 1789. Flank companies to the West Indies, 1793 and present at capture of Martinique, St. Lucia and Guadeloupe, 1794. Rest of regiment to the West Indies, 1794 and took part in capture of St. Domingo. To England then Ireland, 1796; Canada, 1799. During war with the United States gained unique battle honour `Detroit` in 1812. Fought at Queenstown, Frenchtown, Fort Meigs and Miami (another unique battle honour) and Moravianstown (Thames), 1813. *A 2nd Battalion, 41st Regiment formed at Winchester, 1812 and to Canada, 1813. Fought at Black Rock in July. Battalions merged after action at Moravianstown (Thames).* Took part in capture of Fort Niagara and action at Buffalo, 1813; present at Lundy`s Lane and Fort Erie, 1814. To England then France, 1815; Ireland, 1816; Scotland, 1820; England then India, 1822. Took part in war in Burma, 1824-26. Present during actions at Tantabain, Donabew and Seimbyke. Gained battle honour `Ava.` To India, 1826; Burma, 1832; India, 1834. Took part in Afghan War of 1842 and present during action at Hykulzee, battles of Kandahar, Ghuznee and Cabool. To England, 1843; Ireland, 1845; Ionian Islands, 1851; Malta then the Crimea, 1854. Gained battle honours `Alma`, `Inkerman` and `Sevastopol.` To England, 1856; West Indies, 1857; England, 1860; Ireland, 1864; India, 1865; Aden, 1874; England, 1875; Gibraltar, 1880; South Africa, 1881. Became 1st Battalion, The Welsh Regiment, 1881.

69th Regiment

Formed as 2nd Battalion, 24th Regiment (see South Wales Borderers) in Lincolnshire, 1756. Took part in expedition to Rochefort, 1757. Took part in expedition to Belle Isle, 1761 then to West Indies. Present during capture of Martinique, 1762. To Ireland, 1763; Gibraltar, 1768; England, 1775; West Indies, 1780. Serving as marines took part in St. Kitts operations and battle of The Saints, 1782. To England, 1785; Ireland, 1784. Joined Lord Hood's Mediterranean Fleet for service as marines, 1793 and present during siege of Toulon. Took part in attacks on Pharon and Aränes. Fought in Corsica, 1794 and present during the action of Genoa, 1795. *A 2nd Battalion, 69th Regiment formed, 1795 and merged with 1st Battalion at Gibraltar.* To St. Domingo. 1796. Detachments also served with Nelson along the Italian coast and at Cape St. Vincent. also with Howe on the 'Glorious First of June' 1794. Left St. Domingo for Ireland, 1798. Took part in Helder expedition of 1799. To Jamaica, 1800; England, 1802; India, 1805. Present during mutiny at Vellore, 1806. Took part in Travancore campaign, 1809. Present during capture of Bourbon and Mauritius, 1810 and Java, 1811. Flank companies served in Mahratta War, 1817-19. *A 2nd Battalion, 69th Regiment formed, 1803 and to Jersey, 1805; Ireland, 1806; Holland, 1813. Took part in attack on Bergen-op-Zoom, 1814. Moved into Belgium and at Quatre Bras and Waterloo, 1815. To England and disbanded, 1816.* To England, 1825; West Indies, 1831; Nova Scotia, 1839; England, 1842; Malta, 1847; Barbados, 1851; England then Burma, 1857; India, 1862; England, 1864; Channel Islands, 1866; Ireland then Canada, 1867. Served during Fenian Raids, 1867-68. To Bermuda, 1870; Gibraltar, 1873; England, 1878. Became 2nd Battalion, The Welsh Regiment, 1881.

1st Battalion

Formed from the 41st Regiment stationed in South Africa. Took part in operations in Zululand, 1884. To Egypt, 1886. Took part in Suakin expedition of 1888 and present during action at Gemaizah. Took part in Nile expedition, 1889. To Malta, 1889; Wales, 1893; England, 1895; South Africa, 1899. Gained battle honours 'Relief of Kimberley' and 'Paardeberg'

Above - Officer's silver and gilt shoulder-belt plate - 41st Regiment. Introduced after 1831.

Right - Other ranks' brass shoulder-belt plate - 69th Regiment. Introduced after 1782.

and present during battles of Driefontein, Johannesburg, Diamond Hill and Belfast. To England, 1904; Egypt, 1909; the Sudan, 1913; India then England, 1914; France, 1915 and fought in battles of Ypres and Loos. Moved to Egypt in October and in 1916 to Salonika. Served on Macedonian Front. until end of First World War. To Wales then India, 1919; Aden, 1927; England, 1928; Northern Ireland, 1935; Palestine, 1939. Served in Palestine and Egypt, 1939-40; Crete, 1941; Western Desert, 1942; Sicily and Italy, 1943-44; Italy and Austria, 1945. To England, 1947. Served in Korea, 1951-52; Hong Kong, 1952-54; Germany, 1956-57; Cyprus, 1957-59; Libya, 1959-60; Germany, 1961-1963; Hong Kong, 1966-1968. Amalgamated with 1st Battalion, The South Wales Borderers to form 1st Battalion, The Royal Regiment of Wales (24th/41st Foot), 1969.

Above - Officers` shako plate - 69th Regiment, 1816-1829. (H.L. King)

Left - Drummer - 69th Regiment, Gosport, 1864.

2nd Battalion

Formed from the 69th Regiment stationed in England, 1881. To Ireland, 1883; England, 1891; India, 1892; South Africa, 1906; Wales, 1910; England, 1912; France, 1914. During First World War took part in battles of Mons, the Aisne and Ypres, 1914; Aubers Ridge, Loos and Hohenzollern Redoubt, 1915 (Lance Corporal William Fuller awarded Victoria Cross); the Somme, 1916; operations on Flanders coast, defence of Nieuport and battle of Passchendaele, 1917; battles of the Lys, Arras, Hindenburg Line, the Selle and Sambre, 1918. To Ireland, 1919; England, 1923; Shanghai, 1927; Singapore, 1928; India, 1931. Fought in Burma, 1944. Left Burma for England, 1947. Amalgamated with 1st Battalion, 1948.

Badges

The Rose and Thistle within a crowed Garter - in use by 1747. The Prince of Wales's Coronet, Plumes and motto - authorized for the 41st Regiment in 1831. The Red Dragon of Wales - adopted in 1881. A Naval Crown superscribed 12th April, 1782 - commemorates Admiral Sir George Rodney's victory of that date at which the 69th Regiment served as marines.

Above - Badges and motto - `Gwell angau na chywilydd` (Rather death than dishonour) of the Welch Regiment.

Right - Drum-major McKelvey, 1st Battalion, The Welsh Regiment with Regimental Goat, c1897.

Uniform

41st Regiment - blue facings were worn by The Invalids Regiment. Red was adopted in 1789, changing to white in 1822. 69th Regiment - green facings. The Welch Regiment - white facings.

Nicknames

No less than eight nicknames are recorded in Major A.C. Whithorne's history of the Welch Regiment. For the 41st Regiment - `The Old Fogeys` - a name given to the invalids. `Wardour's Horse` - origin uncertain, but probably from the period (1743-52) when Tomkins Wardour was Colonel of the regiment. `The Six Old Corps` - in use c1741. `The Travelling Tinkers` - recalled by an old soldier who enlisted in 1888. The 69th Regiment also had four nicknames. `The Ups and Downs` - from the fact that the number 69 was the same either way up. `The Old Agamemnons` - a name given by Admiral Nelson to the detachment that had served on HMS Agamemnon. `The Lincolnshire Poachers` - from the 1782-1881 title. `The Grass Pickers` - While in Burma, 1858-62, the regiment was required to clear high grass from the parade ground at Tounghoo.

Colours - 1st Battalion, The Welsh Regiment, 1919.

The Oxfordshire and Buckinghamshire Light Infantry

Titles

1741-1751	Known by name of Colonel.	1755-1757	54th Regiment of Foot.
1751-1782	43rd Regiment of Foot.	1757-1782	52nd Regiment of Foot.
1782-1803	43rd (Monmouthshire) Regiment of Foot.	1782-1803	52nd (Oxfordshire) Regiment of Foot.
1803-1881	43rd (Monmouthshire Light Infantry) Regiment.	1803-1881	52nd (Oxfordshire Light Infantry) Regiment.

1881-1908 The Oxfordshire Light Infantry.

1881-1958 The Oxfordshire and Buckinghamshire Light Infantry.

52nd Officer 1826

43rd Regiment

Formed, 1741 and to Minorca. To Ireland, 1747; Nova Scotia, 1757. During the Conquest of Canada fought at Quebec, 1759. To the West Indies, 1761. Took part in capture of Martinique and Havannah, 1762. To England, 1764; America, 1774. During American War of Independence fought at Lexington and Bunker Hill, 1775; Brooklyn, 1776; Rhode Island, 1777 and Yorktown, 1781. To England, 1783; Ireland, 1787; West Indies, 1793. Took part in capture of Martinique, St. Lucia and Guadeloupe, 1794. To England, 1795; West Indies, 1797; England, 1800; Channel Islands, 1801; England, 1804. Took part in 1807 expedition to Copenhagen. To Portugal, 1808. Fought at Vimiera and during retreat to Corunna. Returned to England then Portugal, 1809. Fought at the Coa and Busaco, 1810; Fuentes d` Onor, 1811; Ciudad Rodrigo, Badajoz and Salamanca, 1812; Vittoria, Pyrenees operations, Bidassoa, Nivelle and the Nive, 1813; Toulouse, 1814. To England then America, 1814. Took part in attack on New Orleans. To England, Belgium then France, 1815. *A 2nd Battalion, 43rd Regiment formed, 1804. To Portugal, 1808; England, 1809. Took part in 1809 expedition to Walcheren. Disbanded, 1817.* To England, 1818; Ireland, 1819; Gibraltar, 1822; Portugal, 1827; Gibraltar, 1828; England, 1830; Ireland, 1832; New Brunswick, 1834; Canada, 1838; Nova Scotia, 1844; England, 1846; Ireland, 1848; Cape of Good Hope, 1851. Took part in Kaffir War, 1851-53. To India, 1853. Took part in capture of Kirwe and operations in Bundelkund during Indian Mutiny. To New Zealand, 1863. Fought in Maori War, 1863-66. To England, 1866; Channel Islands, 1868; Ireland, 1869; India, 1872; Burma, 1879. Became 1st Battalion, The Oxfordshire Light Infantry, 1881.

52nd Regiment

Formed, 1755. To Ireland, 1758; Canada, 1765; America, 1774. During War of Independence fought at Lexington and Bunker Hill, 1775; Brooklyn and Fort Washington, 1776; Brandywine, 1777 and Rhode Island, 1778. To England, 1778; India, 1783 and took part in siege of Cananore. During Third Mysore War fought at Bangalore and Arikere, 1791 and Seringapatam, 1792. Present at siege of Pondicherry, 1793. Took part in

Above - Undress cap badge - 52nd Regiment.

Left - Buglers - 52nd Regiment 1862.

Above - Officers` shoulder-belt plate - 52nd Regiment.

Below - 2nd Battalion, The Oxfordshire and Buckinghamshire Light Infantry arriving at Aldershot, 1911.

war in Ceylon, 1795-96. To England, 1798; Took part in 1800 expedition to Quiberon and Ferrol. *A 2nd Battalion, 52nd Regiment formed, 1799. Took part in expedition to Quiberon and Ferrol, 1800. Became 96th Regiment, 1803.* To Sicily, 1806; England, Sweden then Portugal, 1808. Fought at Vimiera and during retreat to Corunna. To England then Portugal, 1809. For remainder of war in the Peninsular and France fought at the Coa and Busaco, 1810; Fuentes d`Onor, 1811; Ciudad Rodrigo, Badajoz and Salamanca, 1812; Vittoria, the Pyrenees, Nivelle and the Nive, 1813; Orthes and Toulouse, 1814. To England then Belgium, 1815. Fought at Waterloo. *A 2nd Battalion, 52nd Regiment formed, 1804. Took part in 1807 expedition to Copenhagen. To Portugal, 1808 and fought at Vimiera. Returned to England, 1809 and took part in Walcheren expedition. To Holland then Belgium, 1813; England, 1815. Disbanded, 1816.* Left France for England, 1818. To Canada, 1824; England, 1831; Gibraltar, 1837; West Indies, 1838; Canada, 1842; England, 1848; India, 1853. Took part in capture of Delhi, 1857. To England, 1864; Malta, 1868; Gibraltar, 1873; England, 1874. Became 2nd Battalion, The Oxfordshire Light Infantry, 1881.

1st Battalion

Formed from the 43rd Regiment stationed in Burma, 1881. To India, 1882; England, 1887; Ireland, 1893; South Africa, 1899. Took part in relief of Kimberley and operations at Paardeberg. To England, 1902; India, 1903; Mesopotamia, 1914. Captured at Kut al Amara, 1916. Later re-formed from drafts. Re-formed in England, 1919 and to North Russia. Returned to England same year and joined by cadre from Mesopotamia then to Ireland. To England, 1922, Germany, 1925; England, 1927. Fought in France and Belgium, 1939-40; North West Europe, 1944-45. Became 1st Green Jackets, 43rd and 52nd, 1958.

OXd BUCKS Lt INFTy ARRIVING AT ALDERSHOT 1911

2nd Battalion

Formed from the 52nd Regiment stationed in England, 1881. To Gibraltar, 1884; Egypt, 1885; India, 1886. Took part in Mohmund campaign of 1887. To Burma, 1889; India, 1892. Took part in Tirah expedition, 1897-98. To England, 1903. During First World War fought at battles of Mons, the Marne, Aisne and Ypres, 1914; Festubert and Loos, 1915; the Somme, 1916; Arras and Cambrai, 1917; the Somme, Hindenburg Line and Selle, 1918. To England, 1919; Ireland, 1920; England then India, 1922; Burma, 1929; India, 1934; England, 1940. Fought in North West Europe, 1944-45. Served in Palestine, 1945-47. Amalgamated with 1st Battalion, 1948.

Badges

A bugle-horn.

Uniform

43rd Regiment - white facings. 52nd Regiment - buff. Oxfordshire and Buckinghamshire Light Infantry - white.

Nicknames

`The Light Bobs.`

The Oxfordshire and Buckinghamshire Light Infantry - officer 1915. Note unique collar badges comprising regimental button and length of cord.

Officer - 56th Regiment 1798.

Facing Page: Top - Cap badge - The Essex
Regiment.

Centre - Officers` shoulder-belt plate - 44th
Regiment 1830-55.

Bottom - 1st Battalion, The Essex Regiment -
shooting team, Bangalore, 1906.

The Essex Regiment

Titles

1741-1751	Known by name of Colonel.	1755-1757	58th Regiment of Foot.
1751-1782	44th Regiment of Foot.	1757-1782	56th Regiment of Foot.
1782-1881	44th (East Essex) Regiment of Foot.	1782-1881	56th (West Essex) Regiment of Foot.

1881-1958   The Essex Regiment.

44th Regiment

Raised by Colonel James Long, 1741. Served in Scotland during Young Pretender`s Rebellion, 1745-46 and present at battle of Prestonpans. To Ireland, 1749; North America, 1755. Took part in first expedition to Fort du Quesne, 1755 and fought at Ticonderoga, 1758 and Niagara, 1759. Left Canada for Ireland, 1765. To North America, 1775 and during American War of Independence fought at Brooklyn, 1776; Danbury, Brandywine and Germantown, 1777. To Canada, 1780; England, 1786; Guernsey, 1787; England, 1788; Ireland, 1792. Flank companies sent to West Indies, 1793 and present during operations in Martinique, St. Lucia and Guadeloupe, 1794. Battalion companies to Flanders, 1794 and fought at Boxtel. To England then the West Indies, 1795. Fought at St. Lucia, 1796. To England, 1797; Gibraltar, 1798; Malta, 1800; Egypt, 1801. Took part in fighting at Mandora and Alexandria. Returned to Malta then to England, 1801. To Ireland, 1802; England, 1803; Malta, 1805; Sicily, 1808. Took part in expedition to Naples and capture of the Ionian Islands, 1809-10. To Malta, 1811; Sicily, 1812; Minorca, 1813. Took part in operations in eastern Spain, 1813-14. Moved into France and then to North America, 1814. Fought at Bladensburg and Baltimore, 1814 and operations in New Orleans, 1815. To Ireland, 1815. *2nd Battalion, 44th Regiment formed in Ireland, 1803. To England, 1804, Guernsey, 1805; Alderney, 1809; Spain, 1810. During Peninsular War fought at Sabugal and Fuentes d` Onoro, 1811; Badajoz, Salamanca and Burgos, 1812. To England then Flanders, 1813. Fought at Bergen-op-Zoom, 1814, Quatre Bras and Waterloo, 1815. To England and disbanded, 1816.* To India 1822. Took part in First Burma War and Arakan operations, 1825. Served in First Afghan War, 1842. Battalion destroyed during retreat from Kabul, making a last stand at Gundamuck Hill. Left India for England, 1843. To Ireland, 1845; Malta, 1848; Gibraltar, 1851; the Crimea, 1854. Gained battle honours `Alma`, `Inkerman` and `Sevastopol.` Sergeant W. McWhiney awarded Victoria Cross. *A Reserve Battalion* *formed in Ireland, 1847. To Malta, 1848 and merged into line Battalion, 1850.* To England, 1856; India, 1857; China, 1860 and present at Taku Forts. Left Hong Kong for India, 1861. To England, 1866; Ireland, 1868; India, 1871; Burma, 1877. Became 1st Battalion, The Essex Regiment, 1881.

56th Regiment

Raised by Lord Charles Manners in the North of England, 1755. To the West Indies, 1762 and took part on capture of the Moro Fort, Havannah, Cuba. To Ireland, 1763; Gibraltar, 1770. Present during siege of 1779-83. To England, 1783; Ireland, 1788; West Indies, 1793. Took part in capture of Martinique, St. Lucia and Guadeloupe, 1794. To England then Ireland, 1795; West Indies, 1796. Took part in operations on St. Domingo, 1796-97. To England, 1798. Took part in Helder campaign of 1799 and present at Schoorl, Bergen and Egmont-op-Zee. To Ireland, 1800; England then India, 1805. Detachment present during capture of Rodriguez, 1809 and operations against Bourbon and Mauritius, 1809-1810. To Mauritius, 1815. *2nd Battalion, 56th Regiment formed, 1804. To Channel Islands, 1806; India, 1807. Detachment took part in capture of Fort Mallia, 1809. Formed part of Poona Subsidiary Force, 1816. To England and disbanded, 1817. 3rd Battalion, 56th Regiment formed, 1813 and to Holland. Fought at Merxem, 1814. Returned to England and disbanded, 1814.* To England, 1826; Ireland, 1827; Jamaica, 1832; Canada, 1840; Ireland, 1842; England, 1844; Gibraltar, 1847. *A Reserve Battalion formed, 1845. To Gibraltar, 1847. Merged with Line Battalion, 1850.* To Bermuda, 1851; Ireland, 1855; the Crimea, 1855. Gained battle honour `Sevastopol.` To Ireland, 1856; India, 1857; England, 1866; Ireland, 1868; India, 1871; Aden, 1877; England, 1878. Became 2nd Battalion, The Essex Regiment, 1881.

Above - Officers` shoulder-belt plate - 56th Regiment c1830.

Below - The Essex Regiment - sergeant in battle order 1919. Note Eagle badge on helmet.

1st Battalion

Formed from the 44th Regiment stationed in Burma, 1881. To India, 1881; Aden then England, 1884; Ireland, 1891; England, 1896; South Africa, 1899. Fought at Colesberg, relief of Kimberley, Paardeberg, Driefontein, Johannesburg and Diamond Hill. To India, 1902; Burma, 1906; India, 1909; Mauritius and South Africa, 1913; England, 1914. During First World War fought in Gallipoli and then to France and the Somme, 1916. Took part in battles of Arras, Ypres and Cambrai, 1917; the Lys and Ypres, 1918. To England then Ireland, 1919, England, 1922; Palestine, 1936; Egypt, 1938. During Second World War served in Egypt, the Sudan, Syria and Libya, 1939-42; India, 1942-43; Burma, 1943; India, 1943-44; Burma, 1944; India, 1944-45. Remained in India then to England, 1948; Germany, 1951; Korea, 1953; Hong Kong, 1954; Germany, 1956. Amalgamated with 1st Battalion, The Bedfordshire and Hertfordshire Regiment to form 3rd East Anglian Regiment (16th/44th), 1958.

2nd Battalion

Formed from the 56th Regiment stationed in England, 1881. To Gibraltar, 1882; Egypt, 1884. Took part in Nile campaign, 1884-85. To Malta, 1887; Cyprus, 1889; India, 1892; Burma, 1897; South Africa, 1901; England, 1902; Malta, 1904; Ireland, 1907; England, 1912. During First World War took part in retreat from Mons, battles of the Marne, Aisne, Armentières and Messines, 1914; Ypres, 1915; the Somme, 1916; Arras and Ypres, 1917; the Somme, Lys, Arras, Hindenburg Line and the Selle, 1918. To England then Malta, 1919; Constantinople and Malta, 1920; Constantinople, 1921; India, 1923; Egypt, 1935; the Sudan, 1936; England, 1937. Took part in D-Day landings, 6th June and fought in North West Europe, 1944-45. Left Germay for Trieste, 1946. To England and amalgamated with 1st Battalion, 1948.

Badges

The Castle, Key and Motto of Gibraltar - from the 56th Regiment. The Sphinx superscribed `Egypt` - from the 44th Regiment. An Eagle - from the 44th Regiment commemorating capture of French Eagle at Salamanca on 22nd July, 1812. The Arms of the County of Essex - worn by the 56th prior to 1881. An Oak Wreath - adopted in 1881 instead of the usual laurel.

Uniform

44th Regiment - yellow facings. 56th Regiment - deep crimson facings changing to purple in 1764. The Essex Regiment - white changing to purple in 1936.

Nicknames

`The Pompadours` - from the facings of the 56th Regiment. The shade of purple taken into use in 1764 was said to be the favourite colour of Madame de Pompadour - mistress of Louis XV of France. `The Little Fighting Fours` - Peninsular war and Waterloo period when the men of the 2nd Battalion, 44th Regiment were small statured Irishmen. In memory of this, the Corps of Drums beat Reveille every year on 17th March - St. Patrick`s Day.

Below - The capture of Derby 1 (first regimental mascot) by the 95th Regiment at Kotah 30th March, 1858. Illustration by Harry Payne.

Left - Colours - 1st Battalion, The Sherwood Foresters. Recently gained battle honours for the First World War are displayed on the King's Colour left.

The Sherwood Foresters (Nottinghamshire and Derbyshire Regiment)

Titles

1741-1751	Known by name of Colonel.	1823-1825	95th Regiment of Foot.
1751-1782	45th Regiment of Foot.	1825-1881	95th (Derbyshire) Regiment
1782-1866	45th (Nottinghamshire) Regiment of Foot.		of Foot.
1866-1881	45th (Nottinghamshire Sherwood Foresters) Regiment of Foot.		

1881-1902 The Sherwood Foresters (Derbyshire) Regiment

1902-1970 The Sherwood Foresters (Nottinghamshire and Derbyshire) Regiment.

45th Regiment

Raised by Colonel Daniel Houghton at Bristol, 1741. To Gibraltar, 1742; Canada, 1745. Gained first battle honour at Louisburg, 1758. Grenadier Company at battle of Quebec, 1759. Took part in capture of St. John's, Newfoundland, 1762. To Ireland, 1765; America, 1775. Fought at Brooklyn, 1776 and operations around New York. To England, 1778; Ireland, 1784; the West Indies, 1786; England, 1794; West Indies, 1795; England, 1801; Ireland, 1802. Took part in expedition to South America,

1st Battalion, The Sherwood Foresters marching through Valetta, Malta prior to embarkation to South Africa 21st November, 1899.

1806 and fought at Buenos Ayres, 1807. Returned to Ireland same year. Fought in Peninsular War, 1808-14. Present at battles of Rolica and Vimiera, 1808; Talavera, 1809; Busaco, 1810; Fuentes D`Onor, 1811; Ciudad Rodrigo, Badajoz and Salamanca, 1812; Vittoria, the Pyrenees, Nivelle and the Nive, 1813; Orthes and Toulouse, 1814. Left France for Ireland, 1814. *A 2nd Battalion, 45th Regiment formed in Nottinghamshire, 1804 and disbanded, 1814.* To Ceylon, 1819; India then Burma, 1825. Took part in First Burma War gaining battle honour `Ava.` To India, 1832; England, 1837; Ireland, 1840; South Africa, 1843. Took part in Kaffir Wars, 1846-47 and 1851-53. To England, 1859. *A Reserve Battalion, 45th Regiment formed in Ireland, 1842. To Gibraltar, 1844; South America, 1845; South Africa, 1846. Took part in Kaffir operations and First Boar War. Present at Boomplaats August, 1848. Merged into 1st Battalion, 1850.* To Ireland, 1862; India, 1864. Took part in Abyssinia campaign of 1868 and present at capture of Magdala. Returned to India same year. To Burma, 1872; India, 1875; England, 1878. Became 1st Battalion, The Sherwood Foresters (Derbyshire) Regiment, 1881.

95th Regiment

Formed at Winchester, 1823. To Malta, 1824; the Ionian Islands, 1830; Ireland, 1834; Ceylon, 1838; Hong Kong, 1847; England, 1850; the

Crimea, 1854. Fought in battles of Alma, Balaclava, Inkerman and Sevastopol. To England, then Ireland, 1856; India, 1857. Took part in operations in Central India, 1858 and present at Kotah-ki-Serai, capture of Gwalior, Powrie, Beejapore and Koondrye. Private Bernard McQuirt awarded Victoria Cross for gallantry at Rowa on 6th January. To England, 1870; Ireland, 1876; England, 1880. Became 2nd Battalion, The Sherwood Foresters (Derbyshire) Regiment, 1881.

1st Battalion

Formed from the 45th Regiment stationed in England, 1881. To Ireland, 1882; England, 1889; Ireland, 1894; Malta, 1898; South Africa, 1899. Fought at Johannesburg and Diamond Hill, 1900; Vlakfontein and Moediwill, 1901. Corporal H.C. Beet awarded Victoria Cross while serving with Mounted Infantry at Wakkerstroom 22nd April, 1900 and Private W. Bees at Moediwill 30th September, 1901. To Hong Kong, 1902; Singapore, 1904; India, 1906; England, 1914. Crossed to France in November and fought at Neuve Chapelle. Victoria Cross awarded to Private J. Rivers. Took part in fighting at Aubers Ridge, 1915 - Victoria Cross awarded to Corporal J. Upton for gallantry near Rouges Bancs 9th May; on the Somme, 1916; Ypres, 1917; Somme and Arras, 1918. To England, 1919; Ireland, 1920; England, 1922; Ireland, 1925; England, 1928; West Indies, 1935; Palestine, 1939. During Second World War served in Palestine and Egypt, 1939-42. Captured at Tobruk. Reconstructed in England 1943. To Germany, 1945; England then Egypt, 1952; Derna, North Africa, 1953; England then Germany, 1955. Served in Malaya, 1958 and later in Singapore before returning to England, 1961. Moved to Cyprus during Christmas, 1963 then to Germany, 1964; England, 1970. Amalgamated with 1st Battalion, The Worcestershire Regiment to form 1st Battalion, The Worcestershire and Sherwood Foresters Regiment (29th/45th Foot), 1970.

2nd Battalion

Formed from the 95th Regiment stationed in England, 1881. To Gibraltar January, 1882 and from there took part in expedition to Egypt. To India October, 1882. Took part in Sikkim expedition of 1888 and present at

Post card published during the First World War illustrating uniforms worn (left to right) - 95th Regiment, 1823; Sherwood Foresters, present day; 45th Regiment, 1741. Art work by Ernest Ibbetson.

capture of Fort Lingtu and the fighting at Gnathong Camp. In Tirah campaign, 1897-98 fought at Dargai. Lieutenant Henry Singleton Pennell awarded Victoria Cross. To Aden, 1898; Malta, 1899. Mounted Infantry Company served in South Africa. To England, 1902. During First World War fought on the Aisne and at Armentières, 1914; Hooge, 1915; on the Somme, 1916; Cambrai, 1917; battles of the Somme, Lys, Hindenburg Line and the Selle, 1918. Left Germany for England, 1919. Served in Egypt and Constantinople then to India, 1922. Stationed in the Sudan and Cyprus, 1934-36 then to Guernsey. To England, 1938. Fought in France and Belgium, 1939-40; North Africa, 1943; Italy, 1943-45. Stationed in Palestine and Syria, 1945-47 then to England. Amalgamated with 1st Battalion in Germany, 1948. Re-formed, 1952 and to Germany. To England and disbanded, 1955.

Badges

A Maltese Cross - the badge of the 95th Regiment. Within an oak-leaf wreath - a Stag lodged - introduced in 1881, the stag from the Arms of Derby, the wreath said to represent Sherwood Forest. The Unified Red and White Rose - introduced in 1881. Arms of the City of Nottingham - worn prior to 1881 by the 45th Regiment.

Uniform

45th Regiment - dark green, later Lincoln green facings. 95th Regiment - Yellow. Sherwood Foresters - white replaced by Lincoln green in 1913.

Nicknames

`The Old Stubborns` - from the fighting of the 45th at Talavera in 1809.

Above - Cap badge - The Sherwood Foresters. The title scroll dates this pattern after 1902.

Right - Booklet published in the 1920s illustrating badge and uniforms for 45th Regiment c1808 (left) and Sherwood Foresters c1923.

The Loyal Regiment
(North Lancashire)

Titles

1741-1751	Known by name of Colonel.	1793-1832	81st Regiment of Foot.
1751-1782	47th Regiment of Foot.	1832-1881	81st (Loyal Lincoln
1782-1881	47th (Lancashire) Regiment		Volunteers) Regiment of Foot.

1881-1920   The Loyal North Lancashire Regiment.
1920-1970   The Loyal Regiment (North Lancashire).

47th Regiment

Formed in Scotland, 1741. Present at battle of Prestonpans, 1745. To England, 1746; Ireland, 1748; Nova Scotia, 1750. Fought at Louisburg, 1758; Quebec, 1759 and Sainte Foy, 1760. To Ireland, 1763; America, 1773. During American War of Independence present at Concord, Lexington and Bunker Hill, 1775. Took part in Saratoga expedition, 1777 and taken prisoner. To England, 1781; Ireland, 1783; Nova Scotia, 1790; West Indies, 1791; England, 1803; Ireland, 1804; Cape of Good Hope, 1806. Took part in expedition to South America, 1807 and present during operations at Monte Video and Buenos Aires. Returned to the Cape then to India, 1808. Flank companies took part in 1809 Persian Gulf operations against Arab pirates. *A 2nd Battalion, 47th Regiment formed, 1803. To*

Above - Cap badge - The Loyal Regiment (North Lancashire).

Left - Officers silver and gilt waist-belt clasp - The Loyal North Lancashire Regiment.

Below - Collar badge - The Loyal Regiment (North Lancashire).

Right - Part of `B` Company, 2nd Battalion, The Loyal North Lancashire Regiment, 1897.

Ireland, 1804; England, 1807; Gibraltar, 1809. During Peninsular War fought at Tarifa, Barrosa, Vittoria, San Sebastian, the Nive and Bayonne. Left France for England, 1814 and disbanded, 1815. Took part in Pindari War, 1817-19 and expedition to the Persian Gulf, 1819-20. During First Burma War of 1824-26 present at Donobya and Napadi and gained battle honour `Ava.` To England, 1829; Ireland, 1832; Gibraltar, 1833; Malta, 1837; West Indies, 1841; England, 1843; Ireland, 1846; Ionian Island, 1850; Malta, 1853; the Crimea, 1854. Fought at the Alma, Inkerman and Sevastopol. To Malta, 1856; Gibraltar then England, 1857; Ireland then Canada, 1861. To Nova Scotia, 1866 and present during Fenian operations. To Barbados, 1868; Ireland, 1870; England, 1872; Jersey then Ireland, 1877. Became 1st Battalion, The Loyal North Lancashire Regiment, 1881.

81st Regiment

Formed in Lincoln, 1793. To Ireland then St. Domingo, 1794; England then Guernsey, 1797; Cape Colony, 1798; England, 1802; Jersey then England, 1803; Malta, 1805; Sicily, 1806. Took part in war in Italy and present at Maida, 1806 and expedition to Naples, 1809. To Spain, 1812. Served in eastern Spain during Peninsular War. To Canada, 1814; England then France, 1815. *A 2nd Battalion, 81st Regiment formed, 1803. To Ireland, 1804; Spain, 1808. Took part in retreat to Corunna then returned to England. Took part Walcheren campaign of 1809. To Jersey, 1811; Holland then Belgium, 1814; England and disbanded, 1816.* To Ireland, 1817; Nova Scotia, 1822; New Brunswick, 1826; West Indies, 1829; England, 1831; Ireland, 1832; Gibraltar, 1836; West Indies, 1839; Canada, 1843; England, 1847; Ireland, 1850; India, 1853. Served on North West Frontier during Indian Mutiny. To England, 1865; Ireland, 1867; Gibraltar, 1870; India, 1874. Took part in Afghan War of 1878-79 and present at All Masjid. Became 2nd Battalion, The Loyal North Lancashire Regiment, 1881.

1st Battalion

Formed from the 47th Regiment stationed in Ireland, 1881. To England then Gibraltar, 1882; India, 1884; Ceylon, 1896; South Africa, 1899. Took part in Defence of Kimberley and present at Graspen and Modder River. To England, 1902; Ireland, 1904; England, 1910. During First World War took part in battles of Mons, the Marne and Ypres, 1914; Givenchy, Aubers Ridge and Loos, 1915; the Somme,1916; operations on the Flanders coast and Ypres, 1917; The Lys, Arras, Hindenburg Line, the Selle and the Sambre, 1918. To Malta, 1919; Ireland, 1920; Constantinople, 1922; North China, 1923; India, 1925; Palestine, 1936; England, 1937. During Second World War fought in France and Belgium, 1939-40; North Africa and Pantelleria, 1943; Italy, 1943-45; Palestine and Syria, 1945. Left Palestine for Eritrea, 1947. Served in Somaliland, 1948; Cyprus, 1949; Egypt, 1950; Triest, 1953; Malaya, 1957-59; Germany, 1960-62; Cyprus and Swaziland, 1963; Hong Kong and New Zealand, 1964; Cyprus, 1965; Malta, 1966-68; Canada, 1969. Amalgamated with 1st Battalion, The Lancashire Regiment (Prince of Wales`s Volunteers) to form 1st Battalion, The Queen`s Lancashire Regiment, 1970.

2nd Battalion

Formed from the 81st Regiment stationed in India, 1881. To England, 1883; Jersey, 1887; Ireland, 1890; England, 1895; Malta, 1899; Crete, 1901; Gibraltar, 1902; South Africa, 1904; Mauritius, 1907; India, 1910. During First World War served in East Africa, 1914-17 Egypt and Palestine, 1917-18. Moved to France and took part in battles of the Marne and final advance into Flanders. Left Germany for Ireland, 1921. To England, 1922; Shanghai, 1936; Malaya, 1938. Captured by Japanese, 1942. Re-formed in England, 1943 and later fought in Italy. Amalgamated with 1st Battalion, 1949.

Badges

The Royal Crest - an old badge of the 47th Regiment. The Red Rose of Lancaster - an old badge of the 47th Regiment. The Arms of the City of Lincoln - from the 81st Regiment.

Uniform

47th Regiment - white facings. 81st Regiment - buff. Loyal North Lancashire Regiment - white.

Nicknames

`The Cauliflowers` - from the white facings of the 47th Regiment. `Wolfe`s Own` - from service of the 47th with General Wolfe in Canada. `The Lancashire Lads.`

Drummer - The Loyal North Lancashire Regiment - overseas service dress.

The Northamptonshire Regiment

Titles

1741-1751	Known by name of Colonel.	1755-1757	60th Regiment of Foot.
1751-1782	48th Regiment of Foot.	1757-1782	58th Regiment of Foot.
1782-1881	48th (Northamptonshire) Regiment of Foot.	1782-1881	58th (Rutlandshire) Regiment of Foot.

1881-1960   The Northamptonshire Regiment.

48th Regiment

Raised in Norwich by the Hon. James Cholmondley, 1741. To Flanders, 1744. Recalled to England, 1745 and then to Scotland. Fought at Falkirk and Culloden, 1746. Returned to Flanders and present at Lauffeld July, 1747. To Ireland, 1748; America, 1755. Fought at Monongahela in July. Present at capture of Louisburg, 1758; Quebec, 1759; fighting at Sainte Foy and capture of Montreal, 1760. To the West Indies, 1761. Fought on Martinique January-February, 1762 then to Cuba. Took part in capture of

158

Fort Moro and fighting around Havannah. To England then Ireland, 1763; West Indies, 1773; England, 1780; Ireland, 1783; West Indies, 1788; England, 1794; West Indies, 1796. Took part in capture of St. Lucia. To England, 1797; Gibraltar, 1799; Minorca then Malta, 1800; England, 1802; Gibraltar, 1805. A 2nd Battalion, 48th Regiment formed in Manchester, 1803 and to Ireland, 1804. Both battalions fought in the Peninsular War - the Douro and Talavera, 1809; Busaco, 1810; Albuhera, 1811 (battalions merged after heavy casualties); Badajoz and Salamanca, 1812; Vittoria, Pyrenees operations and Nivelle, 1813; Orthez and Toulouse, 1814. Left France for Ireland, 1814 and 2nd Battalion disbanded. To Australia, 1817; India, 1824. Took part in Coorg campaign of 1834. To England, 1834; Ireland, 1837; Gibraltar, 1838; Jamaica, 1844; Ireland, 1847; Wales, 1852; Corfu, 1853; the Crimea, 1855. Present during siege of Sevastopol. To Malta, 1856; Gibraltar, 1857; India, 1858; England, 1865; Ireland, 1866; Malta, 1867; India, 1872; Ireland, 1880. Became 1st Battalion, The Northamptonshire Regiment, 1881.

58th Regiment

Raised as 60th Regiment, 1755. Re-numbered as 58th and to America, 1757. Took part in capture of Louisburg, 1758 and Quebec, 1759. Present at Sainte Foy and capture of Montreal, 1760. To Cuba, 1762 (eight companies captured at sea by the French) and took part in operations around

Above - Collar badge -
The Northamptonshire Regiment.

Left - Colonel Charles Donellan - 1st Battalion, 48th Regiment who was mortally wounded at Talavera in July, 1809. Engraving by Paul Hardy.

Machine gun section - 1st Battalion, The Northamptonshire Regiment, Poona, 1908.

Havannah. To England, 1762; Ireland, 1763; Gibraltar, 1770. Present during siege of 1779-83. To England, 1784; Ireland, 1787; West Indies, 1793. Took part in capture of Martinique, 1794. To England, 1795; Jersey, 1797; England then Gibraltar, 1798. Took part in capture of Minorca in November. To Malta, 1800; Egypt, 1801. Took part in landing at Aboukir Bay and fighting at Roman Camp; Alexandria and Rahmanieh. To Ireland, 1802; Jersey, 1803; England then via Gibraltar and Malta to Sicily, 1805. Took part in campaign in Italy - battle of Maida, 1806, siege of Scylla, 1808 and capture of Ischia, 1809. Left Sicily for Spain, 1812. fought at Castalla and Tarragona, 1813. Left France for Canada, 1814. Present at Plattsburg in September. *A 2nd Battalion, 58th Regiment formed in Ireland, 1803 and sent to Jersey. To England then Portugal, 1809. Fought at Salamanca and Burgos, 1812; Vittoria, Pyrenees operations and Nivelle, 1813 and Orthez, 1814. To England, 1814 and disbanded, 1815.* To Belgium then Ireland, 1815; Jamaica, 1816; England, 1822; Ireland, 1824; England, 1826; Ceylon, 1828; England, 1839; Ireland, 1841; England, 1842. Began sailing in detachments with prison ships to Australia, 1843. To New Zealand, 1845. Fought in First Maori War, 1845-47 - present at Ohaiawai, Ruapekapeka and Boulcott's Farm. To England, 1859; Ireland, 1862; India, 1864; England, 1874; South Africa, 1879. Took part in Zulu War and present at Ulundi. In First Boer War, 1880-81 present at Laing's Nek (Lieutenant A.R. Hill awarded Victoria Cross), Wakkerstroom (Private J. Osborne awarded Victoria Cross), Ingogo and Majuba Hill. Became 2nd Battalion, The Northamptonshire Regiment, 1881.

1st Battalion

Formed from the 48th Regiment stationed in Ireland, 1881. To England, 1884; India, 1892. Took part in Tirah campaign of 1897 and present at Saran Sar. To Aden, 1910; England, 1911. Crossed to France and took part in battles of Mons, the Marne, Aisne and Ypres, 1914; Aubers Ridge and Loos, 1915; the Somme, 1916; Ypres, 1917; the Lys, Arras, Hindenburg Line, the Selle and Sambre, 1918. Left Germany for England, 1919 then to Ireland. To England, 1922; China, 1927. Formed part of Shanghai Defence Force. To Malta then Palestine, 1929; Egypt, 1931; Iraq, 1932. Returned to Egypt same year then to India. Served on North West Frontier, 1936-37 taking part in Waziristan operations. Left India for Ceylon, 1942, returning, 1943. fought in Burma, 1945. Returned to England, 1946. Later served in Austria, Germany, Hong Kong and Aden then amalgamated with 1st Battalion, The Royal Lincolnshire Regiment to form The 2nd East Anglian Regiment (Duchess of Gloucester's Own Royal Lincolnshire and Northamptonshire), 1960.

2nd Battalion

Formed from the 58th Regiment stationed in South Africa, 1881. To Hong Kong, 1885; Singapore, 1889; England, 1892; Jersey, 1895; England, 1897; South Africa, 1899. Present at Belmont, Graspan, Modder River, Magersfontein and relief of Ladysmith. To England, 1904; Malta, 1911; Egypt, 1914. To England, crossed to France and fought at Neuve Chapelle, 1914-15; Aubers Ridge, 1915; on the Somme, 1916; Ypres and Passchendaele, 1917; on the Somme, Villers Bretonneux; the Aisne and

Officers - 2nd Battalion, The Northamptonshire Regiment just before leaving for South Africa in 1899. Lieutenant C.W. Barton (standing second from left) wounded, Captain L.G. Freeland (standing first on right) wounded.

Above - Heroes of the First Boer War, 1880-81. Left to right - Colour Sergeant Bridgestock (Distinguished Conduct Medal), Private Osborne (Victoria Cross), Private Godfrey (Distinguished Conduct Medal), 58th Regiment.

Below - Part of 1st Battalion, The Northamptonshire Regiment after return from Iraq expedition, 1932. The battalion was the first to be transported complete by aeroplane.

Arras, 1918. Returned to England then to India, 1919. To the Sudan, 1926; England, 1928; Northern Ireland, 1936. During Second World War served in France and Belgium, 1939-40; Madagascar, India, Iraq and Persia, 1942; Egypt, Syria, Sicily, 1943; Italy, 1943-44; Egypt, Palestine and Syria, 1944; Italy and North West Europe, 1945. Amalgamated with 1st Battalion, 1948.

Badges

The Castle, Key and Motto of Gibraltar - awarded to the 58th Regiment for its service during siege of 1779-83. The Sphinx superscribed `Egypt` - awarded to the 58th Regiment for service during 1801. The Cross of St. George - from the Northamptonshire Militia and A Horseshoe - the old badge of the Rutland Militia. both taken into use, 1881.

Uniform

48th Regiment - buff facings, 58th Regiment - black, The Northamptonshire Regiment - white, 1881-1926 then buff.

Nicknames

`The Cobblers` - in reference to the chief industry (shoe making) in Northampton `The Steelbacks` - the 58th Regiment acquired the reputation of receiving punishment (flogging) often and well. `The Black Cuffs` - from the facings of the 58th Regiment.

Top - Other ranks cap badge. Officers had a special badge comprising the Dragon within a crowned circle of rope.

Bottom - Grenadier - 49th Regiment, 1763.

The Royal Berkshire Regiment (Princess Charlotte of Wales`s)

Titles

1743-1751	Known by name of Colonel.
1751-1782	49th Regiment of Foot.
1782-1816	49th (Hertfordshire) Regiment of Foot.
1816-1881	49th (Princess Charlotte of Wales`s or Hertfordshire) Regiment of Foot.

1756-1758	2nd Battalion, 19th Regiment of Foot.
1758-1782	66th Regiment of Foot.
1782-1881	66th (Berkshire) Regiment of Foot.

1881-1885   Princess Charlotte of Wales`s (Berkshire Regiment).

1885-1920   Princes Charlotte of Wales`s (Royal Berkshire Regiment).

1920-1959   The Royal Berkshire Regiment (Princess Charlotte of Wales`s)

49th Regiment

Raised by Edward Trelawny, Governor of Jamaica from independent companies in 1743. These companies had been in existence for some years and were known as the `Jamaica Volunteers.` To Ireland, 1764; America, 1775. Took part in operations around New York, present at Brooklyn and White Plains, 1776; Brandywine, 1777. To the West Indies, 1778 and took part in capture of St. Lucia in December. To Ireland, 1780; Barbados, 1788; Jamaica, 1792; St. Domingo, 1793. Fought at Tiburon and Acul, 1794. To England, 1796. Flank companies took part in May, 1798 expedition to Ostend. To North Holland for Helder campaign of 1799. Present at Egmont-op-Zee. To Jersey, 1800; England, 1801 and took part in expedition to Copenhagen. To Canada, 1802. Fought at Queenstown, 1812; Stoney Creek and Crystlers Farm, 1813. *A 2nd Battalion, 49th Regiment formed, 1813 and disbanded, 1814.* To England, 1815; Ireland, 1816; South Africa, 1823; India, 1828. Took part in First China War, 1840-42. Returned to India and then to England, 1843. To Ireland, 1845; Corfu, 1851; Malta, 1853; the Crimea, 1854. Gained battle honours - `Alma`, `Inkerman` and `Sevastopol.` Also present during fighting at the Redan. Victoria Crosses awarded to Brevet-Major J.A. Conolly, Corporal J. Owens and Sergeant G. Walters. To England, 1856; Barbados, 1857; England, 1860; Ireland, 1864; India, 1865; England, 1875; Gibraltar, 1881. Became 1st Battalion, The Princess Charlotte of Wales`s (Berkshire Regiment).

66th Regiment

Raised in 1756 as 2nd Battalion, 19th Regiment (see Green Howards) at Morpeth, Northumberland. Became 66th Regiment, 1758. To Ireland, 1763; Jamaica, 1764; England, 1773; Ireland, 1775; St. Vincent, 1785; Gibraltar, 1793; St. Domingo, 1795; Jamaica, 1798; Canada, 1799; England, 1802; Ceylon, 1804; India, 1814. Took part in war in Nepal, 1815-16. To St. Helena, 1817. *A 2nd Battalion, 66th Regiment formed at Winchester, 1803 and to Ireland, 1804. Fought in Peninsular War and present at the crossing of the Douro and Talavera, 1809; Albuhera, 1811. After heavy casualties merged with 2/31st Regiment as 1st Provisional Battalion and present at Vittoria, the Pyrenees operations, Nivelle, the Nive, 1913 and Orthez, 1814. As 2nd Battalion, 66th Regiment returned to England, 1814 and to St. Helena, 1816. Merged into 1st Battalion, 1817.* To England, 1821; Ireland, 1823; Canada, 1827; England, 1840; Ireland, 1843; Gibraltar, 1845; West Indies, 1848; Canada, 1851; England then Gibraltar, 1854; England, 1856; India, 1857; England, 1865; Channel

Above - Officers` shoulder-belt plate - 49th Regiment, 1820-42.

Right - Lieutenant J.A. Conolly who won the Victoria Cross with the 49th Regiment at Shell Hill - 26th October, 1854.

164

Islands, 1867; Ireland, 1868; India, 1870; Afghanistan, 1880. Took part in Second Afghan War and present at Maiwand 27th July. Casualties - 285 killed, 32 wounded. Returned to India in October. To England, 1881. Became 2nd Battalion, The Princess Charlotte of Wales's (Berkshire Regiment).

1st Battalion

Formed from the 49th Regiment stationed at Gibraltar, 1881. To Malta and from there took part in the Egyptian campaign of 1882. To Gibraltar, 1883; Egypt, 1884. Took part in Suakin expedition of 1885 and present at battles of Hashin and Tofrek in March. Fought at Ginnis in December. `Royal` title granted in recognition of distinguished service at Tofrek. To Malta and Cyprus, 1886; Bermuda, 1893; Canada, 1895; West Indies, 1897; England, 1898; Gibraltar, 1900; England, 1902; Ireland, 1904; England, 1910. During First World War took part in battles of Mons, the Marne, Aisne and Ypres, 1914; Cuinchy, Festubert and Loos, 1915; the Somme, 1916; Arras and Cambrai, 1917; the Somme, Hindenburg Line and the Selle, 1918. Left Germany for England, 1919 and then to Mesopotamia. Served in North-West Persia to 1921 then to India. Took part in Waziristan campaign and North-West Frontier operations. To the Sudan, 1934; England, 1935. During Second World War fought in France and Belgium, 1939-40. Served in India and Burma, 1942-46 then to England. Placed into suspended animation, 1947. Amalgamated with 2nd Battalion, 1949. Served in Cyprus and Egypt, 1951; Germany, 1953-56; Cyprus, 1956-59. Amalgamated with 1st Battalion, The Wiltshire Regiment (Duke of Edinburgh's) to form 1st Battalion, The Duke of Edinburgh's Royal Regiment (Berkshire and Wiltshire), 1959.

2nd Battalion

Formed from the 66th Regiment stationed in England, 1881. To Ireland, 1885; England, 1897; South Africa, 1898. Present at Colesberg. Private W. House awarded Victoria Cross for gallantry at Mosilikatse Nek August,

Above - Officers - The Royal Berkshire Regiment, `somewhere in France` during the First World War. Note helmet badges. (Paul Reed).

Left - Painting by Frank Fellar commemorating the stand of the last eleven at Maiwand, 27th July, 1880. Among the survivors of the 66th Regiment can be seen a small dog. `Bobbie` was wounded in the action and later decorated with the Afghan Medal by Queen Victoria in 1881.

Above - Officer's shoulder-belt plate - 49th Regiment, 1843-55.

Below - The Adjutant (Lieutenant David Blake Maurice), Warrant Officers and N.C.Os - 1st Battalion, The Royal Berkshire Regiment - Canada c1896. Note winter clothing. The battalion had recently arrived from Bermuda and the temperature at time of photograph was noted as several degrees below zero.

1900. To Egypt, 1902; India, 1906; England, 1914. Crossed to France and fought at Neuve Chapelle; on the Somme, 1916; at Ypres and Passchendale, 1917; Somme and Arras, 1918. Left Germany for England, 1919. One company served in North Russia, 1919. To Ireland, 1920; England, 1923; Germany, 1926; England, 1928; Palestine, 1934; Egypt, 1936; India, 1937; Burma, 1944; England, 1948. Amalgamated with 1st Battalion, 1949.

Badges

The Dragon of China - awarded to the 49th Regiment for service in the China War of 1840-42. A Naval Crown and coiled rope - both in commemoration of the 49th Regiment's service as marines during the battle of Copenhagen 2nd April, 1801, the latter forming part of the officers' cap badge. A Stag under an oak tree - introduced in 1881 and formally the badge of the Berkshire Militia.

Uniform

49th Regiment - green facings. 66th Regiment - at first described as yellowish green, later as various shades of green. Royal Berkshire Regiment - white facings from 1881 changing to blue after 1885.

Nicknames

The Biscuit Boys - the depot of the regiment was at Reading - also the home of Huntly and Palmer's biscuit factory.

The Queen's Own Royal West Kent Regiment

Titles

1755-1757	52nd Regiment of Foot.	1824-1826	97th Regiment of Foot.
1757-1782	50th Regiment of Foot.	1826-1881	97th (Earl of Ulster's) Regiment of Foot.
1782-1827	50th (West Kent) Regiment of Foot.		
1827-1831	50th (The Duke of Clarence's) Regiment of Foot.		
1831-1881	50th (Queen's Own) Regiment of Foot.		

1881-1920 The Queen's Own (Royal West Kent Regiment).
1920-1921 The Royal West Kent Regiment (Queen's Own).
1921-1961 The Queen's Own Royal West Kent Regiment.

50th Regiment

Formed, 1755. As marines took part in expedition to Rocheefort, 1757. To Germany, 1760. During Seven Years War fought at Corbach and Warbourg, 1760; Velinghausen, 1761 and Wilhelmsthal, 1762. Left Holland for Ireland, 1763. To Jamaica, 1772; North America then England,

1776. Took part in attack on French fleet of Ushant, 1778. To Ireland, 1783; Gibraltar, 1784. Took part in operations on Corsica, 1794. To Elba, 1796; Gibraltar then Portugal, 1797; Minorca, 1799. Took part in Egyptian campaign of 1801. Present during operations at Mandora, Alexandria and Rhamanieh. To Ireland, 1802; England, 1807. Took part in 1807 expedition to Copenhagen, then to Gibraltar. *A 2nd Battalion, 50th Regiment formed in 1804 and disbanded, 1807.* Took part in expedition to Cadiz, 1808 and then to Portugal. Present at Vimiero in August and retreat to Corunna. To England, 1809 and took part in Walcheren expedition. To Portugal, 1810. Fought at Fuentes d`Onor and Arroyo Dos Molinos, 1811; Almaraz, 1812; Victoria, Pyrenees operations and the Nive, 1813; Orthez and Aire, 1814. To Ireland, 1814; Jamaica, 1819; England, 1826; Ireland, 1830; England, 1833. Sailed in detachments (guarding convicts) to Australia, 1834-35. To India, 1841. Took part in Gwalior campaign of 1843 and present at Punniar. During First Sikh War fought at Moodkee and Ferozeshah, 1845; Aliwal and Sobraon, 1846. To England, 1848; Ireland, 1854. Left Ireland same year and stationed in Malta and Gallipoli until moving to the Crimea. Gained battle honours `Alma`, `Inkerman` and `Sevastapol.` To England then Ireland, 1856; Ceylon, 1857; New Zealand, 1863. Took part in Second Maori War and present at Rangiawhia, 1864. To Australia, 1866; England, 1869; Ireland, 1874; Scotland, 1878; England, 1880. Became 1st Battalion, The Queen`s Own (Royal West Kent Regiment), 1881.

Above - Private - 50th Regiment c1740.

Right - Bugler - 97th Regiment, Crimea. Engraving after painting by F.F. Shields, 1857.

Left - Signallers - 2nd Battalion, The Queen's Own (Royal West Kent Regiment) c1896. Note lime-light lanterns powered from inflated oxygen bags for use at night.

Below - Cap badge - The Queen's Own Royal West Kent Regiment.

97th Regiment

Formed at Winchester, 1824. To Ceylon, 1825; Ireland, 1836; England, 1837; Ireland, 1839; England, 1840; Ionian Islands, 1841; Malta, 1847. *A Reserve Battalion, 97th Regiment formed, 1845 and disbanded, 1851.* To Nova Scotia, 1848; England, 1853; the Crimea, 1855. Fought at the Redan and Sevastopol. Captain Charles Lumley and Sergeant J. Coleman awarded Victoria Cross. To England, 1856; India, 1857. During Indian Mutiny present at capture of Fort Nusrutpore, operations at Chanda, Ummeerpore, Sultanpore and siege and capture of Lucknow. To England, 1867; Ireland, 1871; Jamaica, 1873; Bermuda, 1875; Nova Scotia, 1877; Gibraltar then South Africa, 1880. Became 2nd Battalion, The Queen's Own (Royal West Kent Regiment), 1881.

1st Battalion

Formed from the 50th Regiment stationed in England, 1881. To Egypt, 1882. Present at Nefisha and Tel-el-Kebir. Part of regiment stationed in Cyprus, 1882-1884. Took part in Nile expedition, 1884-85 and with Sudan Frontier Force fought at Ginnis. To Gibraltar, 1886; Malta, 1889; India, 1892. Took part in Punjab Frontier campaign, 1897-98 serving with Malakand and Buner Field Forces. Present during action at Agrah and Ghat. To Burma then Aden, 1899. Took part in Ad Daraijah expedition, 1901. To Malta then England, 1902; Malta, 1904; England, 1906; Ireland, 1911. During First World War took part in battles of Mons, Le Cateau, the Marne, Aisne and Ypres, 1914; Ypres, 1915; the Somme, 1916; Arras and Ypres, 1917. Moved to Italian Front November, 1917. Returned to France, 1918 and took part in battles of the Lys, Somme, Hindenburg Line and the Selle, 1918. To England then India, 1919; England, 1938. Fought in France and Belgium, 1939-40; North-West Africa and Egypt, 1942-44; Italy, 1944; Greece, 1944-45. Left Greece for Egypt, 1946. To England, 1947. Served in Malaya, 1951-54; Germany, 1954-55; Egypt, 1956; Cyprus, 1957-59. Amalgamated with 1st Battalion, The Buffs (Royal East Kent Regiment) to form 1st Battalion, The Queen's Own Buffs, The Royal Kent Regiment, 1961.

Colours - 1st Battalion, The Queen's Royal West Kent Regiment, 1930s.

2nd Battalion

Formed from the 97th Regiment stationed in South Africa. Served in Natal Field Force. To Ireland, 1882; England, 1885; Ireland, 1893; England, 1898; Egypt, 1899; England then South Africa, 1900. Took part in operations at Wittebergen, Cape Colony and Transvaal. To Ceylon, 1902; China and Hong Kong, 1904; Singapore, 1906; India, 1908. To Mesopotamia, 1915. Captured at Kut al Amara, 1916. To India then England, 1919; Germany, 1920. Served in Upper Silesia, 1921. To England then Ireland, 1921; England, 1924; Guernsey, 1927; England, 1930; Palestine, 1937; Malta, 1939. During Second World War remained in Malta until 1943 then to Aegean Sea. Captured at Leros. Re-formed from 7th Battalion in England, 1944. To Germany, 1945; England, 1947. Amalgamated with 1st Battalion, 1948.

Badges

The Royal Crest - an old badge of the 50th Regiment. The White Horse of Kent and motto 'Invicta' - adopted in 1881 from the West Kent Militia. The Sphinx superscribed 'Egypt' - commemorates serve of the 50th Regiment in 1801. Duke of Clarence's Cypher and Coronet - authorized in 1828.

Uniform

50th Regiment - black facings until 1831 then blue. 97th Regiment - sky-blue facings. The Queen's Royal West Kent Regiment - blue facings.

Nicknames

'The Dirty Half-Hundred' - At Vimiera in 1808, the 50th fought with blackened faces - a combination of smoke and the dye from their black facings. 'The Blind Half-Hundred' - many of the 50th Regiment suffered from ophthalmia while in Egypt, 1801. 'The Celestials' - from the sky-blue facings of the 97th Regiment.

Below - Cap badge - The King`s Own Yorkshire Light Infantry.

Left - 51st Regiment storming Meeah Toon`s Stockade, Burma 1853. Engraving from Illustrated London News of 26th November, 1853.

The King`s Own Yorkshire Light Infantry

Titles

1755-1757	53rd Regiment of Foot.	1839-1861	2nd Madras European Light Infantry Regiment.
1757-1782	51st Regiment of Foot.		
1782-1809	51st (2nd Yorkshire, West Riding) Regiment of Foot.	1861-1881	105th (Madras Light Infantry) Regiment.
1809-1821	51st Light Infantry (2nd Yorkshire, West Riding) .		
1821-1881	51st King`s Own Light Infantry (2nd Yorkshire, West Riding).		

1881-1887 The King`s Own Light Infantry (South Yorkshire Regiment).
1887-1920 The King`s Own (Yorkshire Light Infantry).
1920-1968 The King`s Own Yorkshire Light Infantry.

171

Officers and Sergeants - Depot, 51st Regiment, Dover, 1867. Captain E.B. Burnaby (seated centre) later commanded 1st Battalion in Burma - May-July, 1887.

51st Regiment

Raised as 53rd Regiment by Colonel Robert Napier at Leeds, 1755. Re-numbered 51st Regiment, 1757. Took part in operations along French coast same year. To Germany, 1758. Gained first battle honour at Minden in August, 1759. Also present at Corbach, Warburg and Kloster Kampen, 1760; Vellinghausen, 1761 and Wilhelmstahl, 1762. To England then Ireland, 1763; England, 1770; Minorca, 1771. Present during siege of 1781-82. To England, 1782; Ireland, 1783; Gibraltar, 1792. Took part in Corsica expedition, 1794-96. To Elba, 1796; Portugal, 1797; India via South Africa, 1798; Ceylon, 1800. Took part in Kandian War of 1803. To England, 1807; Spain, 1808. Present during fighting around Corunna. Returned to England January, 1809 and took part in Walcheren expedition same year. To Portugal, 1811 and fought at Fuentes d` Onor and Badajoz, 1811; Ciudad Rodrigo, Salamanca and Burgos, 1812; Vittoria, Pyrenees operations and Nivelle, 1813; Orthes, 1814. To England, 1814; Belgium, 1815. Fought at Waterloo. To England, 1816; the Ionian Islands, 1821; Ireland, 1834; England, 1837. Accompanied prison ships to Australia from 1837. Left Australia for India, 1846. To Burma, 1852 taking part in Second Burma War and gaining battle honour ``Pegu`.` To India then England, 1854; Malta, 1855; England then Ireland, 1856; India, 1857. Took part in Ambela expedition of 1863. To England, 1867; Ireland, 1870; India, 1872. Took part in Jawaki operations, 1877-78 and in Second Afghan War present at Ali Musjid, 1878 and Khyber Pass operations, 1879-80. Became 1st Battalion, The King`s Own Light Infantry (South Yorkshire Regiment), 1881.

105th Regiment

Formed in India by the Honourable East India Company in 1839 and designated 2nd Madras European Light Infantry Regiment. To Burma, 1856; India, 1857. Became part of British Army, 1861 and designated 105th Regiment. To Aden, 1872; England, 1874; Channel Islands, 1878; Ireland, 1879. Became 2nd Battalion, The King's Own Light Infantry (South Yorkshire Regiment), 1881.

1st Battalion

Formed from the 51st Regiment stationed in India, 1881. To Burma and served in Upper Burma Field Force, 1886-87. To England, 1887; Channel Islands, 1891; Ireland, 1893; England then Ireland, 1899; England, 1902; Gibraltar, 1905; South Africa, 1906; Hong Kong, 1910; Singapore, 1913; England, 1914. Crossed to France in 1915 and fought at Ypres and Loos. Transferred to Macedonian Front in October. Returned to France, 1918 and fought in battles of the Hindenburg Line, Selle and Sambre. Left England for India, 1919. Took part in Mesopotamia campaign, 1920-21. Returned to England then to Ireland. To England then Germany, 1922. To England, 1924; Gibraltar, 1935, England, 1938. Fought in France and Belgium, 1939-40. Served in Norway, 1940; India and Iraq, 1942; Persia, 1942-43; Egypt and Syria, 1943; Sicily and Italy, 1943-44; Egypt, Palestine and Syria, 1944; North West Europe, 1945. Left Germany for England, 1947. Amalgamated with 2nd Battalion in Malaya, 1948. Stationed in Germany, 1951-54; Kenya, 1954-55; Aden, 1955-56; Cyprus, 1956-57; Germany, 1958-61; Malaya and Borneo, 1961-64; Aden, 1965. Became 2nd Battalion, The Light Infantry, 1968.

Band - 51st Regiment - Dover, 1867.

Above - Major C.A.L. Yate - 2nd Battalion, The King`s Own (Yorkshire Light Infantry) just after being captured at Le Cateau on 26th August, 1914. Major Yate was awarded the Victoria Cross for his gallantry and leadership at Le Cateau and was killed while attempting to escape in September, 1914.

Below - 2nd Battalion, The King`s Own (Yorkshire Light Infantry) - Minden Day, Aldershot, 1st August, 1909. Note roses in helmets.

2nd Battalion

Formed from the 105th Regiment stationed in Ireland, 1881. To England, 1883; Malta, 1885; India, 1887. Took part in Zhob Valley expedition of 1890. Joined Tirah Field Force, 1897 and fought at Shin Kamar Pass, 1898. To South Africa, 1899. Fought at Belmont, Graspan, Modder River, Magersfontein, Wittebergen and Nooitgedacht. Private Charles Ward awarded Victoria Cross. To Malta, 1902; Crete, 1904; England, 1905; Ireland, 1910; France, 1914. During First World War took part in battles of Mons, the Marne, Aisne, Armentières and Ypres, 1914 (Major C.A.L. Yate and Lance Corporal F.W. Holmes awarded Victoria Cross); Ypres, 1915; the Somme, 1916; operations on the Ancre, Flanders Coast and defence of Nieuport, 1917 (Sergeant J.W. Ormsby, M.M. awarded the Victoria Cross); battles of the Somme, Amiens and Hindenburg Line, 1918. To Ireland, 1920; England, 1921; India, 1922. Served on North West Frontier operations, 1930-31. To Burma, 1936. Fought through Burma, retreating to India, 1942. To Malaya, 1947. Amalgamated with 1st Battalion, 1948.

Badges

The White Rose of York and A French Bugle-horn - from the 51st Regiment.

Uniform

51st Regiment - green facings changing to blue in 1821. 105th Regiment - pale buff. The King`s Own Yorkshire Light Infantry - blue.

Nicknames

`The Kolis` - from the initials K.O.L.I (title of the 51st Regiment after 1821). `The Koylis` - from the initials K.O.Y.L.I. (after 1881).

The King's Shropshire Light Infantry

Titles

1755-1757	55th Regiment of Foot.
1757-1782	53rd Regiment of Foot.
1782-1881	53rd (Shropshire) Regiment of Foot.

1793-1808	85th (Bucks Volunteers) Regiment of Foot.
1808-1815	85th (Bucks Volunteers) (Light Infantry) Regiment.
1815-1821	85th (Bucks Volunteers) (Duke of York's Own Light Infantry) Regiment.
1821-1881	85th (Bucks Volunteers) (The King's Light Infantry) Regiment.

1881-1882	The King's Light Infantry (Shropshire Regiment).
1882-1921	The King's (Shropshire Light Infantry).
1921-1968	The King's Shropshire Light Infantry.

53rd Regiment

Formed by Colonel William Whitmore as 55th Regiment, 1755. To Gibraltar, 1756. Re-numbered 53rd, 1757. To Ireland, 1768; Canada, 1776. During American War of Independence present at Ticonderoga, 1777. Left Canada for England, 1789; To Flanders and present at Famars,

175

Above - Colonel Manley Power - Commanding Officer, 85th Regiment, 1852-57.

Below - Band and Bugle Band, 85th Regiment, 1852. Illustration by R. Ebsworth.

Valenciennes and Nieuport, 1793; Landrécies, and Tournai, 1794. To England then the West Indies, 1795. Took part in attack on St. Lucia and operations against the Caribs on St. Vincent, 1796; capture of Trinidad and attack on Porto Rico, 1797. To England, 1802; India, 1805. Took part in capture of Fort Adjighion, 1809 and storming of Fort Callinger, 1812 and in Nepal campaign fought at Kalunga, 1814. *A 2nd Battalion, 53rd Regiment formed at Sunderland, 1803. To Ireland, 1804; England, 1807; Ireland, 1808; Portugal, 1809. During the Peninsular War fought at Talavera, 1809; Salamanca, 1812; Vittoria, throughout Pyrenees operations and Nivelle, 1813 and Toulouse, 1814. To Ireland then England, 1814. Accompanied Napoleon to St. Helena, 1815. Returned to England and disbanded 1817.* To England, 1823; Ireland, 1826; Gibraltar, 1829; Malta,, 1834; Ionian Islands, 1836; England, 1840; Ireland, 1843; England then India, 1844. Took part in Sutlej campaign and present at Aliwal and Sabraon, 1846. In Punjab campaign fought at Goojerat, 1849. During Indian Mutiny engaged at the relief and capture of Lucknow and at Cawnpore. Five Victoria Crosses awarded. To England, 1860; Ireland, 1864; Canada, 1866; West Indies, 1869; Ireland, 1875; Jersey, 1877; England, 1878. Became 1st Battalion, The King`s Light Infantry (Shropshire Regiment), 1881.

85th Regiment

Formed in Buckinghamshire by Lieutenant-Colonel George Nugent, 1793. Took part in expedition to Holland, 1794-95. To Gibraltar, 1795; England, 1797; Jersey, 1798; England, 1799. Took part in Helder campaign of 1799. Present at Bergen in October. A 2nd Battalion, 85th Regiment formed, 1800 and with 1st Battalion to Jersey. To England, 1801. First Battalion took part in capture of Madeira, 1801 and then to Jamaica, 1802. Second Battalion to Jamaica and disbanded, 1802. To England, 1808 and converted to Light Infantry. Took part in Walcheren expedition of 1809. Present during siege of Flushing. To Portugal, 1811 and fought at Fuentes d` Onoro and during siege of Badajoz. Returned to England in December after heavy casualties. Returned to the Peninsular, 1813 and fought at San

Sebastian, San Marcial, Nivelle and the Nive. Present during siege of Bayonne, 1814. To America, 1814 and present at Bladensburg, Baltimore and operations at New Orleans. To England, 1815; Malta, 1821; Gibraltar, 1827; Malta, 1828; England, 1831; Ireland, 1833; Canada, 1836; West Indies, 1843; Ireland, 1846; England, 1850; Mauritius, 1853; South Africa, 1856; England, 1863; Ireland, 1865; India, 1868. Took part in Second Afghan War of 1879-80 and present during action at Zawa. To South Africa, 1881 and served in Natal Field Force. Became 2nd Battalion, The King's Light Infantry (Shropshire Regiment).

1st Battalion

Formed from the 53rd Regiment stationed in England, 1881. To Ireland then Egypt, 1882; Malta, 1883. Returned to Egypt and garrisoned Suakin, 1885. To Malta, 1887; Hong Kong, 1892. Awarded special medal for services during plague of 1894. To India, 1894; England, 1903; Ireland, 1910. Crossed to France and took part in battles of the Aisne and Armentières, 1914; Hooge, 1915; the Somme, 1916; Cambrai; 1917; the Somme, Lys, Hindenburg Line and the Selle, 1918. To Aden, 1919; India, 1920. Served on North West Frontier operations, 1930-31. To England, 1938. Fought in France and Belgium, 1939-40. To North Africa, 1943 and took part in capture of Pantelleria. Fought in Italy, 1943-45. Stationed in Syria, Palestine, Egypt and the Sudan, 1945-46. To England, 1948; Hong Kong, 1949. Served in Korea, 1951-52 gaining battle honours for fighting at Kowang-San and Hill 227-1. Stationed in Germany, 1952-54; Kenya and Aden, 1955-58; Germany, 1961-63; Malaysia and Mauritius, 1966-68. Became 3rd Battalion, The Light Infantry, 1968.

2nd Battalion

Formed from the 85th Regiment stationed in South Africa, 1881. To England, 1881; Ireland, 1886; England, 1894; South Africa, 1899. Present at Paardeberg, Driefontein, Doornkop, Johannesburg and Komati River. To India, 1903; England, 1914. Crossed to France and fought at St. Eloi and Ypres, 1915. Transferred to Macedonian Front in November, 1915. To Ireland, 1919; England, 1922; Germany, 1924; England, 1927; West Indies, 1939. Returned to England via U.S.A. and Canada, 1942. Took part in

2nd Battalion, The King's (Shropshire Light Infantry) at Paardeberg February 1900. Illustration by Harry Payne.

Officers and Sergeants - `B` Company, 53rd Regiment - Chatham. 1881.

assault landings in Normandy and fought in North West Europe, 1944-45. Private J. Stokes awarded Victoria Cross. Served in Palestine and Cyprus, 1946-47. Amalgamated with 1st Battalion, 1948.

Badges

A Bugle-horn - adopted by the 85th Regiment when made Light Infantry in 1808. A Rose - taken into use, 1881. A Leopard`s face - authorized in 1934 and from the arms of Shropshire.

Uniform

53rd Regiment - red facings. 85th Regiment - yellow changing to blue in 1821. The King`s Shropshire Light Infantry - blue.

Nicknames

`The Brickdusts` - from the red facings of the 53rd Regiment. When the 2nd Battalion, 53rd accompanied Napoleon to St. Helena in 1815 he referred to them as `The Red Regiment.` `The Old Five and Threepennies` - from the number 53. `The Honeysuckers` - a number of men from the 2nd Battalion, 53rd Regiment were flogged for stealing honey while in the Peninsular. In 1813 all officers of the 85th Regiment (except one) were transferred to other regiments. Their replacements were taken from other units which led to the nickname `The Elegant Extracts.` Both the 16th and 85th Regiments were associated with Buckinghamshire, the latter being given the nickname `The Young Bucks` to distinguish it from the senior unit. `The Stonewallers` - nickname given to the 2nd Battalion by Sir John French after Second Battle of Ypres in 1915.

1912
BAND KINGS LIGHT INFANTRY TRIMULGHERRY INDIA

*Above - Band - 2nd Battalion, The King's
(Shropshire Light Infantry), Trimulgherry,
India, 1912.*

*Left - Staff Officers - 2nd Battalion, The
King's (Shropshire Light Infantry) 1899.
Left to right - Captain A. Willmott
(Quartermaster), Major P. Bulman (Second
in Command), Lieutenant-Colonel James
Spens (Commanding Officer) and Captain
C.P. Higginson (Adjutant).*

The Storming of Seringapatam 4th May, 1799. The attacking force included the flank companies of the 77th Regiment whose casualties during the assault amounted to just over sixty. Painting by Sir R.K. Porter.

The Middlesex Regiment
(Duke of Cambridge's Own)

Titles

1755-1757	59th Regiment of Foot.	1787-1807	77th Regiment of Foot.
1757-1782	57th Regiment of Foot.	1807-1876	77th (East Middlesex) Regiment of Foot.
1782-1881	57th (West Middlesex) Regiment of Foot.	1876-1881	77th (East Middlesex) (Duke of Cambridge's Own) Regiment of Foot.

1881-1920   The Duke of Cambridge's Own (Middlesex Regiment).
1920-1966   The Middlesex Regiment (Duke of Cambridge's Own).

57th Regiment of Foot

Raised 1755, first in Manchester and later in the West Country. To, 1756 and from there detachments acted as marines on service along Spanish coast. To Minorca, 1763; Ireland, 1768; America, 1776. Fought at Charleston and during operations in New York. To Nova Scotia, 1783; England, 1791. Served in Flanders during 1793 and 1794-95. West Indies, 1796. Fought in St. Lucia and Grenada and then sent to garrison Trinidad. To England, 1803; Gibraltar, 1804; England then Portugal, 1809. During Peninsular War fought at Albuhera, 1811, Vittoria, the Pyrenees, Nivelle, the Nive and St. Pierre, 1813. To Canada, 1814. *A 2nd Battalion, 57th Regiment formed, 1803 and stationed in England and Jersey until disbandment, 1815.* To France, 1815; Ireland, 1818. From Chatham accompanied convicts to New South Wales, 1824. To India, 1831; England then Ireland, 1846; Corfu, 1853; the Crimea, 1854. Present during battle of Inkerman. Saw action at The Redan and Sevastapol, 1855. To Malta, 1856; India, 1858; New Zealand, 1860. Took part in Maori Wars. To England, 1867; Ireland, 1871; Ceylon,1873; South Africa, 1879. Took part in Zulu War. To Ireland, 1879. Became 1st Battalion, The Middlesex Regiment, 1881.

The 77th Regiment charging French cavalry during the action at El Bodon on 25th September, 1811. Illustration by Richard Simkin.

77th Regiment of Foot

Raised 1787 for service in India and embarked for Bombay, 1788. Took part in Mysore campaign, 1792 and fighting in Ceylon, 1795-96. During Mysore War of 1790 fought at Seedaseer and at the storming of Seringapatam. Present during actions at Arakeera, 1800; Panjalamcoorchy and Caliarcoil, 1801. To England, 1807. Took part in Walcheren expedition of 1809. To Jersey, 1810; Portugal, 1811. Fought at El Bodon September, 1811 and in Spain took part in storming of Ciudad Rodrigo and Badajoz, 1812. To Ireland, 1814; England, 1820; Ireland, 1823; Jamaica, 1824; England then Ireland, 1834; Malta, 1837; Corfu, 1842; Jamaica, 1843; Canada, 1846; England, 1848; Malta then the Crimea, 1854. Present at battles of Alma, Inkerman and Sevastopol. Also present during attacks on The Redan, 1855. To England then Ireland, 1856; Australia, 1857; India, 1858; England, 1870; Ireland, 1876; India, 1880. Became 2nd Battalion, The Middlesex Regiment, 1881.

1st Battalion

Formed from the 57th Regiment stationed in Ireland, 1881. To England, 1882; Ireland, 1888; Gibraltar, 1892; England, 1895; South Africa, 1896; India, 1898; Aden, 1912; England, 1913. During First World War fought during retreat from Mons and took part in battles of the Marne, Aisne and Ypres, 1914-15. Fought on the Somme, 1916; at Arras and Ypres, 1917; the Lys and Hindenburg Line, 1918. Left France for England, 1919. To Germany then Ireland, 1921; Germany, 1922; England, 1923; Hong Kong,

Another artist's impression of the Middlesex in action, this time by R. Caton Woodville and showing the 57th Regiment at Albuhera on 16th May, 1811. Note the Drummer Boy who's jacket would be in reverse colours to those of the rest of the regiment i.e. yellow with red facings. According to one source, casualties among the 57th at Albuhera amounted to 428 out of a strength of 647.

1927 and later served with Shanghai Defence Force. To England, 1928; Palestine, 1932; Egypt, 1933; Singapore, 1936; Hong Kong, 1937. Captured by Japanese December, 1941. The 2/8th Battalion redesignated as 1st, 1942 and fought in North West Europe, 1944-45. To Hong Kong, 1949; Korean War, 1950; England, 1951; Austria, 1953; Cyprus, 1955; Germany, 1958; England, 1962; Gibraltar, 1963; Northern Ireland, 1965; British Guiana then Northern Ireland, 1966. Became 4th Battalion, The Queen's Regiment, 1966.

2nd Battalion

Formed, 1881 from the 77th Regiment stationed in India. To England, 1898; South Africa, 1899. Fought at Spion Kop, took part in relief of Ladysmith and present at Van Wyk's Hill and Alleman's Nek. To England, 1903; Malta, 1913 England, 1914. During first World War fought at Aubers Ridge, 1915; on the Somme, 1916; at Ypres, 1917 and on the Somme and at Arras, 1918. To Egypt, 1919; Singapore, 1922; India, 1923; England via the Sudan, 1931. Fought in France 1940 and in North West Europe, 1944-45. To Palestine, 1945; Egypt, 1946; Palestine, 1947; England, 1948 and amalgamated with 1st Battalion.

3rd Battalion

Formed at Woolwich, 1900 and to St Helena guarding Boer prisoners, 1902. To South Africa, 1902; Hong Kong, 1906; Singapore, 1908; India, 1911; England, 1914. During First World War took part in Ypres battles of 1915. Embarked for Egypt October, 1915 and from there transferred to the Macedonian Front. To Germany, 1921. Returned home and disbanded, 1922.

4th Battalion

Formed at Woolwich, 1900. Crossed to France August, 1914 and took part in retreat from Mons and battles of the Aisne and Ypres. Fought on the Somme, 1916; at Arras and Ypres, 1917; Somme and Hindenburg Line, 1918. To Gibraltar, 1919; England, 1921; Egypt, 1922. Returned home and disbanded same year.

Badges

A Laurel Wreath - awarded to the 57th for its part in the battle of Albuhera. The Prince of Wales's Plumes, Coronet and motto - granted to the 77th Regiment in 1810 and The Cypher and Coronet of the Duke of Cambridge - in 1876. The arms of the County of Middlesex - used as a badge by the 57th.

Uniform

57th and 77th Regiments - yellow facings. The Middlesex Regiment - white from 1881, then lemon yellow restored in 1902.

Above - Brass shoulder-belt plate bearing the battle honour "Albuhera" worn by other ranks of the 57th Regiment c1836-1855.

Below - Officers' shoulder-belt plate - 77th Regiment. The Prince of Wales's Plumes, numerals, wreath and battle honour is in silver and mounted on a burnished gilt plate. Major H.G. Parkyn in his book Shoulder-Belt Plates and Buttons records this fine item as being in use after 1830.

Three members of The Middlesex Regiment - note their post 1902 yellow collars, cuffs and shoulder straps. The large brass device worn on the right upper arm denotes that the wearer is a 1st Class Scout. The badge, which comprises a fleur-de-lys with bar below was traditionally used as the north compass pointer and of course associated with the Boy Scout Movement.

Nicknames

`The Steelbacks` - at one period in the history of the 57th its men received more floggings than was considered normal in other regiments. The offenders were also known to take their punishment well. `The Die Hards` - at the battle of Albuhera in 1811 the 57th incurred over four hundred casualties. Severely wounded Colonel Inglis inspired his men by shouting "Die hard, 57th, die hard." ``The Pot-hooks` - from the number 77.
The Mids.`

A photograph from the 1904 catalogue of J.R. Gaunt & Son showing badges worn by The Middlesex Regiment. The top section illustrates officers' buttons, helmet plate, collar and cap badges, and at the bottom items as worn by other ranks. Note the variation in the collar badges and that officers' had regimental pattern buttons while those for other ranks (with the exception of one) are the General Service (Royal Arms) type. The item shown as B105 is a helmet plate centre and would have been worn attached to a brass star-pattern back plate.

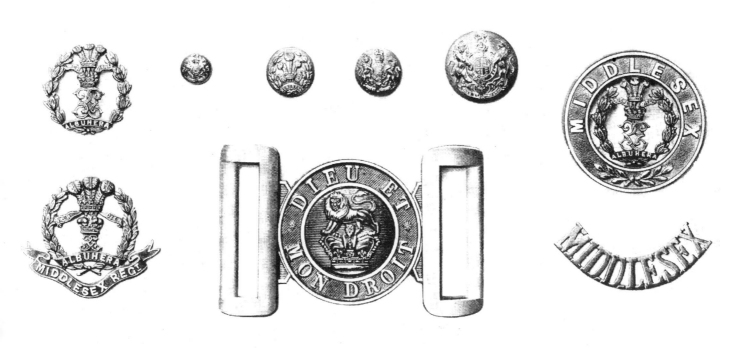

The King's Royal Rifle Corps

Titles

1755-1757 62nd (Royal American) Regiment of Foot.
1757-1815 60th (Royal American) Regiment of Foot.
1815-1824 60th (Royal American) Light Infantry.
1824-1830 60th Duke of York's Own Rifle Corps.
1830-1881 60th King's Royal Rifle Corps.
1881-1920 The King's Royal Rifle Corps.
1920-1921 The King's Royal Rifles.
1921-1958 The King's Royal Rifle Corps.

1st Battalion

Formed in America, 1755. Took part in attack on Ticonderoga and capture of Fort Dunquesne, 1758. Fought in Indian campaign of 1763-64. To Jamaica, 1767. Took part in 1780 expedition to Nicaragua. To Canada, 1786; Guernsey, 1797; West Indies, 1799; England, 1810; Cape of Good Hope, 1811; England and disbanded, 1819. The 2nd Battalion stationed in Canada re-numbered 1st Battalion. To England, 1824; Portugal, 1826; Ireland, 1828; Gibraltar, 1830; Malta, 1834; the Ionian Islands, 1836; England, 1840; Ireland, 1843; India, 1845. Took part in Punjab campaign of 1848-49 and present at Mooltan, Goojerat and Pullee. During Indian Mutiny gained seven Victoria Crosss at Delhi, 1857. Joined Roorkee Field Force, 1858. Private V. Bambrick awarded Victoria Cross at Bareilly. To England, 1860; Ireland, 1864; Malta, 1866; Canada, 1867. Took part in Red River expedition of 1870. To Nova Scotia, 1871; England, 1876; Ireland, 1880; England, 1886; India, 1890. Served on North West Frontier and present at Samana, Hazara and Miranzai, 1891. Took part in Isazai expedition, 1892 and in Chitral operations present at Malakand Pass, 1895. To Mauritius, 1896 and having left half of battalion at the Cape of Good Hope involved in wreck of the Warren Hastings. To South Africa, 1899. Fought at Talana Hill, Lombard`s Kop, Ladysmith and Waggon Hill. To Malta, 1902; Egypt, 1905; the Sudan, 1906; Egypt, 1907; England, 1909. During First World War took part in battles of Mons, the Marne, Aisne and Ypres, 1914; Festubert, Loos and the Hohenzollern Redoubt, 1915; the Somme, 1916 (Sergeant Albert Gill awarded Victoria Cross); Arras and Cambrai, 1917; the Somme; Hindenburg Line and the Selle, 1918. To England, 1919 then Ireland. To England then India, 1922; Egypt, 1938. During Second World War served in Egypt, Libya and North Africa, 1939-43; Italy, 1944-45 then to Austria. Served in Germany then to Cyrenaica, Libya, 1955. To Tripoli, 1956; England, 1958. Became 2nd Green Jackets, King`s Royal Rifle Corps, 1958.

2nd Battalion

Formed in America, 1755. Took part in capture of Louisburg, 1758; Quebec, 1757 and action at Sainte Foy, 1760. To Antiqua, 1772. Six companies took part in operations against the Caribs on St. Vincent, 1773. To Barbados, 1781; St. Vincent, 1785; Canada, 1787; West Indies, 1800; England then the Channel Islands, 1807; England then Spain, 1808. Present at Corunna, 1809 then via Guernsey to the West Indies. To Canada, 1817. Re-numbered 1st Battalion, 1819 (see above). The 3rd Battalion stationed in Nova Scotia re-numbered 2nd Battalion, 1819. To Demerara, 1824; England, 1830; Ireland, 1831; Gibraltar, 1835; the Ionian Islands, 1837; Jamaica, 1841; Canada, 1844; England, 1847; Ireland, 1848; South Africa, 1851. Took part in Kaffir War, 1851-53. To India, 1858; China, 1860. Fought at Taku Forts and Pekin. To England, 1861; Ireland, 1866; India, 1867. Took part in Second Afghan War, 1878-80 and present at Ahmad Khel and Kandahar. To South Africa then England, 1881; Ireland, 1888; Gibraltar, 1891; Malta, 1895; Cape of Good Hope, 1896; India then South Africa, 1899. Fought at Rietfontein, Ladysmith and Waggon Hill. Lieutenant L.A.E. Price-Davies, DSO awarded Victoria Cross. To Ceylon, 1900; India, 1901; England, 1910. During First World War took part in battles of Mons, the Marne, Aisne and Ypres, 1914 (Lieutenant J.H.S. Dimmer awarded Victoria Cross); Aubers Ridge; Loos and the Hohenzollern Redoubt, 1915 (Privates W. Mariner and G. Peachment awarded Victoria

Above - H.R.H. Frederick, Duke of York, KG, Colonel-in-Chief 60th Regiment, 1797- 1827. Illustration by P.W. Reynolds.

Below - Officers` silver pouch-belt plate, The badge bears the battle honour `Martinique` and those for the Peninsular war, 1808-14.

Machine-gun detachment - 3rd Battalion, King's Royal Rifle Corps c1895.

Cross); the Somme, 1916; Ypres; 1917; the Lys, Arras, Hindenburg Line, the Selle and Sambre, 1918. To England, 1919 then Ireland. To Germany, 1922; England, 1925; Northern Ireland, 1932; England, 1935; Palestine, 1936; England, 1937. During Second World War fought in France, 1940; Egypt and Libya, 1942-43; Italy, 1943-44; North West Europe, 1944-45. To Tripoltania, 1946; Palestine, 1947; Egypt then England, 1948. Disbanded, 1948. Re-formed, 1950. Served in Germany and the Middle East. To England, 1956 and disbanded.

3rd Battalion

Formed in America, 1755. Took part in capture of Louisburg, 1758; Quebec, 1757 and action at Sainte Foy, 1760. To the West Indies and present during capture of Martinique and Havana, 1762. To West Florida, 1763; England and disbanded, 1764. Re-formed, 1775 and to America. During War of Independence took part in operations in Georgia and South Carolina. Present at Savannah, 1779 and Mobile, 1780. Disbanded, 1783. Re-formed, 1787 and to the West Indies. To Guernsey, 1793; West Indies, 1795. Took part in operations on St. Vincent, 1795. To Guernsey, 1806; West Indies, 1807. Took part in capture of Martinique and operations on The Saints Islands, 1809. To Nova Scotia, 1816. Re-numbered 2nd Battalion, 1819 (see above). Formed in Ireland, 1855. To India, 1857; Burma, 1861; India, 1865; Aden, 1871; England, 1872; South Africa, 1879. Took part in Zulu War of 1879 (Captain and Brevet Lieutenant-Colonel R.H. Buller, CB awarded Victoria Cross) and in First Boer War present at Laing's Nek, Ingogo River and Majuba. To Malta, 1882; Egypt, 1882 and fought at Tel-el-Kebir. Private Frederick Corbett awarded Victoria Cross. In Suakin expedition of 1884 present at El Teb and Tamai. Lieutenant P.S. Marling awarded Victoria Cross. To Cyprus, 1884; Gibraltar, 1886; England, 1891; Ireland, 1898; South Africa, 1899. Fought at Colenso, Spion Kop and Vaal Krantz. To Ireland, 1903; Bermuda, 1904; England,

1905; Crete, 1908; Malta, 1909; India, 1910; England, 1914. During First World War took part in 1915 battles of Ypres then to Macedonian Front. To England then India, 1919; England, 1922. Disbanded, 1923.

4th Battalion

Formed in America, 1755. Took part in attack on Ticonderoga, 1758 and Niagara, 1759. To England and disbanded, 1763. Re-formed, 1775 and to America. During War of Independence took part in operations in Georgia and South Carolina. Present at Savannah, 1779 and Mobile, 1780.

General Sir Redvers Henry Buller, VC, GCB, GCMG.

Disbanded, 1783. Re-formed, 1787 and to the West Indies. Took part in capture of Tobago, 1793; Martinique and Guadeloupe, 1794. To the Channel Islands, 1796; West Indies, 1797; England, 1805; Cape of Good Hope, 1806; West Indies, 1808. Took part in capture of Martinique and operations on The Saints Islands, 1809. To England, 1810; West Indies, 1812; Demerara, 1816; England and disbanded, 1819. Re-formed at Winchester, 1857. To Ireland, 1860; Canada, 1861; England, 1869; Ireland, 1874; India, 1876; Burma, 1890. Took part in Manipur expedition of 1891 and operations in the Chin Hills, 1891-92. To England, 1892; Ireland, 1898; South Africa, 1901. During Boer War served in Orange River Colony. To England, 1904; India, 1909; England, 1914. During First World War took part in 1915 battles of Ypres then to Macedonian Front. Returned to France, 1918 and took part in battles of the Hindenburg Line, Selle and Sambre. To England then India, 1919; England and disbanded, 1923.

5th Battalion

Formed, 1797. To Ireland, 1798; Surinam, 1799; Nova Scotia, 1803; England, 1805; Ireland, 1807; Portugal, 1808. During Peninsular War gained battle honours `Rolica`, `Vimiera`, `Talavera`, `Busaco`, `Fuentes d`Onor`, `Albuhera`, `Ciudad Rodrigo`, `Badajoz`, `Salamanca`, `Vittoria`, `Pyrenees`, `Nivelle`, `Nive`, `Orthes` and `Toulouse.` Left France for Ireland, 1814. To England then Gibraltar, 1816; England and disbanded, 1818.

6th Battalion

Formed, 1799 and to Holland on Helder campaign. Present at Egmont-op-Zee. Returned to England then to Jamaica. To England, 1817. disbanded, 1818.

7th Battalion

Formed in Guernsey, 1813. To Nova Scotia, 1814. Took part in expedition to Penobscot, 1814 and present at capture of Hampden. Disbanded, 1817.

8th Battalion

Formed in Lisbon, 1813. To Gibraltar, 1814. Disbanded, 1816.

Badges

A Maltese Cross with Crown. A Bugle-horn. The motto `Celer et Audax` (Swift and Bold).

Uniform

The regiment at first wore red jackets with blue facings. When the 5th Battalion was formed in 1797 they wore green jackets with scarlet facings. By 1815 this had become the dress for the whole regiment.

Nickname

`The Green Jackets.`

Bandmaster Mr W.J. Dunn - 2nd Battalion, King`s Royal Rifle Corps.

The Wiltshire Regiment (The Duke of Edinburgh`s)

Titles

1756-1758	2nd Battalion, 4th (The King`s Own) Regiment of Foot.	1824-1832	99th Regiment of Foot.
1758-1782	62nd Regiment of Foot.	1832-1874	99th (Lanarkshire) Regiment of Foot
1782-1881	62nd (Wiltshire) Regiment of Foot	1874-1881	99th (The Duke of Edinburgh`s) Regiment of Foot.

1881-1920   The Duke of Edinburgh`s (Wiltshire Regiment).
1920-1959   The Wiltshire Regiment (Duke of Edinburgh`s).

62nd Regiment

Raised, 1756. Four companies to North America and present at Louisburg, 1758, Cape Breton and Quebec, 1759. Remainder of regiment to Ireland, 1758 and present during French attack at Carrickfergus Castle. To the West Indies, 1764; Ireland, 1769; North America, 1776. Fought at Trois Riviäres, 1776; Bemis Height and interned at Saratoga, 1777. To England, 1780; Ireland, 1784; West Indies, 1791. Took part in operations on San Domingo, 1794. To England, 1798; Ireland, 1800. *A 2nd Battalion, 62nd Regiment formed, 1799 and disbanded, 1802.* To Sicily, 1805. Took part in siege of Scillia, 1808 and operations in Italy, 1809-11. To North America, 1814; Nova Scotia; 1819. *A 2nd Battalion, 62nd Regiment formed, 1804. To Ireland then Sicily, 1805; England, 1810; Portugal, 1813. Fought at Bidassoa, Nivelle, Nive and Bayonne. To Ireland then France, 1815; Ireland and disbanded, 1816.* To Ireland, 1823; India, 1830. Took part in Sutlej campaign and present at Ferozeshah, 1845 and Sabraon, 1846. To England, 1847; Ireland, Malta then the Crimea, 1854. Took part in operations at Sevastopol. To Nova Scotia, 1857; Canada, 1862; England, 1864; Ireland, 1867; India, 1868; Aden, 1880. Became 1st Battalion, Duke of Edinburgh`s (Wiltshire Regiment), 1881.

99th Regiment

Formed in Glasgow, 1824. To Mauritius, 1825; Ireland, 1837. Began escorting convicts in detachments to Australia, 1842. To New Zealand, 1845. Fought in First Maori War, 1845-47. To Ireland, 1856; India, 1858; China, 1860. Took part in capture of Pekin. Served in Japan and to South Africa, 1865; England, 1869; Ireland, 1875; South Africa, 1878. Took part in Zulu War of 1879. To Bermuda, 1880; South Africa, 1881. Became 2nd Battalion, The Duke of Edinburgh`s (Wiltshire Regiment), 1881.

Officers of the 62nd Regiment sometime during their stay in India, 1868-80.

1st Battalion

Formed from the 62nd Regiment stationed in Aden, 1881. To England, 1882; Jersey, 1885; Ireland, 1887; England, 1893; India, 1895; South Africa, 1909; England, 1913. During First World War took part in battles of Mons, Le Cateau, the Marne, Aisne, Armentières and Ypres, 1914; Hooge and Bellewaarde, 1915; Vimy Ridge and the Somme, 1916; Messines and Ypres, 1917; the Somme, Lys, Hindenburg Line and Selle, 1918. Captain R.F.J. Hayward, MC awarded Victoria Cross. To England, 1919; Ireland, 1920; England, 1923; Egypt, 1930; Shanghai then Singapore, 1932; India, 1936. Served in India and Burma during Second World War. Left India for England, 1947. Served in Germany, 1949-50; Hong Kong, 1950-53; Cyprus, 1956-58. Amalgamated with 1st Battalion, The Royal Berkshire Regiment (Princess Charlotte of Wales`s) to form 1st Battalion, The Duke of Edinburgh`s Royal Regiment (Berkshire and Wiltshire), 1959.

2nd Battalion

Formed from the 99th Regiment stationed in South Africa, 1881. To India, 1882; Burma, 1894; England, 1895; Guernsey, 1897; South Africa, 1899. Took part in operations around Colesberg, Wittebergen and Slaapkranz. To England, 1903; Ireland, 1908; England, 1911; Gibraltar, 1912; England,

1914. During First World War took part in Antwerp Operations and battles of Ypres, 1914; Neuve Chapelle, Aubers Ridge, Festubert and Loos, 1915; the Somme, 1916; Arras and Ypres, 1917; the Somme, Lys, Selle and Sambre, 1918. To England, 1919; Hong Kong, 1920; India, 1922; Shanghai, 1928; England, 1930; Palestine, 1936; England, 1937. During Second World War served in France and Belgium, 1939-40; Madagascar, India and Iraq, 1942; Persia, 1942-43; Syria, Egypt and Sicily, 1943; Italy, 1943-44; Egypt, 1944; Palestine, 1944-45; Italy and North West Europe, 1945. Sergeant M.A.W. Rogers, MM awarded Victoria Cross. Amalgamated with 1st Battalion in Germany, 1949.

Badges

The Duke of Edinburgh's Coronet and Cypher - authorized to the 99th Regiment in 1874. A Cross Pattee - from the old Maltese Cross badge of the 62nd Regiment.

Uniform

62nd Regiment - buff facings. 99th Regiment - yellow. Wiltshire Regiment - white restored to buff in 1905.

Nicknames

`The Springers` - given to the 62nd Regiment while serving in America in view of the quickness of its movements in action. `The Moonrakers` - in regard to the old story of two Wiltshire rustics who were seen raking a pond at night for the moon.

Left - Corporal - 2nd Battalion, Wiltshire Regiment. The badges see on the lower left arm indicate that the wearer is best shot in his company (top), best shot in his battalion among corporals, lance corporals and privates (bottom). Note also Queen`s and King`s Medals for South Africa and Cross Pattee collar badges.

Above - Captain R.F.J. Hayward, V.C., M.C.

Right - Post card showing original (city arms) cap badge of The Manchester Regiment.

Below - Fleur-de-lys cap badge that replaced the city arms type in 1923.

The Manchester Regiment

Bottom - Ensign James Hulton Clutterbuck, 63rd Regiment - killed 5th November, 1854 at Inkerman. He was one of three officers killed that day and went into action carrying the Regimental Colour.

Titles

1756-1758	2nd Battalion, 8th (The King's) Regiment of Foot.
1758-1782	63rd Regiment of Foot.
1782-1881	63rd (West Suffolk) Regiment of Foot.
1824-1881	96th Regiment of Foot.

1881-1958   The Manchester Regiment.

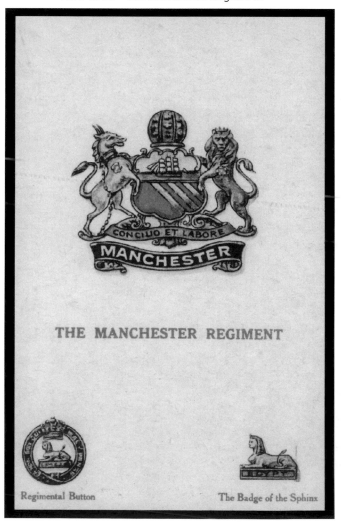

THE MANCHESTER REGIMENT

Regimental Button

The Badge of the Sphinx

Left - Illustration from the Illustrated London News showing the 63rd Regiment passing through New Brunswick on the occasion of the visit of H.R.H. the Prince of Wales in 1860.

Below - Detachment from 2nd Battalion, The Manchester Regiment at Gnatong, Jalep La - Tibetan frontier in 1894.

63rd Regiment of Foot

Formed as 2nd Battalion, 8th Regiment of Foot, 1756. Made an independent regiment and numbered 63rd, 1758. To the West Indies, 1759 and first battle honour gained for capture of Guadeloupe. To Ireland, 1764; America. 1775. Fought at Bunker Hill. Took part in New York campaign, 1776 and present at Brooklyn and capture of Fort Clinton. Went on Charleston expedition, 1780 and fought at Fish Dam and Eutaw Springs. To the West Indies, 1782; England, 1783; Ireland, 1786; England, 1793; Holland, 1794. Took part in Austrian Netherlands campaign and present at Nimeguen and Bommel. To England, then the West Indies, 1795. Engaged during operations at St. Lucia, St. Vincent, the Carib War and Honduras. To England, 1799 then to Holland. Gained second battle honour at Egmont-op-Zee on 2nd October, 1799. To Ireland, 1800. Took part in attack on Ferrol, 1800 then to Gibraltar, 1801; Malta, 1802; Ireland, 1803; Madeira, 1807; the West Indies, 1808. Fought at Martinique, 1809 and Guadeloupe, 1810. *A 2nd Battalion, 63rd Regiment of Foot formed in Suffolk, 1804. Took part in Walcheren expedition, 1809 and disbanded, 1814.* To England, 1819; Ireland, 1820; England then Portugal, 1826; England then Australia, 1828; India; 1833; Burma, 1838; India, 1842; England, 1847; Ireland, 1851. Served in the Crimea and gained battle honours "Alma", "Inkerman" and "Sevastopol." Took part in expedition to Kertch, 1855. To Nova Scotia, 1856 Canada, 1862; England, 1865; Ireland, 1867; India, 1870. Took part in Afghanistan expedition, 1880. Became 1st Battalion, The Manchester Regiment, 1881.

96th Regiment of Foot

Formed in Manchester, 1824 and to Nova Scotia.. To the West Indies, 1825; Nova Scotia, 1828; England,1835; Ireland, 1836; England then New South Wales, 1839. Gained first battle honour "New Zealand" for service during First Maori War, 1844-47. To India, 1849; Ireland, 1854; Gibraltar, 1856; England, 1857; Ireland, 1860; England then Cape of Good Hope, 1862;

Above - 2nd Battalion, The Manchester Regiment at Guernsey, 1904-07. Note full- dress helmet being worn with khaki service dress.

Below - Brass foreign service helmet badge, 3rd Battalion, The Manchester Regiment.

Right - 1st Battalion, The Manchester Regiment during the action at Caesar's Camp 6th January, 1900. Casualties amounted to some thirty-four killed and forty wounded during the defence of this position. Privates J. Pitts and R, Scott, who held their post under heavy fire for fifteen hours, awarded the Victoria Cross. Illustration by R. Caton Woodville.

Facing Page: Top - Illustration showing 1st Battalion, The Manchester Regiment at Givenchy 20th December, 1914. In two-days gallant fighting the battalion's casualties amounted to over two hundred and thirty.

India, 1865; England, 1875. Became 2nd Battalion, The Manchester Regiment, 1881.

1st Battalion

Formed from the 63rd Regiment stationed in India, 1881. To Egypt, 1882 and during war employed on garrison duty at Ismailia. To England, 1882; Ireland, 1888; England, 1894; Gibraltar, 1897; South Africa, 1899. Moved forward to Ladysmith and engaged during October actions at Elandslaagte and Lombard's Kop. Fought at Caesar's Camp (two Victoria Crosses awarded) 6th January, 1900 and in the following August at Bergendal. To Singapore, 1903; India, 1904; France, 1914. Fought at La Bassée and Givenchy and during battle of Ypres, 1915. Moved to Mesopotamia end of 1915. Served in Egypt and Palestine, 1918. To England, 1919. Stationed in Ireland,, 1920-22; Channel Islands, Ireland and England, 1922. To Germany, 1922; England, 1927; West Indies, 1934; Egypt. 1935; Palestine, 1938. Assisted in putting down Arab rebellion and then to Singapore. Captured by the Japanese, 1942. Reformed at home from 6th Battalion and fought in North West Europe, 1944-45. Left Germany for England, 1947. To Germany, 1948; England then Singapore, 1951; England then Germany, 1954; England, 1957. Amalgamated with 1st Battalion, The King's Regiment (Liverpool) to form 1st Battalion, The King's Regiment (Manchester and Liverpool), 1958.

2nd Battalion

Formed from the 96th Regiment stationed in England, 1881. To Malta, 1881; Egypt the India, 1882. Took part in Miranzai expedition, 1891. To Aden, 1897; England, 1898; Ireland, 1899; South Africa, 1900; England, 1902; Channel Islands, 1904; England, 1907; Ireland, 1909. During First World War fought during retreat from Mons and battle of the Aisne, 1914. Took part in Ypres operations, 1914-15, battle of the Somme, 1916, operations on Flanders Coast, 1917, Somme and Hindenburg Line battles,

1918. Left Germany for England, 1919 then to Ireland. To Mesopotamia, 1920 and engaged Arab tribesman at Hillah in July. Captain G.S. Henderson, DSO, MC awarded Victoria Cross. To India, 1920; Burma, 1925; India, 1929; (sent to Burma during rebellion, 1931); the Sudan, 1932; England, 1933. Fought in France and Belgium, 1939-40. To India, 1942 and from there fought through to Burma. Left India for England, 1947 and amalgamated with 1st Battalion, 1948.

3rd Battalion

Formed at Aldershot, 1900. To St. Helena then South Africa, 1902; England, 1906 and disbanded.

4th Battalion

Formed at Aldershot, 1900. To Ireland, 1901; England, 1905 and disbanded, 1906.

Badges

The Brunswick Star - worn by both the 63rd and 96th Regiments, the former, it is said, having received the device as a reward for service in America 1775-81. The Arms of the City of Manchester - were in use from 1881 and until replaced by The Fleur-de-lys in 1923. The Fleur-de-lys was an old badge of the 63rd Regiment and is said to have been awarded after the capture from the French of the island of Guadeloupe in 1759. The Sphinx superscribed ` Egypt` - awarded to the 97th Regiment of Foot. This regiment, however, was disbanded in 1818 (having been re-numbered as

Below - 2nd Battalion, The Manchester Regiment at Guernsey, 1904-07. Note cloth shoulder title (white letters and number on red) - MANCHESTER/2.

96th in 1816) and the Sphinx badge, along with the battle honour "Peninsula" granted to the new 96th in 1874.

Uniform

63rd Regiment - the history of the 63rd Regiment records black facings until 1768 when "very dark green" is the colour noted. This was later described as "deep green" and then as "Lincoln green". 96th Regiment - yellow. The Manchester Regiment - white facings until 1937 when dark green were restored.

Nicknames

`The Bloodsuckers` - from their Fleur-de-lys badge of the 63rd Regiment. The device said to resemble a mosquito. `The Bendovers` - from the number 96 and the fact that it looked the same either way up.

Above - Second Lieutenant James Leach and Sergeant John Hogan, 2nd Battalion, The Manchester Regiment, winning their Victoria Crosses near Festubert 29th October, 1914.

Below - Her Majesty the Queen Mother, as Colonel-in-Chief of The Manchester Regiment, inspecting 1st Battalion in June, 1948.

Below - Cap badge - The North Staffordshire Regiment.

Left - Post First Ward War side-drum shell - 1st Battalion, The North Staffordshire Regiment. The regiment`s badges and combined battle honours are displayed.

The North Staffordshire Regiment (The Prince of Wales`s)

Titles

1756-1758	2nd Battalion, 11th Regiment of Foot.
1758-1782	64th Regiment of Foot.
1782-1881	64th (2nd Staffordshire) Regiment of Foot.
1824-1876	98th Regiment of Foot.
1876-1881	98th (The Prince of Wales`s) Regiment of Foot.

1881-1920 The Prince of Wales`s (North Staffordshire Regiment).
1920-1959 The North Staffordshire Regiment (The Prince of Wales`s).

64th Regiment

Raised at Southampton as 2nd Battalion, 11th Regiment of Foot (see The Devonshire Regiment), 1756. Became 64th Regiment and to the West Indies, 1758. Took part in capture of Guadeloupe, 1759 then to England. To Ireland, 1763; North America, 1768. During War of Independence took part in New York operations, 1776 and present at Brooklyn. Fought at Danbury, Brandywine, 1777; Charleston, 1780 and Eutaw Springs, 1781.

Below - Other ranks brass shoulder-belt plate - 64th Regiment, 1830-55.

Right - Drummer - The North Staffordshire Regiment in foreign service order. Note bugle cords and arm badge.

To Jamaica then England, 1783; Ireland, 1787; West Indies, 1793. Took part in capture of Martinique, 1794. To England then Gibraltar, 1795; Ireland, 1796; England, 1800; West Indies, 1801. Took part in capture of St. Lucia, 1803 and present during operations at Demerara, Essequibo and Bernice. Fought at Surinam, 1804. Left Serinam for Barbados then Canada, 1813. To France as part of Army of Occupation in Paris, 1815. To England, 1816; Gibraltar, 1818; Ireland, 1827; Jamaica, 1834; Canada, 1840; England, 1843; Ireland, 1845; India, 1848. Took part in Persian War, 1856-57 and gained battle honours `Reshire`, `Bushire` and `Koosh-ab.` Returned to India for Indian Mutiny, 1857. Fought at Lucknow, Behar, Cawnpore and Rohilcund. Drummer Thomas Flinn awarded Victoria Cross. To England, 1861; Ireland, 1866; Malta, 1867; Ireland, 1872; Scotland, 1874; England, 1875; Jersey, 1878; Ireland, 1879. Became 1st Battalion, The Prince of Wales`s (North Staffordshire Regiment), 1881.

98th Regiment

Formed at Chichester, 1824 then to South Africa. To England, 1837; China, 1842. Took part in fighting at Ching Kiang Foo and Ma-Kin-Kaon. To India, 1846. Took part in Punjab campaign of 1848-49. To England, 1855; India, 1857. Part of Sittana Field Force, 1858. To England, 1867; Ireland, 1870; Barbados, 1873; Malta, 1875; India, 1880. Became 2nd Battalion, The Prince of Wales`s (North Staffordshire Regiment), 1881.

1st Battalion

Formed from the 64th Regiment stationed in Ireland, 1881. To England, 1883; Barbados, 1884; Natal, 1887; Mauritius, 1890; Malta, 1893; Egypt, 1895. Fought in the Sudan gaining unique battle honour `Hafir.` To India, 1897; England, 1903; Ireland, 1912. During First World War took part in battles of the Aisne and Armentières, 1914; Hooge, 1915; the Somme, 1916; Arras, Ypres and Cambrai, 1917; the Somme, Hindenburg Line and the Sambre, 1918. To Ireland, 1919, England then Gibraltar, 1921; Turkey, 1922; India, 1923. Served in Burma, 1942-43. Left India, 1947 and amalgamated with 2nd Battalion in Egypt, 1948. To England, 1950; Trieste, 1951; Korea, 1953; Hong Kong, 1954; Germany, 1957. Amalgamated with 1st Battalion, The South Staffordshire Regiment to form 1st Battalion, The Staffordshire Regiment (The Prince of Wales`s Own), 1959.

1st Battalion, The North Staffordshire Regiment Band at military funeral in India. Note side-drum covered in black cloth.

Headquarters Wing, 1st Battalion, The North Staffordshire Regiment - India, 1935. Lieutenant-Colonel J.W.L.S. Hobart, D.S.O., M.C. seated centre.

2nd Battalion

Formed from the 98th Regiment stationed in India, 1881. Took part in Zhob Valley expedition, 1884 fighting at Dowlutzai in October. To Aden, 1886; England, 1888; Ireland, 1893; South Africa, 1900 and present at Reit River, Jacobsdal, Paardeberg and Driefontein. Took part in operations at Karree Siding, Spytfontein, Zand River and Johannesburg. To England, 1902; India, 1903. Remained in India during First World War. Fought in Afghanistan, 1919. To Egypt then the Sudan, 1920; England then Ireland, 1921; England, 1923; Gibraltar, 1930; Northern Ireland, 1932; England, 1935; Palestine, 1936; England, 1938. During Second World War fought in France and Belgium, 1939-40; North Africa and Pantelleria, 1943; Italy, 1943-45. Stationed in Palestine and Syria, 1945-46. To Egypt then Palestine, 1946; Egypt, 1947. Amalgamated with 1st Battalion, 1948.

Badges

The Staffordshire Knot - from the 64th Regiment. The Prince of Wales`s Coronet, Plume and motto - from the 98th Regiment. The Dragon of China - awarded to the 98th Regiment for service in China war of 1842.

Uniform

64th Regiment - black facings, 98th Regiment - white, The North Staffordshire Regiment - white from 1881, black restored in 1937.

Nickname

`The Black Knots` - from the facings and badge of the 64th Regiment.

The York and Lancaster Regiment

Titles

1756-1758	2nd Battalion, 12th Regiment of Foot.	1793-1809	84th Regiment of Foot.
1758-1782	65th Regiment of Foot.		
1782-1881	65th (2nd Yorkshire North Riding) Regiment of Foot.	1809-1881	84th (York and Lancaster) Regiment of Foot.

1881-1968 The York and Lancaster Regiment

65th Regiment of Foot

Formed as 2nd Battalion, 12th Regiment of Foot (see The Suffolk Regiment), 1756. To the West Indies, 1758. Gained first battle honour at Guadeloupe, 1759. Also saw action at Martinique and Cuba, 1762. To Ireland, 1764; North America, 1768 and fought at Bunker Hill, 1775. To England, 1776; Ireland, 1783; Canada, 1784; Nova Scotia, 1791; the West Indies, 1793. Took part in operations at Martinique, St. Lucia and Guadeloupe, 1794. To England, 1794; Cape of Good Hope, 1800. Two companies to Ceylon, 1802 and fought in Kandian Wars, 1802-04. Regiment to India, 1803. Engaged during Second Mahratta War and pre-

Other ranks (above) and officers (below) shako plates - 65th Regiment, 1861-69.

Right - The York and Lancaster Regiment c1893.

sent during siege of Bhurtpore, 1805. To the Persian Gulf, 1809 and in operations against Arab pirates at Ras-al-Khaimah. Took part in capture of Mauritius, 1810. Engaged throughout Mahratta and Pindari War, 1817-18. Present at capture of Poona November, 1817. Took part in expedition to Kutch, 1819 and further operations against Arab pirates in Persian Gulf, 1819-20 and 1821. Present at battle of Beni Boo Alli. Left India for England, 1822. To Ireland, 1824; West Indies,1829; Canada, 1838; England, 1841; Ireland, 1843; England then Australia, 1845; New Zealand, 1846. Took part in Maori Wars - Colour Sergeant E. McKenna and Lance Corporal J. Ryan awarded Victoria Cross for bravery during action near Waikato River, 1863. To England, 1865; Ireland, 1867; India, 1871. Became 1st Battalion, The York and Lancaster Regiment, 1881.

84th Regiment of Foot

Raised at York, 1793. To Ireland then England. 1794. Took part in campaign in Holland, 1794-95. A 2nd Battalion, 84th Regiment formed, 1794 and to Cape of Good Hope, 1795. First Battalion to Cape, 1796 and there amalgamated with 2nd Battalion. Present at surrender of Dutch Fleet in Saldanha Bay. To India, 1799. Served on Island of Goa; took part in capture of Mauritius, 1810; Mahratta and Pindari War, 1817-19. To England then Ireland, 1819. *New 2nd Battalion, 84th Regiment formed, 1808 around Preston area and served in Walcheren expedition of 1809. Present at siege of Flushing. To Ireland, 1810; Spain, 1813. During Peninsular War fought at Bidassoa, Nivelle, the Nive and Bayonne. Left France for Ireland, 1814 and disbanded, 1817.* To England, 1825; Jamaica, 1827; England, 1838; Ireland, 1839; Burma, 1842; India, 1845. During Indian Mutiny present at Cawnpore, Lucknow and defence of Alum Bagh, recapture of Lucknow and operations in Behar. Six Victoria Crosses awarded. To England, 1859; Ireland, 1863; Malta, 1865; Jamaica, 1867; Nova Scotia, 1870; Ireland, 1871; Channel Islands, 1873; England, 1874; Ireland, 1880. Became 2nd Battalion, The York and Lancaster Regiment, 1881.

1st Battalion

Formed from 65th Regiment stationed in India, 1881. To Aden, 1882; Egypt, 1884. Present at battles of El Teb and Tamai. To England, 1884; Ireland, 1888; England, 1895; South Africa, 1899. Took part in operations on the Tugela Heights and relief of Ladysmith. Later fought at Botha`s Pass. To India, 1902; England, 1914. Crossed to France January, 1915. Fought throughout battle of Ypres and at Loos September-October. Moved to Egypt and from there to Macedonia. To England, 1919; Ireland, 1921; England, 1922. Served in Germany, 1922-26; Egypt and Palestine during Arab revolt, 1936. Fought in France, 1939-40 and Norway, 1940. Embarked for India, 1942 and later fought in Sicily, Italy and North West Europe. Remained in Germany until 1952. Stationed in the Sudan and Egypt, 1953-55; took part in Suez operations, 1956 and Aden, 1958. Stationed in Germany, 1959-62; Swaziland, 1963-64; Cyprus, 1965-68. Disbanded, 1968.

2nd Battalion

Formed from 84th Regiment stationed in Ireland, 1881. To Egypt, 1882 and took part in action at Kassassin and battle of Tel-el-Kebir. Returned to England and to Bermuda, 1883; Nova Scotia, 1886; West Indies, 1888; South Africa, 1891. Took part in operations in Matabeleland, 1893; Rhodesia, 1896 and Mashonaland, 1897. To India, 1897; England, 1902;

The Alexandra Redoubt - Tuakau, New Zealand. This strong point, which stands on the Waikato River, was seized by a detachment of the 65th Regiment on 13th July, 1863 after crossing in canoes. Engraving from the Illustrated London News.

Ireland, 1911. During First World War took part in battles of the Aisne and Armentières, 1914; Hooge, 1915; the Somme, 1916; Cambrai, 1917; the Somme, Lys and Hindenburg Line, 1918. Left Germany for England, 1919 then to Mesopotamia. Took part in North West Persia operations, 1920. To India, 1921; the Sudan, 1938. Stationed in Palestine and Egypt, 1940. Took part in operations in Crete, 1940-41. Fought in Syria, 1941-42 and then to India. Formed part of Wingate's 2nd Chindit Expedition to Burma, 1943. To England from India, 1947 and amalgamated with 1st Battalion, 1948. Reformed, 1952 and disbanded, 1955.

Badges

The Royal Tiger - awarded to the 65th Regiment for its services in India. The Union Rose and Coronet of the Duchy of Lancaster - were badges of the 84th.

Uniform

65th Regiment - white facings. 84th Regiment - various shades of yellow. The York and Lancaster Regiment - white.

Nicknames

`The Royal Tigers` - from the badge of the 65th. `The Twin Roses` - from the badge of the 84th. `The Cat and Cabbage` - after 1881 from the Tiger and Rose badges. `The Ickety Pips` - the Maori version of "65th."

Above - Drum-major - 1st Battalion, The York and Lancaster Regiment. The sash includes a selection of battle honours recently awarded for the Great War.

Right - Lieutenant-Colonel R. Lloyd who commanded 2nd Battalion, 84th Regiment from its formation in 1808 until his death in the Peninsular December, 1813.

Top - Cap Badge - The Durham Light Infantry.

Bottom - Officers' silver shoulder-belt plate - 68th Regiment 1796-c1810.

The Durham Light Infantry

Titles

1756-1758	2nd Battalion, 23rd Regiment of Foot.	1839-1840	2nd Bombay European Regiment.
1758-1782	68th Regiment of Foot.	1840-1862	2nd Bombay European Light Infantry Regiment.
1782-1808	68th (Durham) Regiment of Foot.	1862-1881	106th (Bombay Light Infantry) Regiment of Foot.
1808-1881	68th (Durham Light Infantry) Regiment of Foot.		

1881-1968 The Durham Light Infantry

68th Regiment of Foot

Formed, 1756 at Leicester as 2nd Battalion, 23rd Regiment. Became independent as 68th Regiment, 1758 and saw first active service during operations along French coast - Cherbourg, St. Malo and the Bay of St. Cast. To Antigua, 1764. Took part in operations against the Caribs in St. Vincent, 1772. To England, 1773; Ireland, 1775; England, 1782; Guernsey and Jersey, 1783; Gibraltar, 1785; the West Indies, 1794. Present during operations at St. Lucia and Grenada. To England, 1796; Ireland, 1797; England, 1800. Divided into two battalions, 1800. To the West Indies, 1801. Second Battalion disbanded, 1802. Took part in capture of St. Lucia, 1803. To England, 1806. Trained and equipped as light infantry, 1808. Took part in Walcheren expedition of 1809 and present at siege of Flushing. To Portugal, 1811 and during Peninsular War saw action at Salamanca, Burgos, Vittoria, the Pyrenees, Nivelle and Orthes. Left France for Ireland, 1814. To Canada, 1818; Ireland, 1829; Scotland, 1833; Gibraltar, 1834; Jamaica, 1838; Canada, 1841; England, 1844; Ireland, 1846; Malta, 1851; the Crimea, 1854. Fought at Alma and Inkerman and during siege of Sevastopol. Victoria Crosses awarded to Captain T. de Courcy Hamilton and Private John Byrne. To the Ionian Islands, 1856; England then Burma, 1857; New Zealand, 1863. Took part in Maori War, 1864-66. Sergeant John Murray awarded Victoria Cross. To England, 1866; Ireland, 1869; India, 1872. Became 1st Battalion, The Durham Light Infantry, 1881.

106th Regiment of Foot

Raised, 1839 in India for service with the Honourable East India Company. To Aden, 1846; India January, 1848. Took part in expedition to Persia, 1857 and engaged during operations at Reshire, Bushire and Kooshab.

207

Transferred to British service as 106th Regiment, 1862. To England, 1873; Ireland, 1880. Became 2nd Battalion, The Durham Light Infantry, 1881.

1st Battalion

Formed from the 68th Regiment stationed in India, 1881. To England, 1887; Ireland, 1893; England, 1898; South Africa, 1899. Fought at Colenso, Spion Kop, Vaal Kranz, Monte Christo, Railway Hill and Pieter`s Hill. To India, 1902. Served on North West Frontier throughout First World War and in Third Afghan War, 1919. To 1920 and then to Germany. Served in Upper Silesia, 1921-22 then to England. To Northern Ireland, 1925; Egypt, 1927; England, 1930; Shanghai. 1937; Tientsin, 1938; Egypt, 1940 and fought in North Africa campaigns. Stationed in Malta, 1942 and fought at Cos in the ígean Islands October, 1943, Italy, 1944-45. Stationed in Greece, 1946-48; Germany, 1949-52. Fought in Korea, 1952-53. Stationed in Egypt, 1953-55; Aden, 1956-57 and to Cyprus, 1958; Borneo, 1966. Became 4th Battalion, The Light Infantry, 1968.

Above - Officers` shako - 106th Regiment 1869-1878. The plate displays the regimental number within a French bugle-horn and carries the battle honours awarded for the expedition to Persia in 1857 - "Reshire", "Bushire", "Kooshab" and "Persia".

Right - Officer - 106th Regiment.
(A. Gavaghan)

2nd Battalion

Formed from the 106th Regiment stationed in Ireland, 1881. To Gibraltar, 1882; Egypt, 1885 and took part in battle of Giniss. To India, 1887; Burma, 1899; India, 1900. Mounted infantry company fought in South Africa, 1900-1902. To England, 1902; Ireland, 1905; England, 1911. During First World War fought in battles of the Aisne and Armentières, 1914; Hooge, 1915, the Somme; 1916; Cambrai, 1917; the Somme, Lys and Hindenburg Line, 1918. Left Germany for England, 1919. To Turkey then India, 1920. To Shanghai, 1927 and served with Shanghai Defence Force. Returned to India same year. Too part in operations on North West Frontier, 1930. To the Sudan then England, 1936. Fought in France and Belgium, 1939-40. Second Lieutenant R.W. Annand awarded Victoria Cross. To India, 1942 and took part in Burma campaign, 1944-45. Stationed in Malaya and Burma, 1945-48 then amalgamated with 1st Battalion. Reformed at Barnard Castle and to Germany, 1952. Disbanded, 1955.

Badges

A Bugle-horn - featured in the badges of the 68th after 1808, a French pattern bugle-horn being worn by the 2nd Bombay Europeans and later as 106th Regiment. The United Red and White Rose.

Uniform

68th Regiment - blue facings were worn as 2nd Battalion, 23rd Regiment and deep green as 68th. 106th Regiment - The 2nd Bombay Europeans at first had light buff but this was changed to white in 1842. The Durham Light Infantry - white facings from 1881, dark green being restored in 1902.

Nickname

`The Faithful Durhams.`

Above - Sergeant - The Durham Light Infantry wearing the Inkerman Whittle and Chain. The scarlet tunic has a green collar and suggests that the photograph was taken some time after 1902.

Below - Officers - 1st Battalion, The Durham Light Infantry 1899. Seated centre is General Sir Reginald Gipps, KCB who was appointed Colonel of The Durham Light Infantry in 1897. On his right is Lieutenant-Colonel A.L. Woodland, Commanding Officer, 1st Battalion, and on his right, H.R.H. the Crown Prince of Siam who had been attached to the battalion. His A.D.C., Captain Sarasiddhi can be seen standing second from the left, middle rank. The battalion later left for South Africa, Major Thomas Roger Johnson-Smyth (seated fourth from the right) being killed in action on 5th February, 1900.

Below - Officer - The Rifle Corps c1801.

Right - Collection of officers` shoulder-belt plates each inscribed with varying selections of battle honours. (John Byrne Collection).

The Rifle Brigade
(Prince Consort`s Own)

Titles

1800-1803 The Rifle Corps
1803-1816 95th or Rifle Regiment.
1816-1862 The Rifle Brigade.
1862-1881 The Prince Consort`s Own (Rifle Brigade).
1881-1920 Rifle Brigade (The Prince Consort`s Own).
1920-1958 The Rifle Brigade (Prince Consort`s Own).

1st Battalion

Formed as `An Experimental Corps of Riflemen` at Horsham, Sussex, 1800. Took part in expedition to Spanish coast and landed at Ferrol. Took part in attack on Copenhagen, 1801. Detachments served in Germany, 1805-1806 taking part in occupation of Bremen. Five companies took part in expedition to South America, 1806-07 and present during operations at Buenos Aires. Took part in expedition to Denmark, 1807-08 and engaged at Copenhagen and Kioge. To Sweden then Portugal, 1808. During Peninsular War present at Vimiera and retreat to Corunna, 1808; Talavera; the Coa and Busaco, 1810; Sabugal and Fuentes d` Onor, 1811; Ciudad Rodrigo, Badajoz and Salamanca, 1812; San Millan, Vittoria, San Sebastian, Pyrenees operations, Vera, Nivelle and the Nive, 1813; Merxem and Toulouse, 1814. To England, 1814; Belgium, 1815. Fought at Quatre Bras and Waterloo. Left France for England, 1818. To Ireland, 1820; Nova Scotia, 1825; New Brunswick, 1829; Nova Scotia, 1832; England, 1836; Malta, 1840; Corfu, 1843; Cape of Good Hope, 1846. Took part in Kaffir War, 1846-47 and expedition against the Boers, 1848. Present at battle of Boemplaats. To England, 1850; Cape of Good Hope, 1852. Served against the Kaffirs and fought at Berea. To England, 1853; the Crimea, 1854. Fought at the Alma, Inkerman, the Redan and Sevastopol. Four Victoria Crosses awarded. To England, 1856; Ireland then Canada, 1861. Rifleman T. O`Hea awarded Victoria Cross for action during Fenian Raids, 1866. To England, 1870; Ireland, 1876; England, 1878; India, 1880; Burma, 1886. Took part in Third Burma War. To India, 1888. Served in Karen Field Force, 1888-89. To Hong Kong, 1894; Singapore, 1896; 1897; England; 1899; South Africa. Fought at Colenso (Captain W.N. Congreve awarded Victoria Cross), Vaal Kranz, Monte Cristo, Peter`s Hill and Tugela. To England, 1902; Malta, 1904; Ireland, 1906; England, 1911. During First World War took part in retreat from Mons, battles of Le Cateau, the Marne, Aisne,

Private Thomas Plunket killing General Colbert - an incident during the Retreat to Corunna, 1809.
Illustration by Harry Payne.

`The First Shot at Waterloo.` Illustration by W.B. Wollen.

Armentières and Meteren, 1914; Ypres, 1915; the Somme, 1916; Arras, and Ypres, 1917; Arras, the Lys, Scarpe, Hindenburg Line, and the Selle, 1918. To England then Mesopotamia, 1919. Active during Arab rebellion. To India, 1921; the Sudan, 1933; England, 1934. During Second World War served in France and Belgium, 1939-40; Egypt, Libya, North Africa and Italy, 1941-43; North West Europe, 1944-45. Left Germany for England, 1953. Served on Kenya, 1954-56; Malaya, 1956. Became 3rd Green Jackets, The Rifle Brigade, 1958.

2nd Battalion

Formed at Canterbury, 1805. Took part in expedition to South America, 1806-07 and present at Monte Video, San Pedro and Buenos Aires. Served in Denmark, 1807-08 taking part in attacks on Copenhagen and Kioge. To Portugal, 1808. During Peninsular War present at Rolica and Vimiera, 1808; Talavera, 1809. Returned to England then took part in expedition to Walcheren, 1809. Present during siege of Flushing. Returned to England then to Peninsular, 1810. Present at Barrosa, Fuentes d`Onor and Tarifa, 1811; Salamanca, 1812; San Milan, Vittoria, San Sebastian, Pyrenees operations, Vera, Nivelle and the Nive, 1813; Merxem, Orthez and Toulouse, 1814. To England, 1814; Belgium, 1815. Fought at Waterloo. Left France for England, 1818. To Ireland, 1820; Malta, 1826; the Ionian Islands, 1832; England, 1837; Bermuda, 1842; Nova Scotia, 1843; Canada, 1846. A Reserve Battalion formed in Bermuda, 1843 and then to Nova Scotia. Disbanded, 1850. To England, 1852; the Crimea, 1854. Fought at the Alma, Balaclava, Inkerman, the Redan and Sevastopol. Four Victoria Crosses awarded. To England, 1856; Ireland then India, 1857. During

Indian Mutiny fought at Cawnpore, 1857; Lucknow and Nawabgunge, 1858. Three Victoria Crosses awarded. Contingent (with 3rd Battalion) formed The Camel Corps and present at Goolowlee, 1858. To England, 1867; Ireland, 1872; Gold Coast, 1873. Took part in Ashantee War and present at Amoaful, 1874. To England then Gibraltar, 1874; Ireland, 1880; England, 1884; Ireland, 1890; England, 1895; Malta, 1897; the Sudan, 1898. Present at Omdurman. To Crete, 1898; South Africa, 1899. Fought at Ladysmith, Ceasar's Camp and Bergendal. Private E. Durrant awarded Victoria Cross. To Egypt, 1902; India, 1905; England, 1914. During First World War fought at Neuve Chapelle, 1914 and 1915; Aubers Ridge and Bois Grenier, 1915; the Somme, 1916; Ypres and Passchendaele, 1917; on the Somme, Villers Bretonneux, the Aisne, Scarpe and Douai, 1918. To England, 1919; Ireland, 1920; England then Constantinople, 1922; England, 1923; Malta, 1933; India, 1938; Palestine, 1939. During Second World War served in Palestine, Egypt, Libya and North Africa, 1939-43; Italy, 1944-45; Austria, 1945. Stationed in Germany, 1945-48. Amalgamated with 1st Battalion, 1948.

Above - Major the Hon. Barrington Reynolds Pellew - 2nd Battalion, Rifle Brigade - wounded during the attack on the Redan, Crimea, 8th September, 1855.

Left - Bandmaster Richardson - 3rd Battalion, Rifle Brigade with his three sons c1896.

Private, Edward Durrant, V.C. - 2nd Battalion, Rifle Brigade, India 1903.

3rd Battalion

Formed, 1809. During Peninsula War present at Barrosa and Fuentes d`Onor, 1811; Badajoz and Salamanca, 1812; San Millan, Vittoria, San Sebastian, Pyrenees operations, Vera, Nivelle and the Nive, 1813; Merxem, Orthez and Toulouse, 1814. Left France for England, 1814 and then to America. Took part in New Orleans campaign and Mobile expedition, 1815. To England then Belgium, 1815. Fought at Waterloo. Left France for England, 1815. To Ireland, 1816. Disbanded, 1819. Re-formed, 1855. To India, 1857. During Indian Mutiny fought at Cawnpore, 1857; Lucknow and Nawabgunge, 1858. Rifleman S. Shaw awarded Victoria Cross. Contingent (with 2nd Battalion) formed The Camel Corps and present at Goolowlee, 1858. Took part in Mohmund expedition and present at Shubkudder, 1864. To Aden, 1870; England, 1871; Ireland, 1878; England, 1882; Gibraltar, 1885; England, 1886; Egypt, 1887; South Africa, 1888; India, 1889. Took part in Tochi Valley expedition, 1897. To Aden, 1904; England, 1905; Ireland, 1910. During First World War took part in battles of the Aisne and Armentières, 1914; Hooge and Loos, 1915; the Somme, 1916; Vimy Ridge, Messines, Ypres and Cambrai, 1917; the Somme, Hindenburg Line and the Sambre, 1918. To England, 1919; Ireland, 1920; England, 1922. Disbanded, 1922.

4th Battalion

Formed, 1857. To Malta, 1864; Canada, 1865. Took part in Fenian operations, 1866. To England, 1867; Ireland, 1872; India, 1873. Took part in Second Afghan War and present at capture of Ali Masjid, 1878. Took part in Waziri expedition, 1881. To Burma, 1888. Took part in Popa expedition, 1889. To England, 1889; Ireland, 1896; South Africa, 1901. Took part in Orange River Colony operations. To England, 1903; Malta, 1905; Egypt, 1909; the Sudan, 1912; India, 1913; England, 1914. During First World War took part in battles of St. Eloi and Ypres, 1915. Left France for Macedonian Front end of year. To India, 1919; Gibraltar, 1921; England, 1922. Disbanded, 1922.

Badges

A Bugle-horn and Crown. A Naval Crown - for service on board ship during attack on Copenhagen, 1801. A Maltese Cross.

Uniform

Rifle-green with black facings.

Nicknames

`The Sweeps` - from the dark uniforms. `The Green Jackets.`

1st Battalion, Rifle Brigade - Belgium, December, 1914.

Appendix A

List of numbered regiments of foot with their 1881 titles. Scottish and Irish regiments have been included (shown in italics). Shortened titles have been used.

Regiment of Foot	In 1881 Became
1st	*Royal Scots*
2nd	Queen's Royal West Surrey Regt.
3rd	Buffs, East Kent Regt.
4th	King's Own Royal Lancaster Regt.
5th	Northumberland Fusiliers
6th	Royal Warwickshire Regt.
7th	Royal Fusiliers
8th	King's Liverpool Regt.
9th	Norfolk Regt.
10th	Lincolnshire Regt.
11th	Devonshire Regt.
12th	Suffolk Regt.
13th	Somersetshire Light Infantry
14th	West Yorkshire Regt.
15th	East Yorkshire Regt.
16th	Bedfordshire Regt.
17th	Leicestershire Regt.
18th	*Royal Irish Regt.*
19th	Yorkshire Regt.
20th	Lancashire Fusiliers
21st	*Royal Scots Fusiliers*
22nd	Cheshire Regt.
23rd	Royal Welsh Fusiliers
24th	South Wales Borderers
25th	*King's Own Borderers*
26th	*1st Bn. Cameronians*
27th	*1st Bn. Royal Inniskilling Fusiliers*
28th	1st Bn. Gloucestershire Regt.
29th	1st Bn. Worcestershire Regt.
30th	1st Bn. East Lancashire Regt.
31st	1st Bn. East Surrey Regt.
32nd	1st Bn. Duke of Cornwall's Light Infantry
33rd	1st Bn. Duke of Wellington's Regt.
34th	1st Bn. Border Regt.
35th	1st Bn. Royal Sussex Regt.

36th	2nd Bn. Worcestershire Regt.
37th	1st Bn. Hampshire Regt.
38th	1st Bn. South Staffordshire Regt.
39th	1st Bn. Dorsetshire Regt.
40th	1st Bn. South Lancashire Regt.
41st	1st Bn. Welsh Regt.
42nd	*1st Bn. Black Watch*
43rd	1st Bn. Oxfordshire Light Infantry
44th	1st Bn. Essex Regt.
45th	1st Bn. Sherwood Foresters
46th	2nd Bn. Duke of Cornwall's Light Infantry
47th	1st Bn. Loyal North Lancashire Regt.
48th	1st Bn. Northamptonshire Regt.
49th	1st Bn. Berkshire Regt.
50th	1st Bn. Royal West Kent Regt.
51st	1st Bn. King's Own Light Infantry
52nd	2nd Bn. Oxfordshire Light Infantry
53rd	1st Bn. King's Light Infantry (Shropshire) Regt.
54th	2nd Bn. Dorsetshire Regt.
55th	2nd Bn. Border Regt.
56th	2nd Bn. Essex Regt.
57th	1st Bn. Middlesex Regt.
58th	2nd Bn. Northamptonshire Regt.
59th	2nd Bn. East Lancashire Regt.
60th	King's Royal Rifle Corps
61st	2nd Bn. Gloucestershire Regt.
62nd	1st Bn. Wiltshire Regt.
63rd	1st Bn. Manchester Regt.
64th	1st Bn. North Staffordshire Regt.
65th	1st Bn. York and Lancaster Regt.
66th	2nd Bn. Berkshire Regt.
67th	2nd Bn. Hampshire Regt.
68th	1st Bn. Durham Light Infantry
69th	2nd Bn. Welsh Regt.
70th	2nd Bn. East Surrey Regt.
71st	*1st Bn. Highland Light Infantry*
72nd	*1st Bn. Seaforth Highlanders*
73rd	*2nd Bn. Black Watch*
74th	*2nd Bn. Highland Light Infantry*
75th	*1st Bn. Gordon Highlanders*
76th	2nd Bn. Duke of Wellington's Regt.
77th	2nd Bn. Middlesex Regt.
78th	*2nd Bn. Seaforth Highlanders*
79th	*1st Bn. Cameron Highlanders*
80th	2nd Bn. South Staffordshire Regt.
81st	2nd Bn. Loyal North Lancashire Regt.
82nd	2nd Bn. South Lancashire Regt.
83rd	*1st Bn. Royal Irish Rifles*
84th	2nd Bn. York and Lancaster Regt.
85th	2nd Bn. King's Light Infantry (Shropshire) Regt
86th	*2nd Bn. Royal Irish Rifles*
87th	*1st Bn. Royal Irish Fusiliers*
88th	*1st Bn. Connaught Rangers*
89th	*2nd Bn. Royal Irish Fusiliers*

90th	*2nd Bn. Cameronians*
91st	*1st Bn. Argyll and Sutherland Highlanders*
92nd	*2nd Bn. Gordon Highlanders*
93rd	*2nd Bn. Argyll and Sutherland Highlanders*
94th	*2nd Bn. Connaught Rangers*
95th	2nd Bn. Sherwood Foresters
96th	2nd Bn. Manchester Regt.
97th	2nd Bn. Royal West Kent Regt.
98th	2nd Bn. North Staffordshire Regt.
99th	2nd Bn. Wiltshire Regt.
100th	*1st Bn. Leinster Regt.*
101st	*1st Bn. Royal Munster Fusiliers*
102nd	*1st Bn. Royal Dublin Fusiliers*
103rd	*2nd Bn. Royal Dublin Fusiliers*
104th	*2nd Bn. Royal Munster Fusiliers*
105th	2nd Bn. King`s Own Light Infantry
106th	2nd Bn. Durham Light Infantry
107th	2nd Bn. Royal Sussex Regt.
108th	*2nd Bn. Royal Inniskilling Fusiliers*
109th	*2nd Bn. Leinster Regt.*
Rifle Brigade	Rifle Brigade

Appendix B

Seniority of infantry regiments. Scottish and Irish regiments are shown in italics. Shortened titles have been used.

Royal Scots
Queen`s Royal West Surrey Regt.
Buffs, Royal East Kent Regt.
King`s Own Royal Lancaster Regt.
Royal Northumberland Fusiliers
Royal Warwickshire Regt.
Royal Fusiliers
King`s Liverpool Regt.
Royal Norfolk Regt.
Royal Lincolnshire Regt.
Devonshire Regt.
Suffolk Regt.
Somerset L.I.
West Yorkshire Regt.
East Yorkshire Regt.
Bedfordshire and Hertfordshire Regt.
Royal Leicestershire Regt.
Royal Irish Regt.
Green Howards
Lancashire Fusiliers
Royal Scots Fusiliers
Cheshire Regt.
Royal Welch Fusiliers
South Wales Borderers
King`s Own Scottish Borderers
Cameronians (Scottish Rifles)
Royal Inniskilling Fusiliers
Gloucestershire Regt.
Worcestershire Regt.
East Lancashire Regt
East Surrey Regt.
Duke of Cornwall`s L.I.
Duke of Wellington`s Regt.
Border Regt.
Royal Sussex Regt.

Royal Hampshire Regt.
South Staffordshire Regt.
Dorset Regt.
South Lancashire Regt.
Welch Regt.
Black Watch
Oxfordshire and Buckinghamshire L.I.
Essex Regt.
Sherwood Foresters
Loyal North Lancashire Regt.
Northamptonshire Regt.
Royal Berkshire Regt.
Queen`s Royal West Kent Regt.
King`s Own Yorkshire L.I.
King`s Shropshire L.I.
Middlesex Regt.
King`s Royal Rifle Corps
Wiltshire Regt.
Manchester Regt.
North Staffordshire Regt.
York and Lancaster Regt.
Durham L.I.
Highland L.I.
Seaforth Highlanders
Gordon Highlanders
Cameron Highlanders
Royal Ulster Rifles
Royal Irish Fusiliers
Connaught Rangers
Argyll and Sutherland Highlanders
Leinster Regt.
Royal Munster Fusiliers
Royal Dublin Fusiliers
Rifle Brigade

Sources of Information

The main source of information for this book has been the `Ray Westlake Unit Archives` which after some twenty-five years now amounts to over 6,000 individual files and some three thousand published volumes. All illustrations, unless otherwise stated, are from the same collection. A work of this type also depends heavily upon regimental records in the form of published `Regimental Histories.` At least one, and on occasion, as many as five books per regiment have been consulted. The total number of volumes amounting to over two hundred and fifty. Official publications such as the `Monthly Army List` have also been put to good use, the Ray Westlake Units Archives fortunately possessing some seven hundred or so of these essential reference tools.

Other sources

Baker, Anthony - Battle Honours of the British and Commonwealth Armies - Ian Allan Ltd, 1986.

Becke, Major A.F. - History of the Great War - Order of Battle of Divisions Parts, 1, 2A, 2B, 3A, 3B - HMSO, 1935, 1936, 1937, 1938, 1945.

Carew, Tim - How The Regiments Got Their Nicknames - Leo Cooper, 1974.

Edwards, Major T.J. - Military Customs - Gale and Polden, 1961.

Frederick, J.B.M. - Lineage Book of British Land Forces, 1660-1978 - Microform Academic Publishers, 1984.

James, Brigadier E.A., OBE, TD - British Regiments, 1914-18 - Samson Books, 1978.

Joslen, Lieutenant-Colonel H.F. - Orders of Battle Second World War 1939-1945 - HMSO, 1960.

Laffin, John - Brassey`s Battles - Brassey`s Defence Publishers, 1986.

Stirling, John - British Regiments in South Africa 1899-1902 - J.B. Hayward, 1994.

King's Regiment (Liverpool)	27
King's Royal Rifle Corps	186
King's Shropshire Light Infantry	175
Lancashire Fusiliers	68
Loyal Regiment (North Lancashire)	155
Manchester Regiment	194
Middlesex Regiment	180
Northamptonshire Regiment	158
North Staffordshire Regiment	199
Queen's Own Royal West Kent Regiment	167
Queen's Royal Regiment (West Surrey)	1
Oxfordshire and Buckinghamshire Light Infantry	144
Rifle Brigade	210
Royal Berkshire Regiment	163
Royal Fusiliers	22
Royal Hampshire Regiment	119
Royal Leicestershire Regiment	61
Royal Lincolnshire Regiment	35
Royal Norfolk Regiment	21
Royal Northumberland Fusiliers	13
Royal Sussex Regiment	114
Royal Warwickshire Regiment/Fusiliers	18
Royal Welch Fusiliers	75
Sherwood Foresters	151
Somerset Light Infantry	46
South Lancashire Regiment	135
South Staffordshire Regiment	124
South Wales Borderers	79
Suffolk Regiment	42
Welch Regiment	139
West Yorkshire Regiment	50
Wiltshire Regiment	191
Worcestershire Regiment	86
York and Lancaster Regiment	203